Between Two Seasons

I. J. Boodhoo

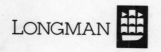
LONGMAN

Longman Group UK Limited,
Longman House, Burnt Mill, Harlow,
Essex CM20 2JE. England
and Associated Companies throughout the world.

Carlong Publishers (Caribbean) Ltd,
P.O. Box 489,
Kingston 10
33 Second Street,
Newport West,
Kingston 13,
Jamaica

Longman Trinidad Ltd,
Boundary Road,
San Juan,
Trinidad

Cover photo taken by Ronnie Joseph.
Title: CARONI, oil on canvas 90cm × 75cm
done in 1992. Painting by author and taken from
the 'CARONI' series, courtesy Robert Las Heras.

First published 1994

British Library Cataloguing-in-Publication Data
A CIP record is available from the British Library

Library of Congress Cataloging-in-Publication Data
Boodhoo, I. J. (Isaiah James), 1932–
  Between two seasons/I. J. Boodhoo.
    p. cm. —(Longman Caribbean writers)
  ISBN 0–582–22869–7
  1. Plantation life—Trinidad and Tobago—Fiction. 2. Carnival—
  Trinidad and Tobago—Fiction. 3. Men—Trinidad and
  Tobago—Fiction. I. Title. II. Series.
  PR9272.9.B57B48 1994
  813—dc20   93–36168
                                                  CIP

Produced by Longman Singapore Publishers (Pte) Ltd.
Printed in Singapore.

ISBN 0582 22869.7

Dedication

For Halima and Farinah, Farhanah, Farah
and Sabina

Biography

Isaiah James Boodhoo was born in a small village in Trinidad in 1932 where his parents owned a few acres of cocoa and coffee. He attended a Roman Catholic Primary School at Upper Guaico, a larger village nearby. With no opportunity for secondary education he became a Pupil Teacher in a now defunct system of teaching and learning. He started to teach at fifteen and was required to take a teacher's examination every year for eight years to become eligible for Teachers' College. He short-circuited the system by taking the Cambridge School Certificate while teaching. After graduating from Teachers' College he entered Brighton College of Art (now Brighton University) to pursue a career in an area in which he had shown special interest and talent. He graduated from Brighton having specialized in Painting and with the Art Teacher's Certificate (Lond). He had completed his studies through a scholarship from the government of Trinidad and Tobago. Upon his return to Trinidad he taught Art at a Boys' College for one year before being appointed Lecturer in Art and Art Education at a Teachers' College where he spent the next thirteen years. In 1968 he took a break and went to the United States to look at American art first hand, and spent a year at Central Washington University completing a Master's Degree. In 1972 he left the Teachers' College once more to do a Doctoral Degree in Art and Art Education at Indiana University. He was appointed Curriculum Supervisor for Art at the Ministry of Education in Trinidad, and in 1978 was put in charge of designing an art and Craft Curriculum for the Caribbean Examinations Council. He is now Chief Examiner. In 1989 he retired from his post at the Ministry to concentrate on painting and writing. As an artist he has had nine One-Man shows and numerous joint exhibitions. He had always written stories along with drawing and painting; in 1962 during his final year at Brighton he wrote the first draft of what was eventually to become *Between Two Seasons*. In 1974, while at Indiana University, he won the 'Best Novel in Progress' award and the 'Superior Writing' award at the Indiana University Writers' Conference for a revised version of this story. In 1989 he decided to re-focus his life and, as mentioned earlier, he retired from his job to concentrate on writing and painting full-time. In January 1991 he began re-working the novel as it stands today, taking time off only to concentrate on a One-Man show in Trinidad.

Chapter 1

Samdaye sat on a jute bag laid on the earthen floor of the hut, sewing on a patch to a pair of boy's trousers made of flour sacking. Her fingers, short and thick like her body moved tiredly, and her elbows with the movement of her arms brushed against her swollen abdomen. From the corners of her eyes she cast a quick furtive glance at her husband who was sitting on a low stool gazing absent-mindedly at the drops of water that leaked from the thatched roof into a tin. The water was almost level with the top of the tin.

Plop. Plo-plop. PLOP. PLOP. Each drop made a small splash as it fell. He seemed to be measuring the intervals of the drops. Sometimes they came fast and the first one had hardly touched the surface when another fell. And at other times the surface had become smooth and placid before being violently broken by an usually large drop.

Now the tin was full and he waited for the drop that would cause it to overflow.

Samdaye sighed irritably and rose. She took the tin and with leaden steps went to the window and threw the water. A gust of wind drove the rain into her face and she wiped her face with the hem of her skirt. She replaced the tin beneath the leak. The plops changed to pings. Again her eyes darted to him. He was still gazing at the tin as if waiting for the plops to return.

The rain was drumming on the straw roof of the hut and like a solid grey fog it connected earth and sky. The heavy drops beat the grass against the ground by the sheer force of their weight and the gathering, gushing rivulets shearing the soil ran down the hillside in yellow streams to

1

the Le Branche River below and to the bay a short distance away.

Samdaye closed her eyes and the crashing of the rain and the wind, and the breakers in Manzanilla Bay filled her consciousness driving out her feelings of irritation and anger. These were sounds that lay behind every part of her life. They were calming sounds and familiar for she had seldom been beyond the sound of the bay.

A small boy squatted peering through the wide cracks of the door at the dropping, dripping palm leaves. His father's shirt swallowed his thin body.

'Get up from the cold ground, Mangal,' she called.

The boy moved to her, snuggling himself to her warmth. She put her am around him.

Roused from his thoughts, Manu muttered about the rain not ceasing. 'I don't know when this damn rain goin' to stop fallin' fallin'.'

Samdaye knew what he was thinking and wished that the rain would go on indefinitely. She waited in the silence of words then said hesitantly, 'You still want to leave?'

He did not reply.

'But you can't leave in this weather.'

'Well, what the hell you want me to do? Stay here and starve?'

'You could go back to the estate. At least you sure you have work here.'

'And beg the damn man for work? All the time I will beg the man. He could haul his potogee arse, you hear. I young and I strong and I could get estate work anyplace. It ain't have a man anywhere could pull a swiper with me. I could cutlass a hundred and fifty cocoa trees before breakfast. Before twelve. And I still fresh. And don't talk about trimmin' cocoa tree. I does make that cocoa-knife sing. I only have to walk to any overseer and they know about me. And pickin' cocoa . . .'

She knew it was no use. For two years they had been living in this place and that seemed to be his limit. It was just like his father before him as he himself said. No place could hold his father for more than two years. From barrack-room to barrack-room his father had moved wife and Manu, with his wife and himself carrying all his possessions from place to place in two jute rice-bags. His father's favourite saying was 'A rollin' stone don't gather moss.'

'A rollin' stone don't gather moss. You want me to gather moss like some stuffed macajuel?'

She could see the signs. They were all there. Since that day one week ago when, arriving from work, he had flung his machete on the floor, mumbling about blasted overseers and kicking at anything that came in his way, she knew that they were about to move again.

'You know where you goin' when you leave here? You know who will take you with your hasty temper? You have house to go to? If you ask me this place is good, you hear.'

'Well I ain't askin' you.'

'Things could never be too bad here. You could always catch a crab or a fish. And Mangal must go to school next term. And the school here not far,' she went on doggedly.

'We goin' to Dorado.'

'You know anybody in Dorado?'

He did not reply.

'And what we will do in this Dorado, eh? Dig for gold?'

'You' father plant gold there?'

'Well, I just askin'.'

The boy's large eyes darted from father to mother. He began a soft whimper.

'But why we can't stay here?' she continued. Her voice had picked up the whine of her son. We could fix up this house. Only the roof need fixin'. And the floor . . .'

He looked at the floor where a pool was forming at the end of a winding trickle coming from under the door.

Outside a calf lowed in misery. Samdaye picked up the half-full tin and looked at the calf with its head hung low and its back arched.

Manu was scratching the ground with a stick. 'Dorado is not too far from here, you know. Is not like we goin' to Venezuela. Is only a few miles past Sangre Grande. Is a nice place with a big estate that always want labourers. And they have a long barracks where we could live in a village near a junction with a shop.'

'A rum shop?'

3

'Yes . . . a rum shop.'

'That will make somebody happy, eh, Mangal, ain't that will make all of us happy? And, to boot, it closer than Mangru shop. It right on the doorstep.'

'Lord, I only mention shop and you jump on my throat.'

'When you say shop we know what you mean, eh Mangal?'

The calf moaned again.

Samdaye moved her hand in two circles on her abdomen and thought about the journey to this new place. 'So when we makin' this great move?'

Without replying Manu rose and took up his swiper. 'I goin' to cut some grass for the cow.' He pulled a file which had a piece of corn husk for a handle from the thatch and holding the long, curved handle of the swiper under his arm, he rubbed the file against the blade.

'I would like to see Mama before we leave . . . if we goin' at all.'

'When?'

'As soon as the weather clear.'

'When the weather clear we leavin' for Dorado. I ain't hangin' round this place.' He looked at the place where the roof leaked and sucked his breath through clenched teeth. 'What you want to see her for? She doesn't come to see you so why you want to see her?'

She had not seen her mother for nearly one year and she lived not more than ten miles along the coast. 'Maybe she doesn't know where we livin'. Maybe she can't keep up with how we movin' about like coal-burners. Or like squirrel on one coconut tree today and on another tomorrow. You think that is some kind of life, eh, running all over the place like crazy ants. You think that good for the children . . . or you not thinkin' about the children. Two of us could hop and skip about but we can't move so with children. And what about family? Here we have my mother not too far away .. and Ranjit Cha Cha . . . and Mangru with his shop where we could get things on credit.' She raised her voice above the grating sound of the file and the soft sound of the rain on the thatch and the whoosh-whooshing of the waves. 'You have family in this Dorado where we could run if anything happen . . . or who we could call when we in trouble?'

4

But he had stopped listening and without another word went out into the rain.

Samdaye watched his figure being swiftly dissolved. In a few seconds his shirt was drenched, sticking to the small of his back, its banana stains disappearing in the wet. His torn trousers frayed at the ends clung to his calves. A lump formed in her throat. He could make such a fine husband if only he could settle in one place. If only he would not be so stubborn. She looked at her son and wondered if he would turn out like his father. Already his hands and feet were large and his knees made large knots. But his face was round and his eyes were filled with liquid black pupils like hers. He was still whimpering and she hugged him tightly.

She remembered the first day she saw Manu. He had passed in front of her house while she was returning from the stand-pipe with a bucket of water on her head. Her back had been turned to him. When she came back to the pipe at the side of the road she could see a stooped figure looking at the ground near the root of a coconut tree. He was still there when she made her third trip. But this time he was upright and was looking boldly at her. She went quickly into the house.

It was only a few days later that he reappeared in a clean shirt and trousers with coconut oil running down behind each ear in the hollow of his neck which had been tied with a handkerchief. Once more he pretended to look for something and dawdled near the stand-pipe. She did not go out.

Not long afterwards she was on the beach with her elder sister when she saw him walking by at the water's edge. From then on he seemed to be anywhere she went.

When Carnival came and she went with her sister to Sangre Grande she was startled when a clown with a long rope and a multi-coloured suit with bells at the tip of the cap and at the ends of the sleeves and the trouser legs, jingled up to her and a voice whispered, 'You very pretty, girl. I like you.'

'Who was that?' her sister had asked.

In the small town of Sangre Grande his clown band of about five or six, with a few children also dressed as clowns, passed several times. And every time he seemed to find her and to tell her something in her ear.

Once he passed around with his wire mask thrown back over his head, and laughing, looked at her straight in the eye. She could not help smiling. He looked very dashing in his shining satin suit, the many mirrors on his chest flashing the morning sun and his long whip cracking ominously.

'You know that fellow playing "diable, diable"?' her sister asked. And when she had shaken her head from side to side her sister had remarked that he seemed to know her.

Late in the afternoon when they were about to take the bus back to Manzanilla he had shouted to her as she sat in the bus, 'Pretty girl, you have a boy-friend?' She smiled and told him no. 'I will marry you, then. I comin' to see you' father.'

He was as good as his word. Two weeks later he went to her father and said that he wanted to marry Samdaye. She was then seventeen.

They were married when she was eighteen.

Her mother had not been too pleased with the match but her father thought that Manu was hard-working and healthy. And although he lived in a barrack-room and had neither property nor parents he could make his way in life. Poverty was the base from which any hard-working man could rise. He had done it and his father before him. Manu had no bastard children and the village people liked him. Samdaye's mother had remarked about his involvement in Carnival as a 'devil' masquerader jumping up and down on the streets like any black hooligan. And the practice of fighting with whips could bring him injury. But her father had seen the light in Samdaye's eyes when Manu was discussed and gave her his blessing.

She thought about going to see her mother and her eyes became bleary. Now that her father had died her mother would be very disappointed if she left without telling her.

For a long time Samdaye stood by the window gazing in the direction in which Manu had gone until she saw him coming through the rain, the bundle of wet grass on his head. She went quickly and lit the kerosene lamp for it had become darker. Sticking a few pieces of damp wood into the earthen stove she began to prepare the evening meal. She boiled rice,

6

made a 'dal' of split peas and roasted the kernel of a nut which she ground with salt and a few bird peppers. 'Look like the rice nearly finish, Mangal.' She saw Manu come in shaking the water from his hair. 'This is the last rice, eh. Rice finish.'

She waited until he had changed into dry clothes then placed the large, chipped enamel plate with a mound of rice covered with 'dal' and with the coconut chutney to one side.

When he had finished she took the plate and without washing it put her food into it and sat down on the stool to eat. 'You know how much money we have? I don't think it come to even one dollar. So what we goin' to do tomorrow?'

'Rain or sun tomorrow we headin' for Dorado.'

'So what about my mother?'

'Well, what about your mother?'

She knew that her mother would help out with a few dollars. Manu did not know but her mother had been sending her a five-dollar bill occasionally. Sometimes she would send a dress for her or a shirt for Mangal. She recalled when she was married how Manu had more than fifty dollars saved after buying his wedding outfit of a long, pink satin gown a pink turban and a crown. But not long after the wedding he had spent most of it on his carnival clown costume: the many half-yards of different coloured satin, mirrors of different shapes, fur to line the edges, bells and a pair of specially made shoes. He also bought leather thongs and wire to make his whip which was nearly six feet long.

'Rain or no rain tomorrow I goin' to see Mama.'

'You will go one way and I will go another. It is time to move.' After a long pause he said, 'Why you don't go and spend one week with your mother and I will go and fix up the place in Dorado?' His voice had softened. 'The barrack room will need fixin'.'

Her eyes welled up again.

'The only thing is the lady will keep you for another month. You remember the last time? I had to go to fetch you. Like you yourself did not want to come back.'

'But I must go to see her. How it will look for me to go just like that without tellin' her anything?'

7

'But I tellin' you, you could go. Go and spend a week . . . two weeks . . .'

'And who will cook for you?'

'So how I eat before I married you? I used to starve? I look starvin' when you see me first?'

'You forget all that now.' She washed the few utensils and put them face down on an open shelf which jutted outside from a windowless space in the wall. She resumed her sewing. Later, her sewing finished, she adjusted the mattress which she had stuffed with coconut husk. On it she spread a sheet with the red letters of 'Canadian Spring Wheat Flour' faintly visible. She waited till her husband had got into bed, then, blowing out the light, she heaved herself beside him. Mangal slept on the far side near the wall. On nights when they had quarrelled she used the boy as a barrier between them. But this evening she was not sure that there had been a quarrel.

She lay on her back and she could make out the great mound of her abdomen. She found a small hole with her toe and pulled the sheet taut to lessen the lump before her.

'We don't need money to go to Dorado, you know.'

'Oh? We flyin'? We will grow wings tonight?'

'Ranjit promised to carry the things in his cart. For nothin, too.'

'So how is that? Ranjit is somebody father?'

'You gettin' me damn vex, you know. I tryin' to explain and you gettin' on like a horsewhip snake.'

She remained silent.

'You will like Dorado,' he said after a while. 'Is a village and Mangal will have children to play with. A boy must have friends to play with. He is stickin' to you too much. I don't want him to be no mama's boy.'

'But here is so healthy. With the sea and the breeze.' After some silence she added, 'I never been out of Manzanilla except for the few times I go to see Carnival in Sangre Grande. I never live anyplace else.'

'You think I don't know?'

'But is hard to move now with the baby comin' and all.'

'It wouldn't be hard. The barrack got big rooms with a wooden floor.'

Big rooms, she thought as she remembered the tiny boxes of the first barrack-rooms into which she moved when they got married. Every sound and movement was public. You could not even whisper. She had been happy moving into their own living space never mind the condition.

'I see the overseer already and he promised me a room when I start to work. In any case we not goin' to be livin' in no barrack-room for long. As soon as we make some money I will get my own piece of land and build a house. I done see the spot already. It got a big rose-mango tree on the front and it right opposite the school.'

'I hope the barrack don't leak.'

'You always thinkin' about the bad side. So if it leakin' it could get fix.'

'And I hope that it not filled with people . . . with a whole heap of children . . . with quarrelsome neighbours . . . with all kinds of stinkin' hogs . . . the dogs . . . and cats that come in the night and mess all over the kitchen . . .' Hearing his snore she stopped. He still smelled of fresh-cut grass.

Outside the rain continued.

'And where the money will come from?' she spoke softly to the sleeping form, 'how we could collect any money if every year it goin' in clown costume?' She nudged him and he mumbled as he turned.

The next morning was the same as the previous one. The wind and the rain and the crashing waves still filled the air. The Le Branche River had risen some more with the high tide. The entire day repeated the previous ones. It was the rainy season. Manu moved about restlessly and Samdaye kept out of his way as much as possible. Later in the day he left in the rain and returned a few hours later with the smell of rum on his breath.

For a brief interval in the late afternoon the sun broke through the shifting clouds. It was the first time it had appeared in two weeks. Quickly the clouds raced over it but the showers had become thinner and the dark sky greyer and by evening the rain had reduced to a drizzle. The rainflies, too, were fewer. Some of them, their fragile wings broken, crawled helplessly. Late that night the rain stopped altogether.

Manu woke early next morning. The sun, like a dazzling white flame burst through the horizon setting the bay ablaze with light. The greyness had gone and every trace of cloud had vanished leaving the sky in a blue wash. The drops of moisture at the tips of the palm leaves glistened like jewels. The flood waters had been sucked back into the sea and all that was left was isolated pools and tiny dry beds of the temporary streams. On the beach lay the debris of gri-gri palm nuts and broken roots and branches which had been brought down by the tide from the forested land to the north. In the distance the horizon was clearly marked where the deep blue of the sea met the paler blue of the sky.

'Aye!' Manu shouted, 'Look at this!'

'The rain over!'

'Which rain? It look like we had any rain? You ever see a sky so blue?'

Samdaye squinted into the light.

'I goin' to find Ranjit,' he announced. 'Pack up in the meantime.' He continued giving directions as he hurried through the palms his voice losing itself in the sound of the waves. There was an increasing hollowness in her stomach and her mouth became dry. She woke the boy then wandered in and around the hut then she walked to the edge of the sea and let the waves wash over her feet as she looked in the direction of her mother's home.

Chapter 2

Samdaye heaped the few belongings. In a wooden box marked 'Fernandes White Star Rum' she put in her kitchen items: two cast iron pots, a chipped blue enamel pot, a ladle, a swizzle made from a twig with five smaller sprouting twigs cut about two inches, a pot spoon, two chipped enamel plates, two enamel cups and one small enamel bowl. She wrapped the two brass plates and brass jugs in a brown paper bag and placed these on top. In another box she stuffed their clothes.

She rolled the straw mattress with the two pillows inside and, tying it with a piece of rope, leaned it against a coconut tree.

In one corner she saw the box with his clown's costume and the coiled whip. She left it there. She picked up the broom made from the spikes of the stripped coconut frond and, without thinking, started to sweep the room. Biting her lip she squeezed a tear.

She looked at the full barrel of water. It was an oil drum tarred on the inside. The water was an undisturbed picture of the blue sky. She tried but she could not overturn the full barrel.

She went back into the kitchen and she fetched a tin bucket, a four-gallon oil tin and a large stone on which she ground her spices. Then she sat on the root of the tree and waited.

'Where we goin', Ma?'

'We goin' for a ride.'

'But why we takin' everything?'

'We not comin' back.'

'Why?'

'Ask your father.'

11

The boy looked puzzled. 'I could take my marble? And my kite? And my "Johnny Walker"?' He ran inside and returned with two marbles, a mildewed kite, and a thread-bobbin into which he had cut a serrated edge and had wound a piece of rubber with a stick so that when the rubber was wound tight with the stick it would crawl like a tracked vehicle. He also brought a few shells, some stones with white veins, the shell of a star-fish and a green bottle.

'And where you goin' with all that foolishness?'

He did not say anything but began putting his things into a shoe box. On top he placed his box of crayons and dog-eared drawing book.

Noticing the bird-pepper tree she went to it and picked it clean – ripe, green and young. She put aside a few very ripe, red ones to make seeds. Then she remembered the ear of corn she had hung over the earthen stove and the few seeds of string beans in an empty condensed milk tin. She did not know if there was any place to plant anything where they were going.

Near the door she had planted some marigold and purple bachelor-buttons. They looked brilliant in the sunshine. She took some of the dried flowers and put these into the tin. She yanked at a marigold plant and flung it against the house.

'Let me root out the rest,' Mangal said as he went to the clump.

'No!' she said roughly and pushed him away. Some distance away she saw Manu striding ahead of the cart.

He took the bucket and emptied some of the water from the barrel then pushed it over and rolled it over to the heap of belongings. He went inside the house and brought out the box with his costume then walked around the hut to see if anything was forgotten. He disappeared at the back of the hut and reappeared leading the calf.

They loaded the cart and set out walking beside it. The wheels of the cart rolled unevenly along the gravelled road leaving parallel lines of powdered pebbles. The donkey pulled reluctantly. Mangal, imitating Ranjit, tapped at its rump with a long, dry straw and echoed his calls. The calf, its rope tied to the cart, walked obediently behind.

Manu walked a few paces ahead. His loose shirt flapped about his trousers which were tied with a rough leather belt from which hung a sheath with his machete. The case squeaked with each step. His felt hat had lost its band so long ago that there was no trace where it had been.

He turned and looked at Samdaye, 'Why you don't go up on the cart? The sun is gettin' hot.'

The sun was swiftly climbing up the sky and the heat rose with it. Manu lifted the boy and put him to sit on the cart and cleared a place at the back for Samdaye.

She sat heavily against the mattress and stared at the large, sad eyes of the calf. Through the palms she could still see the house which had already taken on a shrunken and deserted look. Above the trees where the land sloped downhill she could see the bay but the waves were barely audible above the crunch of the wheels.

Manu had slowed his pace and was now beside her – a grey blur in the corner of her eyes.

'Le Branche flowin',' he teased.

She forced a resigned smile.

'You feelin' good?'

She nodded. Seeing the cow with equally moist and mournful eyes she smiled.

They were approaching Mangru's shop. Manu crossed over to the other side of the road and kept looking straight ahead.

'A-A, boy, Manu, like you movin' out,' Mangru shouted. He was sitting on the shop counter in a sleeveless undershirt, his large belly resting on his thighs. 'Wha' happen, man, like we ain't talkin' or what? How you goin' quiet quiet so? Like a secret. Come, man, and take a little one for the road. You can't go just so.'

Manu was having difficulty trying not to hear.

'And I want to talk to you about something . . . about the little bill that you have outstandin'.'

Manu turned abruptly and rushed into the shop. Samdaye saw them gesticulating. She wondered how much Manu owed. She turned to Ranjit and asked him to go into the shop and buy a penny biscuit and find out the debt discreetly.

Manu emerged his face in a frown. 'Don't worry, Mangru, you will get your six dollars next fortnight,' he shouted as he walked quickly away. As he strode ahead Ranjit quietly told her that it was fourteen dollars. She untied a knot in her waist band and counted eleven dollars. She took out five to give Ranjit to take to the shopkeeper but she carefully put it back. It would serve him right if he did not get one cent more. He deserved nothing for encouraging people to spend their money on rum. And getting fatter and fatter, too.

'I always tell you don't give so much trust,' Mangru's wife came from behind the counter. 'Look how the man runnin' away and he owin' so much money. If every body take your goods and don't pay how you goin' to live, eh? Tell me that. How a honest person will make a livin'? Eh, Mohan, how much he owin'? Call it out loud. FOURTEEN DOLLARS. Let everybody hear. I tell you not to trust them low-class people. Them ain't have no fix place of abode. Them like honey bee suckin' here and suckin' there and makin' life sweet only for themself.'

Soon her voice could be heard no more.

After a while the gravelled road gave way to asphalt which was hot and sticky and Ranjit moved over to the grass verge. In the distance the road shimmered. Manu's shirt clung to his back and a dark streak ran down the middle.

They started up a steep hill and the donkey staggered its way forward. Samdaye alighted. Going down the hill seemed more difficult for the donkey and Ranjit held back the cart a bit to ease the pressure on the animal. Cocoa and coffee trees cast their shadows in purple pools and the donkey dallied in their cool shade and had to be urged forward.

Manu seemed to have regained his good spirits. His sullenness gone he called out to the people he knew as they went along. 'I leavin' this bush, man. I makin' a move. A rollin' stone don't gather no moss.'

As the number of houses increased Samdaye began to feel as though she had been put on a pedestal for inspection. She had climbed back on the cart. Manu had given her his hat and she now rested this against her stomach which stretched her dress in radiating pleats. She began adjusting her hair and to wipe her face frequently.

Ranjit, lean and small, and with a skin that was almost black had climbed up next to Mangal. 'Sangre Chiquito', he called out the name of the village. 'It mean "little blood". They say the Caribs and Spanish had a fight here and some people get killed.' Mangal did not know what Caribs were. He knew Spanish for there was a Spanish man used to pass selling fish.

'Carib is people who used to live in Trinidad long before anybody,' Samdaye explained to the boy. She had been to school up to the third standard and had already started to teach Mangal to read. 'And Spanish is not Mister Diaz who come around sellin' fish. Toobesides he is not even Spanish. He is Potagee. Uncle Ranjit talkin' about when this island belonged to Spain long, long time ago.'

'Before I born?'

'Before you born. Before I born. Before you' Pa born. Before Uncle Ranjit born . . .'

'Before the donkey born?'

'The donkey just a little older than you, you monkey.'

'Before that tree born?'

She wanted to run her fingers through his hair. He was so much like his father. He had already forgotten Manzanilla.

At the top of the high and winding road was a small wooden hospital with the meshed doctor's quarters looming large and mysterious.

'That is where the doctor live,' she pointed the house to Mangal. 'You want to be a doctor when you grow up?'

They passed a large concrete Catholic church with a wide, arched doorway. 'That door is over fifteen feet high,' Ranjit explained. He pointed out the ruins of a building near the church. Moss-covered wooden steps led to a crumbling concrete platform which was almost completely covered with vines and was partly concealed by black sage and other bush. Ranjit told them that the builder had been a rich Indian man named Bhola Nath. He had owned about two hundred acres of land in the area and had even given an acre to the Roman Catholic Church to erect their building. 'Anyway, that is what he tell everybody after he lost everything.' Bhola Nath wanted to build the best house in Trinidad. First, he wanted to put one hundred windows of wooden jalousies but the government stopped him. They said that only the governor house could have so many windows. Then, after he put up the walls and

15

the roof he went to the bank to get all the shillings they had. It turned out that he now wanted to pave the floor with shillings but the police stopped him. The law wouldn't allow him to walk on the king's face. Then the priest put a curse on him. Every night after work was done for the day when the house was nearly finished he would gather with his friends and celebrate. They would sing Hindi songs and beat drums and cymbals and make a lot of noise so that the priest could not hear what he was saying at evening mass and confessions. He even used to curse the priest when he was spoken to. 'And, boy, you can't play with Catholic priest. They work the worst obeah. So the priest shake the cross at him and he never finish the buildin'. He used to come every evenin' and sit down on the steps and drink rum. Now only the step where he used to sit ain't have moss.'

'He still livin'?' Mangal asked.

'He dead long time ago. This is a old story.'

They entered Sangre Grande with its buildings huddled along its single street. At one end stood the police station: an imposing two-storied structure filling the 'Y' at the junction and looking squarely down the street. In the courtyard stood a tall poui tree with dozens of yellow-tail nests hanging like straw clubs and swinging in the breeze.

The smells changed as they passed. The smell of bread and cakes came from a parlour with a small glass case on the counter; curry being cooked floated from the next door; the scent of fabric came from the entrance to a clothing store and from the left came the fragrance of tonka beans and cocoa beans. The stench of urine came from the corner near the rum shop.

Someone from the shop called out to Manu but Manu kept looking ahead.

The houses stopped abruptly for the land was low on both sides of the road. It was still water-logged. The road soon stretched before them flat and straight and shimmering like a river. Above it on either side trees arched like a canopy.

'Why you don't come and sit down,' Samdaye called to Manu. 'You must be gettin' tired. I could walk.' But he merely shook his head and continued with the same rhythm ahead of the cart. 'Is not far again,' he said.

An hour later she could see the village wobbling towards her. Only two buildings were visible at the end of the forest. Beyond the buildings the mountains loomed.

At the junction Ranjit stopped and negotiated with a man to take a few bags of charcoal back to Sangre Grande. 'You see when you have good mind, Uncle, how good things happen to you. You did not charge us and now you get a job to pay for what you lose.'

'Nobody don't lose anything,' Ranjit said. 'It always come back.'

'And I sure you will get something in Sangre Grande to take back to Manzanilla.' She felt less guilty about Ranjit coming all this way for free. He was not even a relative and she called him Uncle because Manu did so. It seemed that he had been a friend of Manu's father.

'You any family to Manu, Uncle?' she asked because she had no idea if she would see him again.

'Child, my father and his grandfather come on the same boat from India. They was "jahaji bhai" – brothers in the journey. They come from the same Bihari village. And they moved from estate to estate together. They was more than brothers. To tell you the truth,' he whispered, 'I really sorry to see you all move. I used to keep an eye on him, you know. Anyhow, if you in any trouble you must send and tell me.' He patted her hand. 'You could say he is the only family I have. Wife dead. Child dead. Father, mother dead. I ain't have nobody. I might come and live here, too.' He turned to Mangal, 'You will mind me, "beta", when I get old?'

The boy nodded.

'You have a good child here,' he remarked.

As they turned the corner in the junction Manu saw the overseer standing beside a brown horse with a white patch on its face. He looked enquiringly at Manu.

'Good evenin', sir. I reach at last.'

'What happen, boy? I thought you not coming again.'

'Too much rain, sir. Too much rain. Flood, too.'

'I was expecting you since last week. More than a week.'

'Well, sir, I had some business to settle.'

'Oho. so we have a regular big shot here. Talking about settling business. And arriving in vehicle.'

17

This was not going too good, Manu thought. 'I ready to work right away, sir. Right away.'

'And only this morning I tell someone to take the barrack room.'

Samdaye felt a dryness in her mouth. She looked at Manu who had a trapped expression and kept glancing from the overseer to his wife.

'And where the hell you think you going with that cow? You did not tell me anything about bringing animals.' He observed Samdaye. 'That your wife?'

Samdaye nodded.

'That woman can't work for at least a few months.'

'She ain't workin' at all. My wife don't work on no estate. She ain't no labourer.' The voice was trembling with rising anger.

'So what we will do now?' the overseer asked.

'I need the room, sir. I pack up everything and come. And I ready to work, sir.'

'Already I have given the place.' He looked at the barrack some distance away. 'O.K. You could move in the last room at the end. You will have to fix it up. I will tell the other fellow to find another place.' He turned to Manu. 'You very lucky, you know'.

'Thanks, sir. Thanks very much.'

'Come up to the yard at six in the morning. Bring your swiper. We cutlassing.'

With a satisfied look Manu headed towards the barrack. When the overseer was out of earshot he muttered about 'all blasted overseers.'

'He don't look like a nice man,' Samdaye said.

'See what I mean about overseers? He better don't play with me of I'll chop off his damn neck.'

Ranjit cautioned him about making threatening remarks. 'Now, son, I want you to behave a good boy. Out here you don't know anybody. Nobody to take your side.' He clapped a hand on Manu's back. 'Soon you will have two children and a wife to support.'

'Tell him about the Devil mask. He should really stop that stupidness. One of these days he will get damage bad. Uncle, you'd better talk to him about that.'

18

'She right, you know, Manu. You have to change.' He embraced Manu as he left when the load was on the ground in the barrack-yard.

It was a long, low one-storied structure. Erosion had removed about three feet of ground so that it seemed raised. The walls were falling apart and the grimy grey boards were missing in some places. The roof of corrugated iron sheets had become brown with rust and pieces were breaking off the edges. Once the ceiling had been used as a drying floor for cocoa and coffee beans and so the roof was designed with two halves which slid one under the other for a few feet and, when open, the halves ran out on rails. Now the rails were rusty and broken and looked dangerous hanging on concrete stumps. The steps leading to the end-room hung more than one foot off the ground which had been eroded.

Samdaye almost rushed to see what the room was like. An underfed dog barked thinly and slunk away from under the steps. She was about to climb the steps when Manu shouted for her to be careful. He came and tested the structure.

With some effort she climbed into the room. It was narrow, less than ten feet but ran the width of the building. In the middle was a partition which rose half-way up the room. It was covered with newspapers brown and crisp and peeling with fragments of news about war. One headline read 'LIES INVADE EUROPE'. The first two letters of 'Allies' were hidden under a curling piece. A cat scampered away from what she supposed was the bedroom.

The roof jutted out a few feet at the back of the building and beneath it stood a row of make-shift kitchens separated by the sides of wooden cartons, flattened tins and old galvanized iron sheets. On the earthen floor of her portion there were several places where dogs had scratched deep depressions. Dried dog droppings whitened like coral rolled about. The only cooking facilities were three stones black with soot.

She sat at the doorway her head in her hands.

'How you like the place?' Manu asked.

'Good. It look good. With a little cleanin' and some paper . . .' She turned but Manu had gone for the broom. From the back of the house she looked across a field that ended at the edge of the cocoa plantation. Towering over the cocoa trees were the imortelle shade trees flaming with orange rooster-shaped blooms that contrasted with the blue-green sky serrated by the Northern Range that ran from east to west as far as the eye could see. She walked round the building and stopped before an almond tree with leaves of red and green. Its branches reached out horizontally on all sides and cast a solid shadow.

Out in the field Mangal was tying the calf to a guava tree. Manu had disappeared. She took out the broom and began to sweep the floor. It was obvious that the room had been unoccupied for a long time. The dust was thick and choking. She swept the walls first and climbing on a box cleaned the ceiling. She dug the cobwebs from the corners and crushed the frail, long-legged spiders.

Manu returned with a hoe and was cleaning out and levelling the kitchen floor.

She called out to the boy to find a few fallen lemons with which she could scrub the floor. He was now gazing at the small groups of children who were returning home from school. He came close to the edge of the road and stared at them. None of them came to the barrack. She called once more and when he answered that there were no lemon trees she showed him one she had spied at the corner of he field.

Two hours later they sat exhausted beneath the almond tree, Samdaye's straying hair plastered over her wet face. 'The place will be good,' she said.

The sun had sunk behind the trees making crowns of gold at the top and the clouds were two gigantic orange brushstrokes across the sky. The hills were sculpted in blue.

'We want some goods from the shop.'

'Make a list,' he said, 'I will try to get some credit from the shop.'

'We only want a few things: oil, rice, flour, potato . . .'

After he left, she took out the broom and swept the earth in front of the building. He soon returned with a carton. 'Is a good Chinee man,' he said. 'He gave me two dollars trust till pay day.'

'We shouldn' take too much credit. And,' she shot a glance at him, 'you shouldn't take any drinks on trust.'

BETWEEN TWO SEASONS

There were four houses in sight. Across the road in front of them stood a wooden house with a struggling hibiscus fence. About a hundred yards away was a small wooden bridge and beyond it was a hut with mud walls and a straw-covered roof. In a corner of the yard was a clump of banana trees with a few tall bamboo poles, flying faded flags. Swinging slowly in a hammock was a man patting a whimpering child. He was singing a hindi song in a monotonous whine.

'It must be hungry,' Manu called. He repeated the statement as the man turned.

'Naw, neighbour,' the voice was a deeper whine than the child's. 'You coun say she always get on so.'

'No work today?'

'Naw, neighbour. You coun say I ain't so well.'

'We jest movin' in.'

'Good, neighbour. Good. If you want anything you must come. You coun say we is neighbours.'

'Give it some suck, Gopaul,' said a voice from around the bend. Laughter came from a smaller group. A bony woman left the group and went and took up the child which immediately became quiet. Four children emerged and surrounded her. An older girl peeped from the kitchen.

The group's talking stopped as they saw the strangers.

Samdaye rose and went into the building. Manu went to the back to attend the calf. Furtive exploratory glances went back and forth.

Soon the smell of burning wood and smoke and a variety of dishes moved with the light breeze. Darkness fell abruptly. Flickering kerosene lamps made feeble indentations in the dark through open windows and doors. Crickets began an interminable shrill buzzing and, from the damp edges of the brook, bullfrogs and smaller frogs carried on a chorus of bell-like trilling and bellowing. Across the field thousands of fireflies twinkled. As Samdaye lay in the bed amid all these sounds the night still seemed empty for there was not the washing of the waves and the rustling of the palm leaves and the clean smell of the wind from the sea.

Chapter 3

The Yard was on a low hill that marked the beginning of a citrus field. On one side stood the overseer's house and on the other two large drying-houses. On the side away from the road was a stable with two horses, a bull and two cows. Manu was the first to arrive and he sat on the steps of one of the drying houses and lit a cigarette.

The sun was not yet visible but its light silhouetted the hills in the east. Some yellow-tails were pecking at the few ripening oranges while other birds swooped through the air or sat on branches whistling and chattering.

The rest of the workers arrived and nodded to Manu. They stood in a group and chatted softly. Gomez, the overseer soon approached and nodded in reply to their greeting.

'What happen? You all ain't know what you have to do this mornin'?' he called to them. 'We cutlassin' as usual.'

'But we thought . . . yesterday you say . . .' one of the men began.

'What I say yesterday?'

'We startin' the orange field.'

'Nuh, we have to finish the cocoa in River Piece. Then we will split up.'

Manu cleared his throat a few times. 'Is day-work we doin' or task-work?'

'Anybody mention task work?' Gomez asked.

'I prefer task-work,' Manu said.

'Nuh. I prefer day-work. Six to six. We ain't have no lazy people here.'

'But you get more done in task work,' Manu persisted. 'You set a man a piece of work and when he done, he done. He could go home and do something else. All about they stop

22

this day-work business. That is real lazy-man work. Whole day you beatin' the bush instead of cutlassin'.'

'Like we have a real debater here,' Gomez said. The rest of the group was becoming increasingly alarmed. 'Like you come here to make trouble,' the overseer continued. 'Like you want to be the overseer. Or maybe you must be some kind of union leader. You ain't do one day . . . not one minute work and already you playin' overseer.'

The workers had become quiet.

'Take him down and show him where you workin',' he turned on his heel and left.

'Don't cross him early in the mornin',' one of them cautioned Manu. 'Gomez is a madman, you know. He could send everybody back home just so and say no work today.'

'But you all don't do task? Day work is a waste of time.'

'Sometimes we do task.'

'Some work like pickin' cocoa is day work. But pickin' coffee is task. Or by the basket. You stop when you feel like it. This six-to-six business finish. It ain't have no estate that still do day-work.'

They passed through the freshly-cut area with the smell of the still-green grass and the damp earth. They each took a width of four cocoa trees and began swinging their curved 'swipers' hooking the grass with their crooksticks in their left hands and with the same motion, pulled the cut grass away.

Back at the barracks Samdaye bathed the boy, poured some coconut oil on his head and rubbed it in then rubbed her greased hands over his face and on his arms and legs including his feet. She sharpened his pencil, wiped his slate clean, put a sheet of brown wrapping paper over the cover of his 'First Primer' reading book, took out a new exercise book and wrote his name carefully in pencil, put everything in a thin bag she had made from left-over khaki, put the bag over his shoulder and said, 'Now Mr Mangal, we goin' to school.' She pulled him over her lap and continued, 'You goin' to be a good boy. You must listen to the teacher and work hard. You must learn your lesson. You must be the brightest in your class. Nobody must be brighter than you. Later, when you come a big man I want you to be a doctor, you hear?

A doctor. Doctor Mangal Hanuman. Eh? Ain't that sound nice? Doctor Hanuman. People will see you pass in your Ford car dress in your white jacket and a briefcase with your name print on it, Dr M. Hanuman. I don't want you to be no labourer on a cocoa estate, getting wet in the rain and burnin' in the sun, workin' like a dog and living from hand to mouth with not even a good pair of pants to cover your backside. I don't want you to live in no barrack in no poor-ass condition. So you goin' to listen to me?'

He nodded.

'And you goin' to listen to your teacher?'

He nodded again. He began to pull himself away from her as he saw some children on their way to school.

'Say yes.'

'Yes.'

'Yes, Ma.'

'Yes, Ma.'

'I will be the brightest boy.'

'I will be . . .' He slipped away and ran to join the group of children . . . 'the brightest,' he shouted.

'Wait. Come back here! Right now!'

He hesitated and returned slowly.

She washed her feet, hands and face, smoothed back her hair with her hands, slipped her feet into a pair of sandals, took a hold of his hand and walked with him to the school a little over a quarter of a mile away.

It was the Dorado Canadian Mission School, a wooden building about thirty-feet square. A short roof jutted just over the door in a feeble attempt to give it an imposing character and the appearance of a church. Along the edge of the road on both sides of the entrance to the school ran an ixora hedge neatly trimmed. Some white rocks lined the entrance. Two circular flower beds one on either side of the pathway lit the front of the building with arrangements of marigold, croton and hibiscus. This contrasted sharply with the rusted roof and the peeling and flaking paint on the greying walls. Pacing in front of the building was a balding, potbellied man who nodded stern-facedly at the arriving students. The small staff of four teachers arrived on bicycles.

Samdaye introduced her son and herself and asked if the boy could be taken in. He was one month short of his fifth birthday. He was admitted.

She returned to the barrack. She decided to plaster the floor of the kitchen. Finding a few cakes of fresh cow-dung she mixed this with clay and water and with her hand spread it on the ground. She repaired the broken stand in a corner with laths and pieces of broken boxes. On this stand she placed a four-inch layer of wet clay. Upon this layer she built an earthen stove with two openings.

She wanted the stove raised off the ground so that dogs would not crawl into the 'chulha' or stove in the night. She must get Manu to provide more privacy for the kitchen. She also needed a shelf for the food items and for the cooking wares. It would be so nice to have a food cupboard with wire mesh to keep out the flies and a glass-fronted portion to put her dishes. But that was for those who had pretty earthenware dishes not for tin cups and chipped enamel wares.

She noticed that nobody stayed in the barrack during the day. Now that Mangal was at school she felt alone. But Gopaul was back in his hammock humming to his child. He also had a daughter who seemed to be about fourteen and would occasionally relieve him of the child holding it astride her hip while she swept the grassless front of the house. Samdaye was about to walk across to meet the girl when she saw another child emerge. This one was about three with stringy, unkempt hair, a runny nose and a face that looked like that of a chicken which had been pecking at an over-ripe mango.

Back in the room she looked at the spaces between the boards in the partition and walls where the paper was torn. She would have to make some cassava starch and get some new paper. The best seemed to be the magazine pages with pretty coloured pictures that had held well and had not become brittle and brown like the newspapers. The coloured pictures advertised 'Lifebuoy Soap' and 'Kellog's Cornflakes'. On some pages were shiny cars and well-dressd men and women. With a far-away expression she passed her hand over the pictures.

She was surprised when she heard the voices of children and saw Mangal returning for lunch with other children.

'He get licks already,' one of the boys called out to her.

'You get licks, Mangal?' she asked. 'Who beat you?'

'The schoolmaster.' The boy continued, 'He screamed in the class. He shouted loud loud "A B C D E". He shouted the whole alphabet and the whole school get quiet.' The boy related how he was asked by the teacher to teach Mangal the alphabet from a large card. He asked Mangal to repeat each letter about five times after he called it. The teacher asked him to make Mangal do the alphabet several times.

'Ma, he make me say it over and over. And I already know the whole alphabet.' The tears started to well.

She hugged him and told him that he must not shout in the school and reminded how she had asked him to be a good boy.

'But, Ma, why he didn't ask me if I know the ABC? You know that I could read the ABC and I could read nearly half the book. But he didn't ask me.' His lips trembled. 'I not goin' back for that fat old man to beat me.'

She fed him and, with her arm around him, took him back to the school. She did not complain to the teacher.

Later when Manu returned from work she remarked how the boy was just like him. He was just as short-tempered.

'I should go and tap up the man. Imagine beatin' the boy the first day he go to school. And he is a schoolmaster. Mang,' he called, 'boy, like school ain't cut out for you and me.'

'Don't put that foolishness in the boy head, you hear,' she said fiercely. 'That boy will finish school even if I have to slave. He won't be like you leaving school in second primer just after two years. He not goin' to end up with a cutlass in his hand.'

'And what wrong with that? That is honest labour. I sweatin' for me livin'. As soon as people get education and put on collar and tie they become crook, t'ief and smart-man.' He had been sitting on the back step eating his dinner. 'No matter how high a man get in life he should know how to milk a cow, dig a drain, use a swiper and plant cassava. If you go up you could come down faster.'

26

'Some people, like when they go up in life, they on a greasy pole. They can't hold on. And sometimes they put the grease on the pole themself. And some people have no ambition. They quite happy to crawl about the ground like a worm. And even if they have wings they move about like chicken, they can't fly. They just go scratchin' and scratchin' in the dirt until somebody chop their neck and put them in a pot.'

He sucked air through his teeth in a long 'steu-u-ps', rose and went outside and sat on the root of the almond tree.

The sun had set but the sky still had a bluish haze. A flock of bats had oozed out from some dark roof and were zig-zagging like children in the schoolyard the first two minutes of inter-mission. Manu lit a cigarette and leaned against the trunk of the tree. He was soon joined by Prince and Gabi. Prince was frail-looking from afar but close up you could see the firmness of muscle in the arms that ended in large hands. Each finger looked like a thumb, thick, snub-ended and with a hard, coarse nail. His tightly crinkled greying hair had receded to the top of his head. From the top of his head to the tip of his bottom lip was an almost unbroken line that sloped about forty-five degrees. His chin fell back sharply. He smelled of rum. 'Come, Gabi, boy,' he invited 'come and meet the new neighbour.'

Gabi, a long-limbed youth of about sixteen, came slowly forward.

'Come and shake the man hand and tell him your name – Gabi, short for gabilan or chicken-hawk. And ask him his name.'

'How, Gabi?' Manu asked. 'I name Manu.'

'Mano?' Prince asked.

'Nuh. Manu. Noo.'

'First time I hear a name so.'

'The whole name is Manchand but nobody ever call me that except the teacher when I used to go to school.'

'I is Prince. And that is my real name. Prince William.'

'His father was King William,' Gabi said jokingly. 'King William of the Congo.' Gabi had to duck a blow from Prince but he was expecting it. 'One of these days you will hit me and I will crank your old tail, you know, Prince.'

'Well, you shouldn't talk foolishness.'

27

'You goin' to stay long?' Gabi asked.

'Mm-hmm. I ain't have nowhere else to go.' He told them about the places he had lived and worked, and how he always seemed to get into trouble with overseers.

'You shouldn't mess about with Gomez, eh. He is a madman. I don't know where the hell he come from. He only come here a few months ago. And he don't know one damn thing about cocoa estate. He doesn't plan the work so you really don't know what you doin' from day to day. You ain't see this mornin'? Yesterday he say that we startin' to clear the orange field today. This mornin' he change his mind. And the bugger like woman too bad. He got wife and children but he does run down any dress. Imagine he make a move on Gopaul wife. Now who in their right mind will get excited over that heap of bone? Nobody but Gomez. And he even try a thing on my wife! My wife who weigh about two hundred pound and have feet like ten-pound ham. No shoes could go around them feet. The heels go back as much as the front part. When she put one foot on the ground it does spread like asphalt in the sun.'

'Why you don't shut you mouth, Prince!' his wife joined the group. 'Why you don't buy a mirror and break it with you looks! Instead of askin' the man if we could help them with anything you tryin' to be funny.'

'I was just goin' to do that. I was just about to ask Manu if they want help to do anything.'

'No. We all right for now.'

'We could give you a hand on Saturday.'

'All I have to do is build a pen for the cow, bar round the kitchen from the dogs and chickens, fix the step and build some shelf. But I could do it little by little.'

'We will give you some help on Saturday. Eh, Gabi?'

'Before one. I have to go to my matinee show.'

'No matinee this Saturday. We have work to do.'

'What! And miss the best war double? "Bataan" and "Back to Bataan"! Man, you must be crazy. Miss John Wayne and Robert Taylor! Rat-tat-a-tat-a-tat.' He rolled on the ground and crouched behind a tree root. 'Pee-ooo pee-oo pe-ooo.'

Hearing the commotion, Mangal came outside.

Prince's wife tousled his head and asked his name and if he went to school.

'He get licks today,' his father said. 'His first day and the stupid schoolmaster beat him. But he is a tough man.'

'John Wayne, Robert Taylor, Anthony Quinn.' Gabi shouted. 'Them is toughmen. Toughmen father.'

'This is Miss Martina, Mangal,' Prince said to the boy. 'And this is Gabi. And my name is Mr Prince. And all of us is friends. Right? Now shake my hand.' He took the boy's hand.

The boy slipped his hand out and from behind his father's ear fired shots with his fingers at Gabi who was calling out the names of films and stars: 'West-of-the-Pecos-Sundown-Jim Hum-phrey-Bo-gart-Doretty-La-mo.'

Mangal threw himself on the ground and tried to imitate the sounds. His mother immediately called out, 'Stop that, Mangal. And come in here right away! And you wash your foot already?' She came down the steps. 'You finish read your lesson for tomorrow?'

The boy dragged his feet and walked backwards in a wide arc to the steps. 'Pee-ow pee-ow,' he shouted as he ran inside.

Samdaye came to the group and was introduced by Manu. She quickly returned to her room saying that she had to help Mangal with his school work.

'So what happen to the last overseer?' asked Manu.

'He left. He gone to Port of Spain and I hear that he open some business – some import business.' Prince pointed to the cocoa field, 'He say cocoa dead.'

'How he mean "cocoa dead"?'

'Is true, man, cocoa dead. It dead dead. Since the war when the Yankee come here and open the base and everybody went for their dollar, cocoa dead. Nobody want to work for the kind of money the planters used to pay. And the Yankees offerin' five dollars a day. I hear that they was goin' to pay ten but our govarment tell them they can't pay so much. But that time the estate used to pay one dollar fifty. Man, everybody left every kind of work: teachin', clerkin', burnin' coals. All man goin' for dollars.' He turned to his wife. 'I tellin' lie, Tina?'

'No. Is true. We was livin' right here. Even we went to work on the base.'

'Well, the base was right here, you know. Look, the entrance was not far from the end of this village. The two big pile of rock and the pine tree by the sentry gate still there.'

'Dorado was a real boom town,' the woman said.

'Boom-Town!' Gabi said. 'Clark-Gable and Spencer-Tracy. Potow-pow!'

'The money used to flow like water. Dorado had a few rum shop. The junction used to be busy with soldiers – black and white. And the girls that used to come here from all over the country . . . all over the islands . . . Grenada, St. Vincent, St. Lucia.'

'And what happen?' asked Manu.

'Gone, all gone.'

'Gone-wit-the-win'. Clark-Gable-Vivien-Leege. That was flim!'

'Why you don't hush you' mouth, Gabi.' Martina said, 'Everything is a filmshow.'

'The money moved through Dorado like a flood in the rainy season. Just how fast the people come and put up shacks and business place just so they leave. With the same speed the Yankee come and gone. All they leave here is chewin' gum and children of all colour. And coco-cola.'

'Rum an' coco-cola kill the Yankee soldier. . .'

'A lotta people get rich but not in Dorado. Here everything went to ruin. The cocoa estate, the barracks, the forest . . .'

They fell silent. The sky was now filled with stars and the only thing that seemed to exist in the liquid dark was the twinkling in the heavens and the echoing twinkling of the fireflies. Not too far away an owl hooted.

'Tomorrow will be hot like hell', Prince observed.

Chapter 4

The sun's first rays melted the mist nestling between the hills and seeped through cracks in the walls. The dew lay white like frost on the grass. Blue smoke rose from the kitchens. From among the almond branches yellow-tails screeched and chattered noisily.

On Saturdays the estate workers had measured tasks. They got into the fields before sunrise so that their work could be completed before eleven o'clock. Some of them would spend their afternoons in the rum shop while others would go to their vegetable plots. Today they had promised to help the new tenants.

Immediately after lunch they began. They nailed strips of an old tyre on the doors to act as hinges and repaired the floor and walls. Newspapers were pasted on the inside with glue made from cassava starch. Samdaye spread another coat of clay and cow-dung on the kitchen floor. Prince split some small branches and wove them to make a wall that reached about half way up to the kitchen. Manu and Gabi mixed liquid clay and grass, and plastered the wall.

They built a lean-to for the calf and covered it with the very large leaves of the 'carat' palm.

The sun had dipped behind the trees when they finally sat down on the almond roots and opened a bottle of rum bought by Manu. A few parrots, homeward-bound, squawked on the wing.

'No drink for you, Gabi. You too young for this,' Prince said.

'I not too young to do the work, though', Gabi protested. 'And I even miss the matinee flim. The best double of the year.'

'We'll let him have one, then', Manu told Prince.

'Thanks, Manu. You could recognize a big man.' He took the bottle and with a flourish unscrewed the cork. He then tipped the bottle and let a few drops fall to the ground. 'For the spirit,' he announced. He passed the bottle to Prince without taking any. 'This is for all-you rum-suckers.'

A shadow of anger flashed over Manu's face. He took the small, heavy one-ounce glass, filled it and threw the rum into his mouth and at the same time tossing his head back in an easy movement in which the glass did not touch his lips. He filled the glass with water and threw it back the same way. He passed the glass to Prince.

'I don't drink no cheap rum,' announced Gabi. 'I drink whisky. Like John-Wayne. Straight from the bottle. I walk up to the bar just so,' he imitated the swaying, slightly sideways walk of Wayne, wrinkled his brows, adjusted an imaginary gunbelt and pretended to pound on the counter. 'Whisky,' he said.

'Gabi, why you don't grow up?' Prince looked at Gabi leaning against the trunk of the tree. 'You ever see a black man with a gunbelt and drinkin' in any bar in a cowboy film?'

'Who said they didn't have black cowboys?' asked Gabi.

'You ever see any?'

'They must have black cowboys. They have black people all over America.'

'But you don't see black people where you have white people. Was the same thing wit' the Yankee soldiers here in the base. Black soldiers and white soldiers didn't stay in the same camp.'

'Well I will be the first black cowboy. And when I buy my six-shooter and my Winchester '73 I comin' like James Stewart an' I drillin' you so full-a-holes you will sink in a basin-a-water.' He had heard this line in some film. 'You hear, Prince, old man?'

'But look at this little boy. You think you ripe! Like your pee makin' froth or what.'

'I want a piece of land to make a garden,' Manu said suddenly. 'I want to plant some corn and cassava. Anybody here make garden?'

'Yes,' Prince replied. 'A few people make garden. Gopaul wife and daughter.'

'What happen to Gopaul?'

'He say he is a artist. He don't do no hard work.'

'He don't do no work at all?'

'Yes. He does make crowns for hindu bridegrooms and decorate their wedding gowns. He does decorate weddin' tents, too. He does also help the pundit with ceremonies. Beat the gong, ring the bell and light the fire.'

'And he go about givin' the weddin' invitations,' Gabi added.

'He make any money out of that?' Manu enquired.

'Looks so. He always got some job to do. And he is good. Everybody say he is the best. When he put them beads and string ixora flowers and stick pieces of glass that crown look like a million dollars.'

'But what about the land?' Manu continued. 'I want about a half-acre. The estate rent any land?'

'They have some abandon cocoa land you could use. They don't charge rent. But I don't know what Gomez will do whether he will ask for rent.'

'The owner have no say?'

'Who, Petit Pierre? Since his father died five years ago I don't know if he come ten times. Old man Pierre used to come every week. He used to ride around the estate on his horse with a machete round his waist like any labourer and a big cork-hat on his head. Any Friday mornin' you could find him somewhere on the estate choppin' a dry branch from a cocoa tree or removin' wild pine. The man knew every piece of the land and you could see how he loved it. The old man was born on this land you know. His father come here from Haiti after the slave revolt he used to say. The British govarment was encouragin' planters and the French had good experience as farmers in Haiti. He get the land for next to nothing. Papa Pierre, so we used to call him, but not to his face, though. We used to say Monsieur Pierre. He say when his father come here the main road was just a dirt track. They had no house, no cultivation, nothing. This place was just forest. He build the house Gomez livin' in about a hundred years ago. And this was one of the slave barracks.'

'You talkin' about Papa Pierre grandfather,' Gabi interrupted.

'How you know?'

'The Old Man tell me so himself.'

'What happen, he was your pal or what?'

'A-A. You know how many time he take me up on his horse. He used to call me "Papa Nice Boy". We used to go all over the bush. He used to tell me all kind of stories. His grandfather was some kind of Comte and had a lot slaves in Haiti. He had lands in France, too. But he had two wife and the one in France take all the land in France.'

'Petit Pierre have no time for land,' Prince said. 'He and some white people open some big business in town. They bringin' in motor-cars and parts. I even hear he want to sell "La Louise". That is the name of this estate.'

'Who could have so much money?' asked Manu.

'It will go cheap,' Prince said. 'Nobody want cocoa estate these days.'

'Miss Martina,' Manu called, 'you not comin' out and fire one? You well help me out today.'

'I thought I wasn't goin' to get invite,' she said as she came and stood. 'I only takin' one. I feelin' tired. Samdaye,' she called, 'you not takin' a little one?'

Samdaye said that she did not drink. Her husband did it for both of them. There was an edge to her voice.

From some distance away toward the junction a dog began barking furiously. From behind the barrack another gave two thin yelps as if to signal its being awake. The barking drew nearer as others took up the relay until crunching footsteps were heard round the corner. A tall, stooping figure appeared.

'Is Compai,' Gabi announced.

The man joined them and they welcomed him with a drink. Manu was introduced to him and his presence was explained.

'You stay long this time, Compai,' Gabi remarked.

'Well, the old man does lose track of time. I intend this time to spend about two-three days as usual.'

'But you was gone nearly two weeks!'

Manu wondered if the old man was the one promised

the room. He asked Prince who seemed surprised. Nobody had asked for any room. Gomez was lying as usual. Compai shared with Gabi. Manu felt his conscience cleared and he took another drink.

Prince explained Compai's name which was really Pacheco but he called everyone 'compadre' but with his missing teeth it came out as 'compai'. He was a real 'pagniol' from Venezuela and was the oldest head in the village.

Compai had given several stories about how he came to Trinidad and how he ended up in Dorado. The one most repeated was that he had been brought in a pirogue from Guiria in Venezuela just across from Cedros in South Trinidad. He had been brought by his mother who was from Trinidad. His father, a Venezuelan fisherman, had settled in Cedros where he had met his mother, got her pregnant and took her to Venezuela where Compai was born. After a few years his mother was left to fend for herself and two little children, the other being a baby girl. So she had returned to Cedros.

Compai had become a fisherman like his father. Later he became a sailor on a Venezuelan boat working the Caribbean coast up to New Orleans in the United States, and Cuba and Santo Domingo in the east. It was after one of his trips that had lasted for over one year that he had returned to find that his mother had died and that his sister had married a visiting Venezuelan sailor just as his mother had done. An argument had ensued and Compai had been driven out of the house. His boat had left Port of Spain so he could not go back to sea for two months so he decided to put distance between himself and Cedros. This is how he ended up in Dorado. His brother-in-law had long since left his sister with one daughter. And now and then Compai would visit her and spend a few days.

He could not live in Cedros. The call of the sea was too strong there and he was bound to go back to the life of a fisherman. The alternative was working on a coconut estate and he had seen too many people with missing fingers from having to chop open hundreds of thousands of nuts.

In Dorado he was living rent-free. He had learned the simple skills required of a worker in the cocoa estate. He could swing the long handled 'swiper' in rhythmic circular movements of the arm while in his left hand the crook stick gathered the grass and brush to be cut, and removed them after they were cut with the same continued movement. In the cool shade of the cocoa field he could soon work with the best. He could manipulate the cocoa rods deftly pushing the blade end or pulling with the hooked portion the richly-coloured ripe pods or the spoilt black pods or the twigs and branches to be trimmed or removed. At a glance he could tell which branches had started to develop 'witches' broom', which branch would grow and not bear, and which branches should be 'thinned'. He knew the angle he should pull a laden coffee branch so that the beans could be got at without the branch breaking. He knew how to run the drains in the citrus field to conserve water or to prevent water-logging; when it should run in contour line and when it should go down a hill.

He had cleared forest trees and underbrush, burnt them, and had grown pigeon peas, corn, cassava and yams. At crop time he had taken these to sell them wholesale in the Port of Spain Market leaving at seven o'clock in the evening so that he could be sure to get a good location for the vegetable vendors at five in the morning.

Going deep into the forest at the foothills of the Northern Range he had burnt charcoal pits and had tasted both the success of pulling a full pit of coals, and the disappointment of having a pit 'burst' and see the black smoke rushing through the thick clay covering, signifying the reduction of the wood to ashes, and the loss of his labour.

And when he had started to feel the result of advancing age, when his shoulder joint had become stiff and he was no longer able to swing the swiper in a complete circle, and he did not have the strength to lift a bag of cocoa pods or a basket of wet beans, he had worked the drying-house raking the beans in the sun and picking out the bad ones. This was now the only work he did except growing a few vegetables for his own use. But he was never short of food. Like so many of the estate workers he would take whatever he wanted from the estate – bananas or breadfruit – whenever the need arose.

'So we have a new tenant, eh? Well, what I will tell you? Welcome. You livin' alone?'

'He got a wife,' Prince said.

'Pregnant,' Martina added.

'And a son,' Gabi said.

'Wife in the family way, eh? Prince, we will have a grand-child soon. Martina, I think that you forget how to mind child. You will have to remember how to tie diaper and sing lullaby. I don't know what Gabi could do.'

'Catch chicken for chicken soup,' Prince cut in.

'Why you don't hush your mouth, Prince,' Gabi snapped.

'I never tell you how Gabi does thief chicken, Manu. He is the best fowl thief in the world. The quietest.' Prince turned to Gabi. 'What about a chicken pelau tonight, Gabi.'

'One of these days I will wring your neck, Prince.'

'Good thing you didn't bring any chicken, Manu. You see Saturday night? Watch out for your chicken. They don't make a cluck. He got a way with them. Like they follow him as soon as they see him. He always go about with corn on Saturday night.'

'Leave the boy alone,' Compai said. 'You always provokin' him. One of these days he will break your tail.'

'Tell him that, Pops. He don't know I could fix him up good already.'

'Oh ho ho!' Prince laughed. 'But look at my crosses! Wait till you become man.'

'That will be sooner than you think,' Compai cut in. 'You know how time fly.'

'But it is true. Gabi is the best chicken-holder. Here, tee tee tee, here,' he pretended that he was feeding chickens. 'Pax! Pax!' He caught imaginary chickens. 'Every Sunday and sometimes late Saturday night you could smell chicken stew in Gabi kitchen.'

'O God, Prince you could lie!' Gabi looked at Compai the whites of his eyes enlarged in the dark. 'Pops, you could say that is not true.'

'Tee tee tee.'

'Enough, Prince.'

'Come. Come .. ah.ah.tee.tee.tee.pax .. pax!' Prince lunged at Gabi and grabbed for his pocket. 'Show Manu your corn, boy.'

Gabi was caught in a firm grip.

'Puck-puck-puck-aaaak-puck-puck.'

Manu began to get concerned when Gabi tried to grip Prince's neck. 'Leave him, Prince. Gabi ain't want to make joke tonight.'

But the wrestling continued. Prince's slight build was deceptive. He had Gabi firmly in his grip. The boy's arms were flailing in rising anger. After a while the man let the boy go. 'You really gettin' strong, fella. You will really break my tail soon.'

'You can't worry with those two,' Compai advised. 'Every day they get on so.'

'You ain't see that I don't take them on,' Martina said.

Gabi had got up and was dusting himself. He went across to the steps leading to Manu's room. 'Mangal,' he called. 'Mangos, is too soon to sleep. Come and talk to me.'

The boy appeared in the doorway. 'Come and sit down,' he shifted and made a place beside him on the step. Mangal had his book in his hand. 'Let us play "picture or no picture"', the little boy said. Gabi agreed. He closed the book and asked Mangal, 'Picture or no picture.' And when the reply was 'picture' he admitted that he had lost and passed the book to Mangal whose turn it was to ask the question. Gabi knew that every page had a picture in the First Primer so he called out 'no picture' and the boy's laughter rang in victory. Gabi soon discovered that Mangal also knew that every page contained a picture for he always called correctly, 'picture'.

An engine and the grinding of tyres on the gravel was heard before the light of a car appeared round the bend. A small cloud of dust followed the car, lit by the reflected light. A soft gurgle of the liquid in the glass and the smacking of lips sounded occasionally. The voices rose in proportion to the diminishing of the contents of the bottle.

A few passersby were invited by Prince for a drink. He loudly introduced Manu and clapped him on the back saying what a good fellow he is. 'And he is rebellious, too. He want Gomez to give everybody task-work if they want.'

'That is better for everybody,' Manu said. 'The estate will get more work done and we could get more time to do things to make extra dollars. This is a damn foolishness dragging you'self for the whole day for a few dollars.' Manu's voice was rising. 'We have to change some t'ings. We not sheep or cattle. The base come and gone, the money come and gone, and we back with the same condition from overseers. The day for the slave and the bound-coolie done. If we threaten strike –'

'See what I tell you?' Prince pointed out.

'A revolutionist,' Compai said, 'bravo, a revolutionist!'

'Fire one drink for the revolution . . . for the rebel,' Prince raised his glass. 'Next t'ing you will form a union.'

'And what wrong with that?'

'Bravo!'

'That will cause trouble. Big trouble.'

'For who? For the estate. Not for me. Not for you. We could find labourer work anywhere but is not easy to find people to work cocoa for this little money.'

'We have to be t'ankful for what we got,' Prince said.

'True,' Martina added. 'We can't jump about and make trouble. I mean, we livin' free. We gettin' fig and breadfruit, and orange and thing, for nothing. We have to add that up. Is not only the wages, you know.'

Manu was shaking his head. 'That is how they ride us. A little something here, a little something there. And we get fooled.'

'The boy is right,' Compai said. 'Workers have to fight for a better deal. Nobody will give you anything just so.'

'Especially estate owners,' Manu agreed. 'I not askin' for more money – and God know we deserve more – I just feel we would do better workin' task-work. The estate would get their work done and the worker could have more time for himself. Just now I will have two children and I have to see about them. I can't bring them up in the barrack especially if I have more.' He lowered his voice. 'My wife will kill me. She want her own house.'

'So what about your father-in-law?' Martina asked. 'He ain't give you land? All Indian people does give their son-in-law something. You ain't get dowry?'

Manu laughed. 'My father-in-law, poor fellow dead now. He was a labourer on a coconut estate in Manzanilla. He had a little house but no land. And he had five children to bring up.'

'So when you makin' this move about task-work?' Prince asked. 'We have to do things together.'

'I givin' Gomez one more week.'

The sound of a bell was heard and a voice calling, 'Come to the meetin'. Come and hear the words of the Lord.' The Gopaul baby began a loud bawling. 'Repent! O sinners, repent!' The voice rose above the clanging and the crying.

'Have a drink first, Sheppy,' Prince invited.

'Don't be rude, Prince. Come and save your soul.' He looked at the group. 'Martina, you have to help in the singin'.'

Prince explained to Manu that Shepherd had a job with a road-working gang, weeding the grass verges and clearing the road-side drains. His name was really Richardson . . . something Richardson . . . or Richardson something. However, on Saturdays he preached at the junction. He was a Shouter Baptist. Most villages had them. This evening Sheppy was preaching under Japan's shop in the junction.

'You alone, tonight, Shep?' Martina asked.

'Nah. Some people comin' from Arima.' He shook his bell. His long white gown seemed luminous in the dark. 'Come down to the junction, all-you.'

Half an hour later the group followed. Japan's shop was still open, the gas light hissing, but there were only three men in the rum-shop area, sitting on heavy wooden stools with an empty bottle before them.

With the gathering of the people Japan closed the shop then went to a window that he had cut into the wall, and from which he could serve late-comers. His pale face, back-lit and framed by the small window, looked like a portrait.

Shepherd had been joined by two women preachers. Spread on the ground before them was a piece of white cloth on which stood a small Indian brass jug in which was stuck sprigs of marigold and hibiscus. On both sides of the cloth, flambeaux made with bottles filled with kerosene and topped with cloth wicks, threw waving flames with thin black lines of smoke. Shepherd's white gown was tied at the waist with a cord that dangled to the ground. He stood barefooted, Bible in hand. The women wore white gowns with white head-ties. Each had a hibiscus twig with a few red flowers.

Martina signalled a refusal to an invitation from Shepherd to join the group. He understood. She had probably taken a drink of rum.

Shepherd waited till the talk and laughter lessened then, clearing his throat noisily, he began as he always did, 'Brothers, brothers and sisters, I ain't have a voice like an archangel and I can't preach like Paul. I just come to bring the words of the Lord.' He welcomed them and introduced the 'sisters' who would soon address them. He began a prayer which was punctuated by the women with loud shouts of 'Amen' and 'Yes, Lord.'

Manu whispered to Prince that he could do with a drink. The bottle had been finished. Before Prince's objection could be heard, he went to the window which was at the side of the building away from the preaching and returned with a small, square bottle which held about four ounces of rum. 'I bring a nip.' They moved from the group and went a few yards away to a low concrete wall at the side of the road. This was not before Martina shot a fierce scowl at Prince.

'We could hear the preachin' from here just as good,' Manu said.

A soft breeze wafted by bringing a heavy scent of perfume. This was followed by a woman whose body stretched tightly her large-flowered dress.

'Good night, Doris,' Prince greeted her.

'A-A Prince, how you sitting down in the dark so?' she replied. 'You 'fraid the Bible? You is Satan, or what?'

'I with my friend, Manu. He new here. He just come to live in the barrack.' He nudged Manu. 'This is Doris, the nicest woman in Dorado.'

'Don't worry with Prince, mister. He full of flattery.' She put her hand under Prince's chin. 'You better don't let Martina hear you.'

As she continued to the meeting Prince said, 'Now you will see some bacchanal. Before half an hour you will see Gomez. That is his woman.' He explained how the woman had a husband who worked in a Port of Spain hotel. 'Boy, that Gomez is a real devil.'

'Somebody will do for his ass one day,' Manu said.

It was not long afterwards that Gomez arrived. The woman

41

spent a few more minutes then walked silently by. With heads bowed as Shepherd prayed they did not see when Gomez passed. Only when the prayer was over did Prince dig Manu in his ribs and point to the two dark shapes merging in the distant pitchy shadow.

The group had dispersed and Shepherd had collected the few coins thrown on the white cloth, wrapped up the cloth, thrown the sprigs of flowers, blown out the flambeaux, and taken up his bell which clanged as he lifted it. Japan had closed his window and the junction joined the darkness.

Samdaye looked at Manu who said, 'I had to treat the people, you know. They worked hard whole day. Is just one bottle I take on credit.' When she did not take her eyes away from him he added, 'and a little nip for Prince at the junction'.

Manu lay on his bed, his arms folded behind his head. He settled himself more comfortably, the liquor giving him a warm flush of well-being. As he closed his eyes his head spun in an increasing rhythm and he opened them quickly to steady the movement. He could not understand how Samdaye could grudge his taking a little drink. A man needed a drink on a weekend especially after a week of hard work. As his eyes became accustomed to the dark he watched the regular rise and fall of his wife's abdomen. Now that was another problem that would soon arise. How could a man make progress when mouths were increasing in his house. And what is this constant harping on getting one's own house. This place was comfortable. It was at least better than the little hut in Manzanilla. He certainly was not going to kill himself with work. A man must be satisfied sometime. He had seen so many people slave themselves to make more and more, and the more they made the less they seemed to be content. At forty they had become old. It must be Samdaye's mother who was pushing her to get her own house and land. Where the hell was he supposed to get all that money to buy land and build house. Not on fifteen dollars a fortnight. He closed his eyes again but the roof still spun.

The crow of a cock broke the stillness. It was the start of a chorus of echoing crows. Now that gave him an idea. He could have Samdaye mind some chickens which meant that he would have to plant some corn. And suppose his chickens get stolen. That is just looking for worries and who the hell want to have to worry about losing chickens on top of everything.

The more you had the more you worried. He thought he nodded with that bit of wisdom.

'Prince,' he called.

'What?'

'You sleepin'?'

'Mmm mmm.'

'The more you have the more you does worry.'

Samdaye stirred and mumbled something.

Now suppose he had the money to buy land, where is the piece to buy? He began to visualize all the vacant places where he would like to build a house. The best piece was near the school where the land rose near a clump of mango trees. But it might cost a couple hundred dollars and that was too much to think about. Suppose the calf gets pregnant and has a bull, he could sell it and might make fifty dollars. He shut his eyes tight and fell asleep.

Chapter 5

Manu rose in the pink wash of dawn. A grey mist hung between the trees. Moving quickly in the cool stirring of a morning breeze he took the calf out and tethered it to a tuft of grass, then he cleaned out the pen. At the edge of the field he found a few twigs from which he broke a piece, chewed one end and began to brush his teeth. At the end of the brushing he split it and scraped his tongue making loud, hawking noises. The sweetish pith of the wood left an improved taste in his mouth. He turned to find his son at his elbow. He broke a piece of the wood and gave it to him and took the rest to Samdaye who had already lit the fire.

From across the road came the sound of loud shouting and the crying of a child. Gopaul's wife was whipping one of her sons. 'Out,' she screamed, 'out! What you mean by still sleepin'? You have the yard to sweep and to get things ready. The pundit comin' early. German, boy, you really lazy, yes. Poland, you go and get the fig leaf. Stalin! Sta-a-lin. But where this boy gone already?' She moved around the house whip in hand shouting orders. 'Aye,' she called her husband, 'move quickly, man. You ain't bathe yet?'

Gabi was rubbing his eyes and squinting at the sky. 'O God, that woman mouth big. And she so skinny. A man can't sleep on a Sunday mornin'.' He spied Manu. 'How you get up so early? Your bed wet or what?'

A small brown dog with a large head came shyly forward its head lowered and its tail wagging furiously. Gabi bent and patted it on the head.

On being asked whose dog it was Gabi replied that he really did not know. He saw it wandering in the junction so he gave it a piece of bread. It then followed him home and has been back twice. 'I call him Mussolini. Come, boy, Musso.'

Mangal edged toward the dog. 'It ain't have no owner?' Gabi shook his head from side to side. 'I could have it?' His pointed finger cautiously neared the animal.

'Is not mine, you know,' Gabi said.

'I could have it, then?'

'Suppose somebody claim it.'

'I won't give it. Why they didn't mind it? If they mind it good it wouldn't run away with anybody.' He was now touching the dog which was rubbing itself against the boy's leg. 'It like me.'

'You could afford to mind dog, son?' Samdaye called.

'I ain't get it yet, Ma.'

'You know what?' Gabi said, 'We will mind it together.'

'Well . . . but I must give it a name, too.'

'How you could have a dog with two name.'

'People have two name.'

'But Mussolini is already a long name for a little dog.'

'Musso Lini is not two name?'

'We could make it in two. I call it Musso and you call it Lini.'

'I don't like that name. I like Hero. I know a dog name "Hero". Hero,' he called. 'Hero.' The dog shook its tail more vigorously. 'You see how it like that name. I will call it "Hero".' He ran about the house calling the dog by the new name while the dog chased him.

'It doesn't stay here all the time, you know,' Gabi said 'The first day he follow me here then he went somewhere. Only this mornin' I see him again. I think somebody will come for him.'

'I won't let anybody take him,' the boy said defiantly. He stooped and rubbed his hands under the chin of the dog which curled itself trying to get between his legs and under him.

'Mangal,' his mother called, 'what you doin' with that stink dog? That dog is smellin' from here. That dog look like it got mange.'

'Gabi,' Manu called, 'where you get that pot-hound from? What you don't chase it away? Mash, dog.' He threw a stick at the animal. 'Mash!' He stamped his foot on the ground. The dog slid its feet forward and, stretching its head, rested it on its paws. It kept wagging its tail and now began a mournful whine. 'Gwan!' Manu yelled.

The boy held onto the dog and began to cry.

'You finish washing your mouth?' Manu asked the boy who did not reply. 'Go and finish washin' your mouth and wash your hands.'

Gabi looked on helplessly while Manu pried the boy from the animal and led him in the house while he kicked and yelled then hung his legs limply.

Manu returned and chased the dog away. It went to the edge of the road and, tilting its head, looked appealingly at Gabi.

After a while Gabi picked up a stone and threw it at the dog which retreated slowly with a demeanour of total rejection. He turned to see Mangal peeping through a crack in the wall. 'Go dog. Go on you stinkin' dog,' he said loudly as he threw another stone. He had one stone left in his hand and he threw it at a yellow-breasted bird on the rose-mango tree in the centre of the field.

'Stalin! Sta-a-l-a-a-in! Your bring the flowers?'

'Comin', Ma.' The boy passed quickly with a spray of crimson bougainvillea, a few hibiscus flowers and some ixora.

'German, you bring the milk?'

Mangal came out with a bucket and a calabash. He went to the barrel and filled his bucket. He splashed the water and rubbed his naked body angrily with the cake of blue washing soap. He was still crying. His crying grew louder as soap got into his eyes. He threw the soap into the field.

'I watchin' you, boy, I watchin' you.' Manu warned. 'You goin' for that soap right away . . . right away.'

The boy went and retrieved the soap.

Compai appeared in the doorway. 'You make coffee yet, Gabi?'

Gabi went inside.

Prince came out in his underpants. 'This place noisy, yes. And the sun just comin' up. Gabi, what was all that noise about? Somebody killin' somebody? All this bawlin' on a Sunday mornin'.'

'Laziness will kill some people,' Gabi announced. 'If some people didn't drink rum late in the night they could get up early. And their face wouldn't look so ugly.'

Prince and Gabi carried on their usual banter while Compai laughed loudly at anything that was particularly funny.

Who-o-o-p. Who-o-o-o-p. A conch shell sounded from Gopaul's house. This was followed by the banging of a small gong and the tinkling of a bell.

'Gopaul havin' puja again,' Prince said. 'As if we don't have enough noise.'

'Your mouth watering for the "prasad", though,' Gabi said.

On hearing the sounds of the prayers Samdaye went to the front of the building and looked over the half-door. She fancied she could smell the incense and the burning cedar chips. The rising and falling of the pundit's drone was a soothing sound and she could imagine her mother sitting on the earth like Gopaul's wife in a white dress and 'orhni' draped over her head and her open palms filled with flowers. She could see the 'tharia' – the brass plate with flowers and bits of fruit, bananas and coconut and the small fire with the scent of burning ghee rising with the curling smoke. Above their heads the flags were weakly stirring on the long bamboo poles: red flags, and blue, and white. On poles that had been planted one year apart. Her mother would have had more poles than years for she offered prayers on every occasion she considered important. She must have a 'puja' for 'divali' the festival of lights, when every corner of the house would be cleaned and fresh cow-dung plaster would be applied; when new curtains would be hung and new clothes made, and when flowers would be put under the portrait of Lakshmi Mata and good fortune entreated of her.

Her mother would suddenly decide to have a 'puja' and, when questioned about the reason would reply, 'Beti, you don't have to have reason to pray to God. If I could afford I go have 'puja' every morning. Is a nice feelin'. All-you must have 'puja' too when all-you get married and go in your own house. You must not forget God. And you can't forsake the religion. Religion is the only thing to give you strength to face this life.'

Samdaye could hear her mother's voice clearly with her

frequent admonitions to have the pundit visit and hold prayers. She had been married more than five years and had never once heeded that advice. Manu had never practised the religion and she had neglected to make any effort to have him find a pundit and invite him to visit. She wondered what her husband would say if she invited the pundit.

She strained her ears to catch the sanskrit recitation that she could not understand but which filled her with an indescribable feeling and created a knot in her stomach. She craned her neck to see what the pundit was doing now. And then she closed her eyes to hear the mixture of the chanting and the ringing of the gong and the bell and the breakers in Manzanilla.

The mud hut with the thatched roof and the flags in the corner with the freshly-swept yard, with the mango tree at the side and the golden-apple tree at the back, with the clump of banana trees near the bamboo poles; with the straggling hibiscus plant and the cluster of marigolds; all gave her a sense of yearning for a place of her own like this.

'Wha' happen, lady? Like you forget breakfast or what?' Manu's voice broke into her reverie.

After breakfast Manu sat on the steps smoking a cigarette. He saw the pundit approaching pushing his bicycle. He looked much younger than in the distance although his head was balding and his hair greying. His thick, handlebar moustache covered his upper lip. It was his round, metal-frame glasses that gave him an older appearance. He leaned the bicycle at a sharp angle to prevent his dhoti becoming entangled in the unprotected chain.

'Ram Ram Sita Ram, beta.'

'Sitaram, pundit.' He quickly dropped the cigarette and put his palms together. He rose and went down the steps, and, relieving the man of the bicycle took it and leaned it against the tree. He wondered if he should remove the heavy bag hanging from the handlebar of the bicycle.

Samdaye saved him the embarrassment of finding a seat for the pundit. She came beaming down the steps wiping her hands on the hem of her dress, then joining them together, she greeted him with bowed head. He blessed her and she invited him inside. She had no table or chairs and offered him the small bench while she sat on the floor. Her husband sat on the low stool. Mangal shied from the strange-looking man and sidled up to his mother.

'What is your name, son?' he asked the boy.

'Mangal, tell "Baba" your name,' Samdaye urged.

'Mangal . . . Mangal . . .' he mused. 'Mangal what? Come, tell "Baba", Mangal what.'

The boy was now standing at the back of the woman resting his chin on her shoulder. 'Mangarram-mm-nn,' he mumbled moving the upper part of his head.

'Hanuman,' Manu offered. 'My name is Manchand. Samdaye,' he pointed to his wife.

'Gopal Ramdass say you come from Manzanilla. Who is your family there?'

Manu gave his father's name but it was unfamiliar to the pundit. Samdaye then said who her father was. A light of recognition lit the man's face. 'Yes . . . Yes,' he nodded. 'Raghu "bhai". Ain't he dead now? Yes. Yes. I remember him well. I do a few puja for his wife.'

'That is my mother,' Samdaye said.

'Oh what a good lady. Every year she had "puja".' He turned to Manu. 'You is Hindu?'

Manu hesitated before nodding.

'Like you not sure,' the pundit twiddled his big toes. He had left his slippers by the door. He raised his eyes, 'I used to know a Hanuman Singh in Fishing Pond. But that was long ago. The last time I hear of him he had moved to Cumuto. Big, strong man with one son. He used to be movin' a lot.'

'I think that is himself,' Manu nodded. 'My father was just like that.'

'Dasheen don't bear tannia,' Samdaye said. 'This one,' she pointed with her head to her husband, 'is jest the same. He can't stay in one place.'

Manu flashed a quick scowl which did not escape the priest who told him that his family was now getting bigger and that he should begin serious planning. He must think about the children. They were the future and must get a better break than their parents. Each generation must improve conditions. He told him that his wife had come from a good Hindu family and that he must keep up the religion for the sake of the

49

children, at least. You have to give children guidance in religion or they will have no religion and that there was nothing worse than not having a religion. That was being a 'no-where-ian'. And the Presbyterians were converting more and more Hindus. Some were becoming Roman Catholics and some had fallen away completely. He told them they had good Hindu names; Hanuman was of great help to Ram when he was in exile and had all the best qualities of man and monkey and could fly through the air with the greatest speed. The Hindus had to fight on every front or they would disappear. Isn't it possible that the coming of the Hindus to the New World was not accidental; that it had very little to do with planting cane? Imagine these were the first children of India to come across the Atlantic to meet others who were wrongly taken for the children of India. Did the Indians not come to take their rightful place as West Indians and so stretch their strain from east to west; to bring their unique culture and to teach their ancient religion; to spread the great wisdom of the gods to those who would never have encountered this? What a betrayal it would be if Hindus were not only to fail to make use of this unique opportunity but to desert and abandon their 'dharma'.

He then began to explain the main pillars of Hinduism: action and belief.

Manu began to feel uncomfortable. His eyes wandered through the window to the rusty brown flowers and the soft green young leaves of the rose-mango trees. He could not take responsibility for the whole of the Hindu religion. He had enough troubles of his own. In fact he did not know if he really was Hindu. He shifted in his seat.

The pundit became silent.

The boy whispered something in his mother's ears and giggled. The giggle stopped as he felt his mother's pinch.

The pundit rose and blessed them, then he went to the door. Manu was already at the entrance his palms joined in farewell. But before the man could depart Samdaye had come with a brown paper bag in which she had put about two pounds of rice and a pound of potatoes. She offered this to the man who joined his palms with the bag clutched between and offered gratitude. When he had disappeared round the corner on his bicycle the boy asked, 'Why the man dress so funny?'

Samdaye slapped him across the mouth.

'Why you give him all the food?' Manu asked.

'The man is a priest. The man can't come to your house and leave empty-handed. And you, Mangal, don't ever let me hear you laugh at no pundit, you hear?' She waved a pointed finger at the boy. 'The next time I will mash-up your mouth.' She gazed across at Gopaul's house. 'One of these days I have to do a "puja". We have to stop livin' like animals.'

'So now we livin' like animals?'

'How you call this . . . this movin' from place to place. Even the 'gouti got a hole of his own. We must start to find a real home. This is the last time I movin' to anybody else place. The next time we move is in a place we own.'

'So where we gettin' this money to buy house and land? We goin' to thief? Or we goin' about like the pundit and collect from house to house?'

'We goin' to save. Work and save. Rum-drinkin' and playin' devil mas' will send us down the drain. All about the country people work and save to make a better life . . .'

Manu sucked his teeth in a long s-s-t-e-u-u-ps and went down the steps and sat beside Compai who was drinking a cup of coffee alternating putting the cup to his lip with blowing into it. Manu lit a cigarette and leaned against the tree expelling the smoke from the side of his mouth.

'She right, you know,' Compai said.

'She crazy, yes. I gettin' tired of this naggin'. I just reach here. I ain't get my first pay yet and she want to buy house and land.'

'What happen? She don't like here?' Prince had joined them. 'Man, is a good thing I have a wife who don't worry about house and land. We livin' here now . . . how long, Compai? . . . fifteen years? . . . le' me see . . . sixteen years. Anyway it was before the last war. I see money come and go and I right here and I not goin' anywhere. In any case I too old.'

'Look who talkin' about old!' Compai said. 'Prince you's a little boy to me. But seriously, Prince, you don't think the woman right? You wouldn't like to have your own place?'

'Why? You think I would live better? Eat better? I would have to pinch and starve myself to save. Look, I have a roof over my head and food on my plate and a dollar for a drink when my throat get dry.'

'You is a fool, Prince. Life is plenty more than that.'

Compai had become increasingly aware that he might be at the end of his life and there was a growing disappointment with not having accomplished anything. His hands were no longer steady and he had to hold the cup with both hands. At the back of his hand the skin had become thin with every delineated vein snaking under a million creases and wrinkles. Even his palm had wrinkles. He was not sure what his age was – maybe sixty-five or sixty-eight. As he looked over the years there seemed to be no traces of his passage. Only a few years ago he was a young man thinking there was time enough for marriage and a family; for roots and a fixed place for home. It was as if time had just flown past like a thief leaving its marks in pencilled lines and sucking up his flesh leaving his skin like that of a goat hanging on a line at Christmas. The present moved so fast; the past day seemed to be no more than an hour and in the distance, years, months and weeks had become massed and confused, featureless and unremembered. For so many individual years there was not a single memory. He did not want anyone else to have such an unremarkable and almost useless existence.

He thought of Gabi. The boy had become a sort of son – more of a sort of grandson. But it was more like one would mind a pet one would get to like. He was not even sure that the boy liked him like a father or a grandfather. They shared the same room, cooked for each other and washed each other's clothes but he just could not bring himself to openly show affection to the boy. Maybe he was just not capable of love. Maybe in his own way he loved the boy.

He had brought the boy from Cedros when he was about five or six. One more child of a visiting fisherman. Or maybe the father was a fellow on a day-trip from Port of Spain. In any case the mother did not even know neither did she care. The boy was left with his grandmother who had died leaving him homeless. He had been visiting with his sister when he heard about this and immediately decided that he would take

52

the boy with him. The boy had turned out to be very helpful, a good companion and extremely trusting and trustworthy.

He had sent him to the Presbyterian school nearby and had taken him out when he had one more year to go because he was not earning enough for both of them. Also he was finding it more and more difficult to spend long hours in the field. In any case the boy was not particularly bright.

Maybe he should have let him finish school. Maybe he should have sent him to learn a trade – mechanic or carpentry. Shoemaking was not a bad trade. You did not need a lot of tools and you worked alone. You did not have to depend on anyone.

He looked at the boy playing with Mangal. Gabi was still childish. He had not complained when he had been taken out of school and seemed to welcome the idea of making some money. He had often worked in the estate on weekends and during vacations when it was coffee-picking time and had helped with the raking of the drying beans. But, although the boy was not lazy, he had not really liked estate labour. But there were no other jobs in the village and in the nearby towns there was nothing to do but work as a clerk or a porter in a store. And that was not easy to obtain. In any case the boy was too young to be anything but an apprentice somewhere.

He could feel his ears getting hot as once more the feeling of panic was rising. Suppose he should die tonight what would be the fate of the boy? What would the boy inherit? A few old pots and pans; some patched trousers and used clothing; an old shoe-box in which he had his seaman's papers, some coins from different countries along the Caribbean coast and some useless odds and ends.

A soft breeze shifted the shadows away from the slanting, hardening light and dislodged a leaf which floated slowly down zig-zagging to the ground. Compai picked it up and looked at the crimson glazed and polished side. The other side was yellow. There was no moisture at the end of the stem which showed that the leaf had died and was just waiting for any stirring to be released. He did not know when the stirring would come and break the fragile thread of his life.

Prince was sharing Manu's cigarette. After a few puffs he offered it back but Manu waved it away.

Compai looked at Prince. Prince had a son somewhere in America. He had no idea where the son was and did not seem particularly worried. The boy had been left with his mother where he was born in Grenada before Prince had come to Trinidad and long before he had taken up with Martina. 'Wha' your boy name again, Prince?'

The question startled Prince and he stuttered, 'A-Antoine.' He turned to the old man. 'What make you ask?'

'I just wanted to know. You ain't talk about him a long time.'

'Well, I ain't hear from him a long time. He must be doin' well. The last time he send a picture of himself in front of a big American car. And he was standin' up wearin' a big overcoat and hat. You remember the picture?'

'The one with the coat open and the zoot suit swell up like a balloon?'

'That is the last one.' He took a deep draw on the cigarette. 'He is happy, yes. Drivin' big Yankee car and wearin' jacket and tie every day. Livin' in New York is not like livin' in this ketch-ass place.'

Compai looked long at Prince and wondered how he could show so little interest in his own son. He often regretted that he had not married. By now he would have had children and grandchildren. It was difficult to imagine such a life.

A tiny wisp of smoke snaked upwards past the chipped blue enamel rim of the cup. He passed one hand over the week-old stubble on his face shifting the sagging flesh. The smell of the coffee briefly engaged his drifting thoughts which went back to imagining a life with a family. It must be the dream which had triggered this.

The night before he had dreamt of his father. This was very strange since he had no image of his father who had remained in Venezuela when his mother had brought him back as a baby. In the dream his father was being buried. All around him were people dressed in white, none of whom he could recognize. They were all throwing clumps of earth on the coffin, making horrible hollow thuds. Their arms were moving in exaggerated arcs as though they were dancing and there were expressions of pleasure on their faces. From his face tears were falling in a great gush which was filling up the hole. He was now looking up at the people raining earth on him as he lay drowning in his own tears. He had just got hold of the cover and was pulling it over his head when he woke breathing heavily with the sheet in both hands held protectively.

'Wha' happen, Pops?' Gabi had asked. 'Having a bad dream?'

'A nightmare, yes . . . a nightmare.'

'I tell you that you musn't drink coffee so late.'

He went over the dream again in an effort to unearth any feature of his father's face. All he could recall was the two gold teeth separated by a line of black residue and the rough large hands with jagged broken fingernails.

Chapter 6

'Poland, come back here!' Mrs Gopaul screamed. 'How much parcel you have?'

'Five, Ma.'

'You can't count? Come back for one more. Like school is a waste of time for you, yes.'

The boy soon approached with a few greasy fragments of a brown-paper bag which he distributed.

'That is what you was waitin' for, eh, Prince?' Gabi opened his and found what he expected: some sweet flour preparation looking like dough and greasy with ghee, half of a ripe 'chiquito' banana still in the skin, a few small cubes of coconut, one prune and some parched rice-flour. He was hoping that Mrs Gopaul would have called them over for a curry lunch. He could smell the various dishes: curried pumpkin, curried green jack-fruit, green mango curry and 'dal'. With a hot sauce of chopped raw pepper and lime. He swallowed. But this was not to be today. Normally when it was an evening 'puja' there would be feeding of the village. But this was something small for some private reason.

'How you so quiet this mornin', Compai?' Prince asked. 'Look, you' coffee gone cold.' He turned to Manu. 'On a Sunday mornin' Compai used to tell endless stories about all the places he had been to: Havana, Barranquilla, Miami, Kingston . . .'

'He never tired talkin' about Jamaica "reds" – those red-skinned Kingston women of mixed blood. You see the old man lookin' quiet quiet –' she winked at Compai. 'I sure he was a handsome, tall saga-boy.'

'Like Gary Cooper?'

'Boy, how you stupid so?' Prince said. 'How you expect a white man to look like some cocoa-pagniol?'

'See how you ain't know nothing,' Gabi shot back. 'White people and 'pagniol people is the same. Columbus was a white man.'

'We ain't talkin' 'bout Columbus.'

'But Columbus was 'pagniol.'

'Puck puck aarrgh.'

'Ignorance, Prince –'

'Mister, boy, mister.'

'Ignorance, Mister Prince, is a sickness. It does make you talk gibberish.'

Gopaul, still in his white dhoti and short-sleeved undershirt was approaching. His vest was stretched tight across his protuberant belly and hung loose over the top of the dhoti. Holding on to his hand was a little girl of about two.

'Mornin' mornin',' he said to Prince and Compai. 'Sita Ram,' he said to Manu.

They returned the greeting.

'You had early prayers this mornin', man,' Prince said.

'What he want to say, Mr Gopaul, is the "prasad" taste nice,' Gabi said. 'And he want some more.'

'Say 'mornin', Ramkallia,' Gopaul coaxed the child who buried its coconut-oil-slicked hair in his dhoti. He tried once more to encourage the child. 'I don't know how she shy this mornin'. And she is a real parrot. You can't stop her talkin'. Whole day she chatterin' with me like she eat parrot bottom.' He pushed the child forward. 'Go give this new "ka-ka" a kiss. That is a "ka-ka" a uncle. Come, go give him a hug and a kiss.'

Gopaul and Manu were appraising each other. Gopaul would have invited Manu to the 'puja' but his wife told him they should wait awhile. It was too early to tell what kind of Hindu they were. Already she had heard stories about the man, that he was a drunk and that he takes part in Carnival jumping up all over the street and making a spectacle of himself. That was not the way decent Indian people behaved. It had nothing to do with riches or poverty.

Samdaye had heard the greeting and had come down the steps in order to show that Gopaul was welcome. She approached the little girl and extended her hands and the child came to her.

57

'Good girl,' Gopaul said, 'That is a "ka-ki" you know, Rami.'

Samdaye took the girl up the steps and disappeared into the room.

'Rami! Rami!' Gopaul's wife shrieked. 'All-you come for breakfast. All-you ain't hungry?'

Gopaul took the hint and called the child then they went, he in his slow, short steps with the sandals flipping fine pebbles at his calves. After a few yards he turned and coaxed his daughter once again to blow a kiss at her new uncle.

'Rami, all-you comin'?'

'Comin'.'

Gopaul's wife, her white "orhni" tucked into the waist of her new white dress and draped over her head, came to the side of the road and picked up the girl. She whispered something to her husband and marched back into the house with a twist of her hips.

Samdaye had heard the calling while she was searching for something to give the child. Peeping through a crack in the wall she had seen how the woman seemed to snatch the girl into her arms and walk off exaggeratedly. She could not understand the insult. For some reason the woman did not want the child visiting her. Maybe it was because they had had prayers said and should not mingle. But she made a mental note not to forget the episode.

A car passed by and stopped at the Gopaul's. It was a faded blue with one dark blue door and several dents and aged patches. But it had been washed clean and polished. The occupants spilled out and Gopaul's wife emerged to give them a loud welcome.

'A-A! But how all-you late so?' she addressed them loudly. 'The puja finish long time. The pundit done gone already.' She looked at the new white triangular flag that shook weakly. 'Pola-a-and! German! Stalin! Look all-you "mausi" come. And look Fred and Tommy!' She stuck her hand in their hair and hugged them in turn. 'But look how they gettin' big man.' She kissed their averted faces then she embraced her sister. 'Girl, you gettin' fat! And look at my brother-in-law, nuh. Boy that is a real roti-belly you wearin'. Like all-you have life good.'

'You coun say that,' Gopaul added. 'So how the taxi-work goin'?'

'Good. Good. But I have to get a new car.'

'He does say that every time he come,' Prince told Manu.

'He should tell him the taxi work goin' up and down,' Gabi suggested.

Prince explained that Gopaul's wife's sister lived in Chaguanas or Felicity. Somewhere in Central. And that the man was a taxi-driver with his own vehicle.

The man and his wife flashed golden smiles. More gold shone from round her neck, hanging from her ears, stuck on her nose and jingled on her arms.

The boys had already got together and had scampered across the road into the field and were running about before they could settle into some game.

From the house the loud conversation and laughter grew louder.

'Tommy! Fred! Come and show "mausi" and them your toys what you get for Christmas.' Gopaul's wife's sister had a voice to compare with her sibling.

Mangal heard the invitation and began to edge towards the house. He stopped near the car as the boys opened the door and brought out a small, black plastic gun and a roll of caps. Fred inserted the roll and began to shoot, pointing the gun at his cousins. Tommy took out a tiny plastic car which he wound and set on the ground. One of them shook a box of marbles which opened and spilled on the ground. The new marbles sparkled.

Mangal gazed at the marbles so carelessly spilled on the ground and the gun pop-popping and the little red car rolling relentlessly over the ridges and valleys. He picked up a marble. The blue and green veins and clear, speckled light-green enclosed a world of lights and colours and the shiny surface was painted with the trees and the sky around. It was so smooth and shiny. He once had a marble that his father had found in the road and had practised pitching at various beans and small pebbles.

The boys returned and gathered the marbles. Fred drew a circle and a line about ten feet away. A few marbles were put in the ring. One after the other they stood astride the line and, lifting the marbles to their eyes, dropped them to determine who should pitch first. Furthest from the line went last. The object was to see who could knock out most marbles from the ring.

The air rang with shouts of 'every' when the ground was smoothed so that there was no impediment to prevent one's marble being hit by the person pitching, and 'ups' if a marble came in contact with someone's foot, and 'farts' if one's marble came to rest in the ring.

'Ups,' cried Stalin as Tommy's marble struck Mangal's foot. 'Fen' taw ped,' Tommy cried. 'I said "fen' taw-ped" before you said "ups".'

'You lie!' screamed Stalin. 'Go back to the line!'

'No,' Tommy insisted. 'Eh, Poland?' he appealed to the others, 'ain't I say "fen taw-ped" before he said "ups"? Seeing that he found no support he went across to Mangal and pushed him. Losing his balance Mangal fell and the marble slipped from his hand. 'A-A! This boy is a thief.' He tried to draw attention from the issue. 'Thief! Thief!'

Mangal was still on the ground when Gopaul's wife came out from the house. 'Never see, come see,' she said looking at Mangal.

Samdaye was observing all this. 'Mangal,' she called, 'come back here.' She leaned over the half-door. 'And all-you ain't see the boy crossin' the road to play with them ruffians!'

'Let the boy learn to take care of himself,' Manu said.

'Right,' Gabi added as he went to where the boys were.

Shanti, Gopaul's eldest daughter stood outside the area of play, her last sister astride her hips which stuck out and exaggerated their fullness. She caught Gabi staring at her hips. She turned towards him and shifted the child with an upward thrust. One leg of the child's was pressed against the front of her thigh between her legs emphasising the line from the bowl of her small belly to the joining of her thighs. She smiled at him as he greeted her.

'You practisin' from early,' Gabi said to her.

'What?'

'Mindin' child.'

'It ain't so early as you think,' she countered as she started to walk away.

'Wha' happen? Why you runnin' away? You think I want to bite you?'

'You won't get so near, Gabi.' Her small black eyes narrowed in a teasing smile which stretched thin lips that seemed to have been made by a razor slice.

'Come inside, Shanti,' Gopaul's wife called. 'I don't know what you doin' paradin' yourself outside.'

'You have to be straight with your girls,' her sister counselled. 'I don't have any so I have no worry.'

'You see me,' Gopaul's wife added, 'I don't make joke. He,' she jerked her head towards her husband, 'he always say girl children is dog-meat.'

'They could bring shame on a house,' Gopaul explained. 'I tryin' to bring them up as decent Hindu. You coun say that I doin' everything. I does pray every day that my girls behave theyself and that I get good boys for them.'

'Is hard to get good boys today. Too much rum-drinkin' and playin' creole,' the sister-in-law said.

'Not like our time, eh, Dolly?'

'In our time? In our time? Man, you couldn't look at a boy. Talk? Talk? We never talk to a boy until we married. You don't know brother-in-law, how we peep at you when Papa say how you come to see "didi". All we know was that you was from good family and how he know your father and mother. Is after you done gone he ask me if I like you. Not didi. Me. He know that we will discuss you and what I say is exactly what didi want.' She poked at his exposed knee as he folded his legs in the hammock, his arms behind his head. 'And look how things turn out.'

'She coun do better, eh, Dolly, girl?'

'You right.' She turned to her sister whose protruding teeth pushed out through her lips in a smile.

'Don't flatter him. He already does spend so much time in the looking-glass trimmin' his moustache and smilin' at heself.'

'But the man is a artis',' Dolly's husband said. 'And when he put on his dhoti and get the "tikka" mark on his forehead and on the side of his head as he got it now and he all in white with his greyin' hair combed back in "Caruso" and the black moustache turnin' up, the man does look like any pundit – like a "dharmacharya" – the archbishop of pundits.' He laughed loud and long at his own observation and rubbed his belly.

61

'Was the same thing with you and Dhanpal,' Gopaul's wife said.

'Right.'

'You didn't see Dhanpal until the day of the "tilak" when he father and uncle and a whole carload come to engage you.'

'Not true, you know,' Dolly said. 'I did see him after I hear Papa and Mama talkin' about him. I hear them talkin' about where they from and how the boy does drive taxi and they make the mistake and describe the car.' She poked Gopaul's knee 'From then I start to look out. And one day I see the bugger. Was not hard because he was starin' but I didn't let him know that I recognise him.'

'She jest walk away. Jest, so, cool, cool,' Dhanpal said. 'And I jest goin' to call her and ask her to go for a ride.'

'Ride . . . **ride**? You did want my father to put me out!'

'Talkin' about pundits, Dhan, how all-you goin' with the Ramayan readin'?' Gopaul's wife had risen and was standing outside. Her voice had become louder. 'How many pundits you havin' this time? The last time you had four.'

'And the time before that three,' Dhanpal said. 'The way Dolly goin' we will soon have all the pundits in Trinidad. This time we havin' six!'

'We have the Dharmacharya openin' and closin' the Ramayan and we havin' five others, one for each night. But I invite all for every night.'

'And we cookin' every night. We feedin' everybody. And we makin' "prasad" too. In fact, that is the real reason we come today. Was not only your puja. We come for you and brother-in-law to help plan. We want brother-in-law to arrange for the pundits. We know he know all of them especially the dharmacharya.'

The boys were squabbling again. Gabi had taken Mangal back to the barracks where his mother was giving advice about playing with older boys.

A car rumbled past with a white-shirted chauffeur and a white couple in the back.

'Petit Pierre,' Prince said to Manu. 'He come up this time with Madame.' He waved to Gabi, 'Look out you will get the call any minute.'

62

'I hope he give me some dollars – greenback – moolah – for workin' on Sunday.'

'You get pay enough ridin' in the big car.'

The call really did come soon and Gabi went to the Yard. In a little while the car passed with Gabi in the front seat. He waved imperiously as he went by his elbows sticking out through the window.

It was normal that when the estate-owner came for a visit Gabi was asked to pick fruits and vegetables that were in season.

An hour later Gabi emerged grinning from the car with a few oranges and grapefruit, and a large hand of bananas which he shared around. The estate owner alighted and came towards the workers who stood as at a given signal.

'Mornin', Mister Pierre, mornin',' Prince said. 'Long time you didn't come this side.'

'Busy, Mister Prince. Busy.'

'And how is the mistress?'

'I left her up in the Yard. You know how she is afraid of snakes.'

'But the orange field got no snakes, Boss.'

'She don't believe that.'

'Man, Boss, you must bring her around. And you must come more often. This place will go to ruin, you know. And the Old Man worked hard to keep it in good condition. Hard hard. And he used to be here every week.'

'I know when he used to come by train in the old days,' Compai said.

'So how is Compai?' He did not wait for a reply. 'And how is my girl-friend, Martina?' He raised his voice.

'Me heart break, boy, since you married that pretty Miss Robertson. You forget the old lady now.'

He looked quizzically at Manu.

'The new man,' Prince said.

'How you like it?' Pierre asked.

'Good. But we could make some change.' Manu waited for some encouragement. Prince had opened his eyes wider. Compai looked at the ground.

'Like what?' Pierre asked.

'The hours we work. Only estate labourers work seven

to five. Every day except Saturdays. We want to see more task work so a man could do a good days' job and go and do something else like gardening. Because you don't make enough as a estate labourer.'

'What do you say, Prince.'

'I ain't know. I see nothing wrong in day work. And I don't know if any of the other workers want to see this change.'

'Compai, what you think?' Manu searched for support.

'I think Manu right, Master Pierre. You can't make progress with this kind of income. Manu is a fellah with ambition. He not sayin' he want to work less, he just want to do what he got to do on the estate and go off and do something else to make a extra penny.'

'I find day-work all right,' Prince insisted.

'Day-work is for lazy people,' Manu said.

'No so,' Prince disagreed. 'Gomez does come and check how many trees you clear at the end of the day.'

'Well, that is what I mean. Tell us how many trees you want done and we will work to suit. If we finish early we leave. You work at your own speed.'

Pierre did not seem too interested in the discussion. He seemed to be looking at the rusty cone-shaped mango flowers on their red tree-like stems and the limp young leaves some pink, some lemon-yellow. Suddenly, he said, 'I have the estate for sale, you know. I really can't manage it again. The income is too small and the cost of labour is going up all the time. I don't mind keeping a few acres with some fruit but these hundreds of acres is a load on my head. The price of cocoa and coffee keeps going up and down. Up and down. I really can't take on all this worry. You see in my father's time land was wealth; cocoa, coffee, citrus, bananas was money in the pocket. But I don't understand what is happening myself. The British government pay what they want and they don't give a damn how you fare with your plantation.'

Manu realized that Pierre was not really concerned and he sat down.

But Pierre was still standing in the silence, his unfocused eyes wandering over the landscape. The boys had abandoned their game of marbles and were about to start a game of cricket. One of them was making a bat out of a coconut branch while another had picked some green sour-oranges to be used as balls. During the rainy season the field had become overgrown with weeds and the cricket pitch was covered with the snaking grass planted on lawns. Two boys were pulling these out.

Mangal stood looking at them hoping that he would be asked to join in the game. He was soon called in order to make up numbers. Gabi also joined the group.

Without another word Pierre turned and left.

Some more boys joined the players and two teams were formed with two captains making alternative selections for the sides. Gabi, being the biggest, was asked to play 'both sides'. He was to bat, field and bowl for both teams. Since only half the length of the pitch was cleared it was decided to bat only at one end where three stakes were hammered into the ground to serve as wickets. At the other end a small log marked the bowler's delivery point.

Samdaye kept an eye on Mangal who, although he was on the fielding side screamed, applauded and shouted exultantly at anything.

'Look out for bottles and "pickers",' she called to him.

Tufts of sensitive plant infested the field and could cause severe scratches and numerous prickles could produce sharp stabs.

Down the street Gomez came walking in his quick steps with his shoulders swinging and his short neck tilting his head from side to side. His thick, wavy hair, glistening with 'brilliantine' was parted in the middle and stuck straight out on both sides making a flattened. 'V'. His long-sleeved shirt was tucked into his trousers which were pulled above his navel and sloped from front to back.

Loud greetings came from Gopaul's house as he entered the narrow open verandah. Gopaul rose from the hammock and introduced his wife's sister and her husband.

'But, Ma Gopaul, you did not tell me you had such a pretty sister,' his small eyes sparkled at the woman who pulled at the top of her dress above the parting of her breasts.

'Didi, my sister, tell me about the new overseer, how he so nice. But you is a young man to be overseer for such a big estate.'

'You have nice family, girl. I treat this house like my own. I feel welcome anytime I come.'

Gopaul beamed. 'Boss, you coun say you is one of we.' He turned to Dhanpal, 'The boss is jest like family. He does come here all the time.' He scratched the white fungus blotches spreading all over his neck.

'And what about my girl friend, Shanti?' Gomez craned his neck to peer into the house. 'Shanti, girl, where you hidin'?'

'Shanti, **beti,** look the overseer callin',' Mrs Gopaul called.

The girl came through the doorway the inevitable child on her hips.

'Your daughter really gettin' big, Gopaul. And she is already a lovely young woman,' he winked at Gopaul who had already sunk into the hammock and was now rubbing between his toes. 'Soon it will be time for **sohari.** You better look around for a nice boy. Eh, Shanti?' Gomez was looking straight at her star-apple breasts gently swelling the thin, white dress. 'We start pickin' coffee again tomorrow. Shanti, you helpin' out?'

Shanti looked at her mother.

'But who will mind the baby? And little Ramkallia, too.'

Gomez was mentally stripping the girl. 'I was thinkin', you could send her to learn some sewin' with my wife. My wife is a good seamstress and she used to teach sewin'. It is good for the girl to learn something. That is after the coffee crop.'

From across the narrow road Prince was observing Gomez. 'Compai,' he said 'like we have another Benito Marin. You remember Benito Marin?'

'Benito Marin?' Compai replied, 'who will ever forget Benito Marin. That man, he like too much woman, yes. Benito, he left one string-band of children all about where he went. That man life like a story-book. He come here straight from Venezuela where he used to look after one big cocoa estate. I don't know how Papa Pierre find him but just so one mornin' Benito Marin arrive big, wide leather hat and leather boots and all. And his eyes wider than his hat. He don't bring no wife, though somebody say he had one in Curupita. But he came with hand swingin'. No wife, no pickney. In two weeks he got some woman in the house he say is housekeeper. Well it didn't have two-three months she belly big.'

66

'I remember her good,' Prince said, 'she was uglier than Martina. Then he bring in a young Indian woman who used to work on the estate. Right inside the house with the pregnant one. And in no time she, too, get in the family way. I forget some of the story. I think the Indian woman had some children for him.'

'Three,' Compai said. 'She reigned in the Yard for some years while Benito, he bring two-three more women and had more children.'

'Wha' happen, Papa Pierre didn't know?' Manu asked.

'I really don't know. He was only concerned with his estate.' He looked up at the sky. 'Boy, that 'pagniol was a terror! Talk 'bout drink! He used to bring some **caca-poule** white rum by the gallon from Venezuela and on Saturdays he used to take out his cuatro and with some of his 'pagniol friends from Arima he used to sing and drink-up all night. People used to think he was dealin' with the devil because sometimes the whole place dark and everybody gone to sleep and suddenly his whole house light up and full with white people singing and cookin' and dancin'. Nobody see anybody come. They ain't hear anybody come. But the house full and is one set of noise. But is no devil. I used to get invite because of my Venezuelan connection and because I could understand Spanish. Boy, talk 'bout **parang**! He had **parang** not only at Christmas but whole year!' His eyes became glazed. 'Is just like it happen yesterday. How time fly . . . how time fly.'

'I remember when he dead,' Prince said. 'Just so one mornin' the man dead.'

'Right. And everybody had to clear out of the house. Woman, child, everybody. They get nothing. Not one damn thing.'

'What I remember most about him was his hair. He had red hair. Like rusty galvanize. And he used to beat, eh. He used to beat them women especially when he drunk. He used to beat them and chase them out of the house and throw their clothes after them.'

'And in the mornin' he used to beg them to come back.'

'That was one crazy 'pagniol.'

'It look like Gomez is another Benito Marin.'

The shouts of advice and the squabbling of the cricketers

mingled with the quarrelsome chattering of the yellow-tails and the occasional crying from Gopaul's child. A heavy, black cloud scraped the eastern hills and a distant rumble sounded like corn rolling on the drying floor.

'It might rain tomorrow,' Manu said.

'Nah,' Campai replied. 'That is just a passing cloud.'

Chapter 7

Samdaye lay on her back, her arms behind her head and looked up at the ceiling where the kerosene lamp threw a dancing light. Manu lay beside her in the same position. He shifted himself a few times and began to mutter. Samdaye knew the signs: he was going to pray aloud.

'God,' he began, 'give us wisdom, knowledge and understanding. And keep us from all harm and evil. Keep us healthy and strong. Guard us and protect us, Father. **Hey, Ram**, life is not easy. The load is heavy. Help us to bear it, Father. And help us to prosper, **O Ram**, help us to prosper.' He went on for a few minutes more repeating most of what he had said before. Then ended with a loud 'Amen'.

Samdaye had asked him once where he had learnt the prayer and he had replied that the Principal of the Roman Catholic school where he went prayed aloud and said more or less the same thing after the interminable 'Hail Marys' and 'Acts of Hope, Charity, Contrition and what else.' Only, Manu had added the addresses to Ram. This was his recognition of Samdaye's Hindu background and the fact that he had been married 'under bamboo', that is, in the Hindu faith under a bamboo tent attached to the bride's house, as is the practice, and not in a church. He also, for reasons he could not identify, felt closer to Ram.

After a deep and almost mournful sigh he turned and blew out the lamp. 'Son,' he called to Mangal, 'you play plenty today? You make a lot of friends?'

'Yeh, Pa.'

'And who is your best friend?'

'Gabi . . . and Stalin and Tommy . . . and . . .'

'Those boys too big for him. He could get damage playin'
with them. They play too rough,' Samdaye said.

'You 'fraid any of them, Mangal?' Manu asked.

'No, Pa.'

'Good boy. You don't have to 'fraid any body.'

'What kind of advice is that?'

'The boy got to grow tough. He can't be like no "pap" . . .
softie, softie. You got to beat your way in the world.'

'With what? Devil whip?'

'What wrong with devil whip?'

'Nothing. But that is not how I want him to beat anybody.
Sonny,' she sometimes called him Sonny, 'I want you to beat
people with your brains. Beat them in test. Beat them in
Readin' and Writin' and Sums. Beat everybody in your class.
You hear?'

'Yeh'mm.' He yawned.

'And what happen if anybody fight him in school?'

'You have to look for fight to find fight.'

'In life you have to learn to defend yourself. Not only
that, you have to fight all the way. Sometimes is you against
everybody. You can't be a coward or people will run all over
you. They will mash you up.'

'So what you want Mangal to grow up to be?'

'Strong.'

'But you must want him to be something.'

'I want him to grow up tough. To do anything. If after all
the schoolin' he ain't make no subjects he could fall back on
any kind of work.'

'I don't want him to be no labourer. I say that before and
I will say that everyday to him. He must come out to be
something.'

'I only hope that after you fill up his head with all this
"doctor" talk, if he can't take too much learnin' he wouldn't
become a loafer, feelin' that nothing is good enough for him.
All I hear you tellin' him is how you want him to be doctor.
You think it easy to be doctor? You think it cheap? You can't
study doctor here, you have to go to England. For years –
four, five, six years. You know how much money that take?'

'God will provide.'

'God will provide? God will provide? And why He ain't

provide yet for me? So far I ain't see anything He provide for me. I in the cocoa field since I was twelve. My father say, "Boy, you think school will give you food? You think school will give you clothes. You think Columbus will give you help? And all this present tense and past tense?" So he just went and buy a swiper and make a "poniard" case for me and we take off for Santa Maria Estate.'

'And this is what you want for your son?'

'I didn't say that is what I want. Don't be foolish.'

She became quiet as she saw the argument developing but an irritability grew until it found edge in her voice. 'I only want us to make a fresh start here. To put down some root. To start making for the children. There must be something more than workin' and eatin' and sleepin' and goin' the same way every day every month every year for generation after generation.' A whine had developed. 'I have a child goin' to be born next few weeks. I have to know how you thinkin' about the children and I don't know how much more God will give us.'

'Well, I don't know what you want me to do.'

'**You** don't know what **I** want you to do? **I** don't want you to do anything. You have to do what **you** have to do.'

'Now I don't know what the hell you talkin' about.'

'You know well what I talkin' about.'

'If you have nothing to say you better keep quiet and let me sleep.'

'We have to start savin'. Not this fifty-cent, one dollar business.'

'And where we will get twenty-dollar, hundred-dollar?'

'I will have to work.'

'You must be —'

'Wait. Don't get vex —'

'Not my wife —'

'What kind of pride is that? We livin' ketchin' tail in a barrack and I want to work to come out from here and you talkin' about "no wife of yours" like you must be Raja Dasrath or King George. Tomorrow coffee-pickin' startin' and I could make two or three basket a day. That is fifty . . . seventy-five cents a day.'

'In your condition? You want to kill yourself?'

'You think I don't know how to take care of myself?' When
he kept silent she knew she was getting him to agree. She
pressed on, 'The estate will need all the people it could get.
You know if the coffee don't get pick in two three weeks it
will drop to the ground. I will not tote any basket. I will
pick in a bucket and fill the basket and you could carry
the basket. We two could pick eight . . . nine . . . even ten
basket in one day.'

There was a light rustling outside as the last of the sea
breezes swept down from the hills and filtered through
the many cracks in the wall. Soon the land would become
cooler and the land breezes would reverse the direction of
the blowing. Two smooth hoots came from an owl as it flew
over the building.

'They say when owl cry over your house somebody goin'
to die,' he said. Then he added, 'I don't like this business
about workin'. I don't like it at all.' In what seemed to be a
casual, almost accidental movement his hand brushed against
her belly and stayed there with his elbow resting on the bed.
With an equally seemingly accidental movement she shifted
and let her hand rest against his.

Her eyes were open but there was nothing she could
see in the liquid blackness. But she could hear the myriad
sounds of the night activity so absent in Manzanilla, where
the waves incessant noise with the swishing of their rolling
into one another to their thunderous rising and smashing
themselves on the beach drowned everything else except the
occasional cricket that found itself in the house and made its
teeth-edging 'zee-ing'. Here the frogs clinked and plinged
and croaked and bellowed, cocks crowed and dogs barked,
and the sounds travelled far through the silent air. The owl
hooted again and a dog bayed long and sorrowfully. She
stiffened. All day she had felt discomfort and sometimes she
was not sure that she had felt or imagined a sharp pain. She
had a whole month more so it could not be the baby but the
heaviness was excessive and the pain seemed to be recurring
more frequently. And there was the sound of the owl over
her bed, it seemed. And now the baying of the dog. Manu
had become unusually still and seemed expectant and alert.

'Wha' happen?' he asked. 'You ain't feelin' well?'

'Mus' be a bad stomach.'

'Pain?'

'Is nothing.'

He waited till she fell asleep.

He had no idea what time it was, or indeed, where he was when something woke him up. He had not yet got accustomed to waking up in Dorado and sometimes he would be puzzled at the morning stillness. But now he had become wide awake listening to his wife's groaning increasing in loudness. He felt around for matches and quickly lit the lamp. Her face grimaced in pain and her fists were clenched.

'You think is the baby?' he asked.

Her eyebrows raised in an expression of doubt.

'I better call Miss Martina,' he suggested.

She shook her head feebly.

'Prince,' he called. 'Prince. Wake up Miss Martina.'

Prince mumbled an answer and he repeated the request. His wife, he said, was in pain.

In a few minutes Martina arrived. She had never delivered any babies, she said. She herself had not had any so she had absolutely no experience. 'Prince,' she called, 'take Manu and go for Ma Motilal.'

'How far is that?' Manu asked.

'About two . . . three miles. Not far.'

'Nobody got a bicycle we could borrow?'

'Toussaint son got one but is more than one mile so.' He pointed in the opposite direction. 'By the time we reach for the bicycle it will be mornin',' he attempted some humour.

Manu stood perplexed. Mangal had been born at his mother-in-law's. It was the practice for daughters to go to their mother's home to have babies. There they were taken care of until it was time to return. He should have sent her to her mother's home instead of bringing her to Dorado. Now it may be too late. He would have to send a message to Manzanilla.

'Come on, man, move quick,' Martina called. 'Don't look so worried. Makin' child is not a sickness. Is only man does get worried. Gopaul's wife make them like bread.'

Manu felt a bit relieved. He hugged himself in the cold night air.

The inky-black, cloudless sky was filled with stars that lessened the darkness on the land, and the gravelled road appeared as a grey snaking band. The screams and the commotion had aroused the neighbours and their opening doors cut swathes of yellow into the dark. A dog, disturbed from its sleep, emitted two high-pitched yelps as if to give notice of its watchfulness. A yellow-tail fluttered its wings in protest. The owl hooted again.

'Bad sign,' Manu said.

'Quiet,' Martina said. 'Don't say that.'

Dark forms began to gather hushed and yawning. A cock crowed and others picked up the cry.

'Come on, Prince,' Martina urged. 'All-you ain't leave yet? This business don't wait for nobody, you know. All-you should be comin' back by now.'

Prince stretched and yawned before moving stiffly into the darkness.

'Gabi,' she called, 'wake up, man. Go and call Ma Gopaul.' But Gopaul's wife was already close by. She suspected what was happening and was rushing over. Whispering anxiously the two women hurried up the steps. Martina soon emerged leading a lethargic and unwilling Mangal through the door. She pushed him to Gabi.

Gopaul's wife ran back to her house and returned with a large basin and some rags. Her husband stood by the door with one arm raised as he scratched under it.

Compai sat on his steps his head heavy on his chest. It was during these periods between waking and sleeping that he had begun to hear voices and see images. They were very clear. It was only last night as he was about to fall asleep that he heard very distinctly, 'I still love you, Pablito.' It was the voice of Dolores. There was no mistaking. The voice had startled him. It was a familiar sound about forty years ago. He did not know what to make of it. But it came to him in a sharp and easily identifiable whisper into his ear, 'I still love you, Pablito.' He thought he also heard 'and I miss you'.

He could not determine the meaning of this. Was it that Dolores was calling from another world? Or was she still alive and she was communicating with him somehow? Or was it all a dream and figment of his mind losing sense of reality? Is this what old age and senility was about? He remembered seeing old people talking to themselves – sometimes quite loudly – and gesticulating. Had he become like that?

He could see her so clearly half reclining before him her elbows on the side of the boat, her long hair blowing this way and that and the way she tilted her head to keep it from flowing across her face with that small mouth just a bit wider than her nose; with the glinting bronze fuzz on the side and on her chin on which there was this brown mole. He felt his chin with his forefinger.

His ship was in Kingston Harbour taking cargo – an exercise that would take at least two days. He had borrowed a row-boat and was leisurely leaving the shore with Dolores growing larger against the towering Blue Mountains casting a bluer shadow over the city. It was a good day to visit the sunken city of Port Royal. The water would be clear and he would be able to see the top of the spire of the church.

The sun was still behind the hills and the air was made cooler by the light breeze sailing across the bay and playing with her hair.

The heat rose rapidly as the sun cleared the hills and they had pulled into the shade of the mangrove where they had rum and made love – one of the many times that day. It was the laziest of days, being a weekday, there was no one about. They swam away from the city below for Dolores was fearful of the thousands of ghosts that must be lying in the whitened skeletons, where they had suddenly gone down in that terrible earthquake that had sliced the city like a piece of cake and dropped it into the sea.

Every minute of that day with Dolores was etched in his mind. And now he had heard her call. But there was no point in dwelling on that for even if he had the opportunity to see her he would not want her to see him – not with his shrunken body, balding head and almost toothless mouth, now slack and crooked. And that wrinkled bit of skin which was once smooth and full.

'Foolishness,' he was mumbling. 'Foolishness,' when a mosquito droned into his ears and he slapped it involuntarily and woke.

In the room two doors away Samdaye gave loud intermittent

groans and Martina peered over the half-door anxiously.

In the east the hills were being delineated by the lightening sky and there was now a chorus of crowing when Prince and Manu arrived in a car with the midwife who hurried wordlessly into the room.

'Gabi,' Prince called. 'You make coffee?' He waited a few seconds then called again, 'Come, boy, get up and make coffee.'

After about one minute Gabi looked through the door. 'And what you mean by ordering me so? Wha' happen you ain't have any of your own?'

'Wha' happen, Compai, like you been sittin' here all this time! You shouldn't be out here in the dew, you know.'

'Is all right, Prince, I couldn't sleep anyhow. Not in this noise. Too besides, somebody had to remain up.'

Just then the groaning stopped and they all looked toward the door. A dryness filled Manu's mouth and he rushed up the steps. Martina shooed him out. 'This is woman's business,' she said. 'Go outside; everything will be all right, please God.'

Manu began to curse his luck. How could this happen just now when he needed to work hard especially with the coffee coming in he could have made some extra money? If only he had sent her to her mother's. He did not know how he would cope. He had no idea how long it would be before Samdaye would be up doing her chores. She had stayed two weeks at her mother's when Mangal was born. She had stayed past the twelfth-day ceremony when there was the ritual bathing and the making of 'halwah', when relatives were invited – especially the women and they had sung and danced keeping rhythm with the 'dholak' and the lotah beating it with two spoons. They had sung suggestive 'chutney' songs and with no men to see them the women had made appropriate gestures and rolled their hips with their hands spread wide and their dresses and 'orhnis' swirling. Manu recalled their loud cheering and laughter. He could probably send her to Manzanilla after a few days: maybe her mother would come and take her. He now began to worry about what his mother-in-law would say: that she should not have travelled so far in the state she was in and that she should not have exerted herself so much in fixing up the room; that it was his fault entirely if anything should happen. He would be in a real soup if something should happen to her and he was left with not one but two children to bring up. Silently he began to recite his prayer. He stopped short because his mind would not work. He lit a cigarette and sat on the steps next to the old man.

'Life ain't easy, Compai. Life ain't easy.'

Compai, who had been sitting on a higher step, placed his hand on the younger man's shoulder. 'God is good,' he said and immediately wondered why he said that.

The smell of coffee blew from Gabi's kitchen. He came round the house with three enamel cups with black coffee in which sugar was added but no milk. The morning star twinkled white and luminous in the faintly spreading, rising dawn.

'Well, Manu,' Prince said, 'you will have to stand your hand when the child born. Is the first one that will be born in the barrack as far as we know, eh Compai?'

'Nah. We had plenty children born here. You know how much people live in the barrack? You know how old this place is?'

'In any case is a long time.' He turned to Manu. 'What you expectin' – a boy or a girl?'

'And how he goin' to know that?' Gabi asked.

'Hush, boy. You'd better learn to make a good cup of coffee.'

'I didn't think about it; it was too early. This thing happen soon – too soon.'

'But what you prefer?'

'You know Indian men,' Compai said, 'to them all girl children is trouble. You have to mind them well and then find some man for them before they run away wit' some saga-boy and bring shame on your house. And you have this dowry business. You can't send them off just so. You have to give the husband so much money, so much tharia and lotah and cow.'

'You sound just like my father,' Manu said. 'He used to say that girl children is trouble. They can't really help to build you up but they could bring you down easy, easy.'

Martina appeared at the door. 'Is a girl,' she said, 'and both of them all right.'

Chapter 8

Samdaye lay in the light silence of the morning. Her thoughts zig-zagged through a range of conflicting emotions: one moment she was smiling with a feeling of relief; another, she sighed deeply in despair when she looked at the tiny girl and thought about what might be in store for her. She was almost amused at the suddenness of it all; how quickly the crisis developed and how soon it was over. A knot of anxiety began to grow into fear when she thought about her mother whose arrival would bring some confrontation with Manu. She imagined her mother's voice accusing Manu of unnecessarily risking Samdaye's health at such a late stage in her pregnancy and of being concerned only with his own mad impulses. Her mother could not understand Manu whose gloom could be so dense but who could effervesce so quickly at some trifling amusement. He tried so hard; no one could accuse him of laziness yet he seemed to her to be too easily satisfied.

She had persuaded him to go to work since there was nothing for him to do and she could see the quick relief on his face as he feigned reluctance. Of course she was exhausted and could not get up but the midwife was there and would spend the day at least.

She smelled the tea which Martina had left and which had long gone cold. Several times she had attempted to put the cup to her lips but she just couldn't. Martina was so kind and motherly and she almost drank from the cup because of that but she had smelled the things being cooked next-door: the beef and pig-tail and pig-snout and a strong sense of revulsion prevented her from drinking the tea. Gopaul's wife had sensed this and had attempted to transfer the tea to one of Samdaye's cups but Martina had quickly objected saying that she did not need the cup and that they should not soil too many dishes. Gopaul's wife had softened in this common plight and had even said that she should be called 'didi' – big sister.

The midwife had rummaged around looking for things to cook. She wanted eggs for breakfast – two eggs, she said, and milk, and she liked fried 'roti' after any delivery. She also wanted fresh home-made cocoa 'with the grease floating thick'. Gopaul's wife had sent two eggs and a bottle of milk. That was this morning. What would happen later . . . and tomorrow? Manu had not yet received his wages and would not for a few days.

The midwife had fried both eggs and had added some shredded salt-fish with a piece of red pepper. She had made three fried 'roti' and after she had grated the cocoa bar Gopaul's wife had also sent, she boiled it with spices she carried in her large cloth bag. She had eaten it all sitting on the step facing the kitchen and looking out into the field. The scent of the food made Samdaye hungry but she was too exhausted to eat. She only felt thirsty.

She looked long at the baby with its eyes shut tight and both fists clenched, its tiny arms moving involuntarily. She wanted to hold it to her bosom and nurse it. She tried to call the midwife but her voice did not come out; she only managed a hoarse whisper.

At the back of the building the midwife was bent over a tub washing the soiled clothing and the faded flour-sack sheet. In the homes of the well-to-do she would get a room of her own and the servant would do the dirty work. She would be treated like a special guest and would be invited to stay at least up to the twelfth-day feast. She would give orders as to what she would like to eat and the various visiting relatives would give her money and gifts, especially if it had been a boy. It was as though the birth of a boy was her own doing. But this family had nothing. There would be no gifts here, no special sweets, no quality cloth to make new dresses, not even a flour-sack here. The least she would collect in most houses was ten dollars, not counting the presents. She remembered when she attended to Ratan Singh's wife. What a lovely lady that was and what a generous man. After eleven years Ratan Singh had his first child – a boy. What a celebration that was! She was not allowed to leave for two weeks. She had been given forty dollars, a gold bracelet and a pair of gold earrings and her cloth bag was stuffed with colourful cotton prints to make dresses and yards of georgette to make 'orhni'. Ratan Singh had taken her to his store in Sangre Grande and had asked to take whatever cloth she wanted but she was overwhelmed and could take nothing. Ratan Singh never had another child and up to now she could not pass the store without him giving her something. She wondered why she ever came here. It was only because the man said that it was the daughter of Raghu Ram. But she did not know that the girl lived in a barrack. There was no place for her to sleep here. She would leave this afternoon if only there was someone who would continue to care for the woman. The woman was strong and she could foresee no complications. So she made up her mind to leave after she got her money. She decided that she would ask for five dollars, that is if they could afford even this pittance.

Nearby a chicken had scratched a hole and was nestling in it and stirring up a cloud of dust with its wings and feet. She chased it away. A mangy dog lurked a few feet away its head bowed and its rheumy eyes unblinking. It gave off a smell of sickness and decay.

Mrs Motilal, the midwife, seldom stayed in her own house. She was almost always at someone who was either having or had had a baby. Her eldest daughter had looked after her husband and her seven children until she was married, then her second daughter had taken the place of the first. Now she had only a son and two daughters at home. Her husband had died years ago so she really had no responsibility. She never really assumed responsibility for her husband and family. By the time she was twenty-two and had had two children she acquired the skill of delivering children from an aunt who had come from British Guiana. She became very good and had never lost a child or a mother so she was always in demand. So she did not need to work in these conditions and for such meagre fees. But she was getting on in age.

Moreover, more and more people were going to doctors and nurses as if they knew more than her. She smirked when she heard about the number of caesarean babies and the women who developed complications in hospitals. Those things happened when you did not take care of the patient before delivery. That was the key. Taking this case was risky. It was a good thing that everything turned out right but this was not the time in her life when she should be taking chances. It was certainly not the time of her life when she should be doing washing and other menial tasks. But there was not even one relative in the house – no mother, no sister. And, it seems that there was not a relative nearby. It was obvious that this marriage did not have the support of the woman's relatives. She resolved never again to find herself in such a situation. She grumbled to herself as she rubbed the worn-down cake of brown washing soap on the item stretched on the scrubbing board. She would have to change the water which had become grey and smelly but she would have to fetch water herself from some well God knows how far away.

She emptied the tub and dumped the clothes on the grass. The hen had returned and was stirring a cloud of dust. Angrily she ran after it with a stick. Two beads of perspiration rolled down her temples. A fly buzzed round her face. The heat rose. She flung her fists about and some of the water splashed on her face. She retreated to the kitchen and slumped on the steps. Her throat shook with a dry sob.

She was truly too old for this occupation but she did not know what she would do. She would have to mention this to her children. Bissoon, her eldest son, had once suggested that she go to live with him but that entailed looking after his three children and probably cooking and cleaning. He had such a lazy wife. That, she concluded, was no improvement.

She did not know how long she had been sitting when she heard a car stop, several calls and footsteps coming up into the room. This was followed by whispered greetings and anxious enquiries. The woman's mother had arrived.

Samdaye looked at the spider with its tiny body and frail, long legs dangling at the end of its silken string.

She wondered how it could get there; it was only a few days ago that she had brushed the roof clean. The white sunlight intensified the dark and made stars of the holes in the roof. Through one especially large hole dust particles played in the spotlight.

In a sudden alarm she decided to count the baby's fingers and toes; they were all there. Nothing so far looked abnormal. There were little red spots on the cheeks and on the nose. It looked like a flower – a little 'phool'. She would call her 'Phulandaye'. She sounded the name in her mind for her voice would no longer come through her throat. 'Phulo,' she said silently. She wondered if Manu had chosen a name. Whatever he thought, she had decided on her own name. She wanted her to open her eyes and she touched them lightly but the heavy-looking lids wrinkled as they closed more tightly. She was filled with relief, satisfaction, elation, joy. She felt as if she was floating about in the room. She was smiling to herself when she heard the car stop and her mother's voice.

She watched her mother enter as if she were a third party and was unconnected with the two bodies in the room. She looked at the expression of concern and felt the kiss on her cheek, felt her head nod in assent and shake from side to side negatively and unintelligible sounds came from her. Yes, she was all right. No, she was not sick with anything. Yes, she had everything. No, it was not Manu's fault. She had worried about her mother's visit but now she was strangely very calm in the face of her mother's agitated expressions. 'Having children is very ordinary business,' Martina had said. And she remembered the comment about Gopaul's wife making them like bread. She smiled.

'You smilin'! You think this is a joke,' her mother said. 'You don't know how you get your sister and me frighten. We didn't know how you was livin' here. Who was takin' care of you.' Her eyes wandered about the room. 'But why you didn't come to see me before you leave Manzanilla? All-you was so busy?'

She nodded.

'You couldn't send a message?'

She shook her head.

'Manu had to reach here on that day and no other day?'
She nodded.
'And you couldn't wait one more day?'
She shook her head.
'You, Samdaye, will kill me, yes. And you will kill your
sisters and drive everybody mad. I don't know how you get
so stubborn – so own-way. Like you don't listen to anybody
anymore. You doin' exactly what you want to do and is
nobody else business.' She sat on the bench. There was not
a chair in the room. 'You really feelin' well?'
She decided against making any more gestures.
'You don't think we should go and see Doctor Lee Young?'
'For what?' she croaked.
'How you mean "for what"? To make sure everything all
right.' Her head turned to the child. 'I hope the baby . . . that
nothing wrong with the baby.' She went over and counted the
fingers and toes. She peeled open its eyes and peered into it.
She poked and prodded then, satisfied, she nodded her head
slowly. 'You lucky everything all right.' Her face softened as
she saw a tear running down the side of Samdaye's face and
she wiped it away with a handkerchief she had clenched in
her fist. 'You lucky you's a strong girl. You's the strongest
of all my children. None of them could take what you takin'.
God know what He does do. He don't give you what you can't
bear.' She rose and went to the window. 'But it not fair for
you. None of your sisters have it so hard. Rajendaye going
good. Real good. Her husband workin' in Bata. Man, you
should see him in collar and tie goin' to work. Long-sleeve
white shirt, black pants. She got two children and they doin'
good in school. She say how long she ain't see you. Must be
two years. It can't be so long. You didn't see her for my last
puja? That was, le' me see . . . April last year.' She seemed
to be merely filling the room with sound as though nothing
there was real; that it may vanish like a dream; that it really
was a dream. In the cool half-dark of the room nothing
seemed substantial. 'Basdaye doin' good, too. She and the
husband open a little shop in Mayaro. She ain't have it so
hard.' She went outside and brought a cardboard carton. 'I
bring two chicken. One start to lay already.' She placed the
carton in a corner and went to the back door. A women with

a bucket was walking to the edge of the field. 'Who deliver the child? Motilal wife? I thought it was she I see goin' with the bucket. She put me to bed with Basdaye, you know. And Rajendaye, too. But she couldn't come when it was your time. She ain't tell you that?'

Samdaye shook her head.

She returned to the bench. 'You lookin' pale. You had anything to eat?' When Samdaye shook her head and said that she was not hungry her mother said that she was going to make some soup. She descended into the kitchen. Taking some items from a bag that she had brought she put a few pieces of wood in the clay stove and started a fire all the time shaking her head in sympathy as she thought of the conditions in which her daughter lived. The girl had inherited the same luck she had, for as a child, she experienced almost the same conditions. But she did not want any of her children to go through that. 'Where Manu?' she called. 'He gone to work?' The boy was not that bad. It was just his luck. She would have to give him a good talking-to. 'And how Mangal? He gone to school?'

Samdaye wished she could get up and do something. She was not yet ready for a visit from her mother. She lay back listening to her mother's account of the state of health as well as the progress of various relatives, and grunted replies to the many questions.

Producing a bottle of bay rum her mother filled her cupped palm many times and splashed the cool but pungent liquid over Samdaye's face. She slapped her forehead generously and the liquid ran down behind her ears and tickled. She shuddered and tried in vain to lift her heavy arm to wipe it. Soon her mother brought a cup of hot lime-bud tea and soup. She looked at her mother's veined hands and felt her still-rough palms. Her mother had never complained about her lot and although her life had not been easy she was always willing to do whatever she could for her children. She was so filled with emotion as she saw her blowing over the spoon of hot soup her eyes began to swim. She wished she could be like her mother. There was always an expression of peace over her face now framed by her flowing 'orhni'. It was what she imagined the various Hindu goddesses would look like. The soup finished, her mother sat holding her hand.

Outside Samdaye could hear the splashing as the midwife resumed the washing. Her mother went outside and greeted the midwife, and the conversation that began with enthusiasm soon grew into soft whispers. Her mother was probably apologizing for Samdaye's straitened circumstances.

Mangal came home for lunch to find his mother and the baby asleep. 'Nani. Nani,' he cried as he saw his grandmother who hugged him and gave him a wet kiss on his cheek. He was going to ask what she had brought him but stopped because his father had warned him about begging. He went over to the baby and hesitantly touched its cheek and little hands.

'You like your sister?' the old lady asked.

'But she so small.'

'You was small so, too.'

He did not believe that and shook his head. 'When she goin' to grow? And walk . . . when she goin' to walk?' He did not wait for a reply and went to see what there was for lunch. After he had finished the soup his grandmother gave him he returned to look at the baby. He remembered his mother's screams and cries and wondered how she might have been cut up to get the baby. Gently he touched his mother's arm and she shifted. So she was not dead. But he still felt sorry for her.

'Look what I have in the box for you,' his grandmother led him to the carton.

He saw the chickens and his eyes sparkled. He wanted string so he could tie their legs and so prevent them from running away.

'They won't run away,' she assured him. 'We will have to take them out of the box and let them go.'

He was not sure that it was a good idea to set them free and asked her to keep them in the carton until he had returned from school. 'You goin' to be here when I come back?'

'Yes,' she said. 'And I will spend the night with you.'

Hearing the other children on their way to school he ran off.

Manu returned early from work to meet his mother-in-law sweeping the room. He was greeted warmly with an embrace and a kiss on the cheek. He looked anxiously at Samdaye who smiled.

'You finish early,' Samdaye said.

He nodded. He went beside the bed. 'How you feelin'?'

'She little weak,' his mother-in-law said. 'And she lookin' pale. She want some good tonic to build her up.'

'I woulda have tonic but I didn't expect the baby so soon.'

'And whose fault is that?' His mother-in-law asked. 'If you was not in so much hurry to leave Manzanilla.' She looked up into his eyes. 'The girl coulda dead, yes. Was too much for her to travel so far and do so much work and she in that condition. You take a great risk . . . great risk. Walkin' all that distance in the hot sun. And then havin' to clean up this place.'

'Well she didn't dead,' he said.

'But it was too dangerous,' she shook her head. 'Why you didn't send her home to have the baby?'

'I tell her to go but she say is too soon.'

'But you coulda wait a while –'

'I didn't have work –'

'But you was workin'. What happen, you left the estate? Boy, why you don't settle in one place? You always movin'. You can't do that again. Your family getting bigger. Now you have a daughter and have big responsibility. Is not like a son. You have to provide for a daughter. It doesn't look like you will ever be ready for responsibility.' She saw the long whip hanging in a corner. 'And you still with this carnival stupidness? You will have to give that up. It have no profit in that. I can't see what business you have playin' mas'. It was all right before you was married. Even before you had Mangal. But now, with two children you can't afford to waste money on this childishness, not to mention the danger.' She sat down on the old bench with exaggerated care and looked pointedly about the room. 'You satisfied livin' in this place? You have no ambition for better? You want your children growin' up in barrack-room?'

Manu went and looked into the carton with the chickens. He hated the idea of accepting gifts from his mother-in-law. Every present was accompanied by a lecture on his shortcomings. Each gift was a tightening of the noose of dependency and a belittling of his ability to provide for his family. He leaned against the door-frame and lit a cigarette in a sort of defiance. What did she expect of him? How can anybody save money on estate wages, enough to build house and buy land? You had to have some outside income, or working sons, or some start inheriting land and house.

'That is the one thing about Indian people: they don't like to pay rent; they don't like to live in other people house. They must have their own house no matter how small. They add on as the children come.' She went to the window. 'They have any land 'round here? You should start looking for a piece you could pay down on and think about a house.'

Manu thought about the piece of land near the school with the big mango-rose tree.

'You shouldn't leave Manzanilla. You coulda get a piece near by me. You coulda add a piece to my house until you get your own.'

Manu groaned softly.

'You could still leave this place and come and live by me until you could start your own.'

Manu was too accustomed living on his own to even think about that. A man must have no pride at all to get married and go and live in his in-laws' house. He would have no independence. He stopped listening to her. He looked past the old woman turning over the clothes to catch the last heat of the afternoon sun. A few blackbirds hopped among the grass pecking at the earth their white-rimmed eyes standing out against their glossy black feathers. On the leafless imortelle tree with the orange blooms yellow-tails ducked in and out of their long, swinging nests.

His mother-in-law was now carrying on with Samdaye who was protesting things were not as hard as they seemed and will improve as soon as they settled down. She was now questioning Samdaye about whether Manu still played carnival clown and whether he still drank. Samdaye, also, after a few replies, had grown quiet.

He took his 'swiper' and crook-stick and headed toward the cocoa field to cut a bundle of grass for the cow. He passed Mangal who was chasing a brown dove with a stick. 'Look out for bottles in the grass,' he called out. The boy ran to him, an earnest look in his eyes. 'Pa,' he said, 'I want shoes.'

'What?'

'I want shoes. Nearly everybody in the school have shoes.'

'But look at my crosses! You think I rollin' in money?'

'But Pa –'

'Look, boy, I don't have a good pair of pants to cover my backside and you want shoes!'

'But Pa,' he whined.

'Stop this playin' now, you hear? And go and sharpen my cutlass.' He strode off leaving the boy standing with a puzzled look on his face.

Later, when he had returned with the grass and had brought the cow into the pen he saw the boy sitting on the back step, his reading book in his hand. He went up to him and, pushing his hand through his hair said, 'Don't worry son, you will get shoes but not right now. Right now things a little hard but it will get better and you will have shoes and everything.'

Mangal had forgotten about the shoes. Now, reminded of it, he went to his mother and asked why he couldn't get shoes. He got the same reply from his mother. He thought of asking his grandmother but his father would not like it. Maybe Gabi would buy him shoes. He went back to his reading book.

Samdaye heard Manu call Prince and listened to their footsteps becoming less distinct as they went towards the shop. She knew that he was avoiding her mother. She only wished that he did not come home drunk because then he could become quite talkative and noisy.

The midwife had left saying that she had another delivery which was expected that night. She seemed very pleased that Samdaye's mother was staying. She collected five dollars from Samdaye who had her mother bring her the knotted handkerchief with the eleven dollars. The woman's face brightened a little when her mother gave her an additional two dollars.

Gopaul's wife and Martina came over to visit. The former brought a few oranges and was at pains to point out to Samdaye's mother that she had her own house and had just

88

had a 'puja'. She indicated the now faintly visible flag on the pole.

Martina explained that Prince and Manu had gone to the Junction to celebrate the baby's birth.

'That boy does drink too much,' Samdaye's mother said.

'Well,' Martina said, 'he entitle to take something to celebrate.'

'He should stop drinkin' complete. And he should not keep company with people who encourage him to drink.' She paused briefly. 'And that . . . that man he went with . . .'

'That is my husband,' Martina said.

'Oh.' Samdaye's mother fell silent.

It was much later in the night when Manu returned. Samdaye heard the loud voices and louder laughter. She heard him swear as he missed a step. He was speaking softly to himself as he pushed the top of the unlocked door and it banged against the wall. She heard him feel his way in the dark then lie down on the bag and sheet which had been spread on the floor. In a very short time he was snoring.

Chapter 9

Manu had become quite attached to the baby. He would hold the little bundle close to his chest and walk about the yard tickling its cheek and talking to it. He made a hammock with an empty jute rice-bag and hung it in the kitchen. He would hug the child in the hammock and sing the few lines of a hindi song that he had heard.

'You soundin' just like Gopaul,' Samdaye said. 'If you spend so much time with the baby you might get a belly just like him.'

'You hear what your Mama say, baby? Your Papa will get a fat belly like the neighbour . . . a fat, fat, bel . . . ly. She look to me like she hungry.'

'You always sayin' that. Left to you, you will feed the child whole day.' She was very pleased with the way Manu was spending so much time with the child. It was one week he had not gone to the shop to drink. Maybe this added responsibility would curb the drinking.

'Listen to your Mama. She don't want to feed you. She don't want you to grow up quick so you could make tea and 'roti' for your Papa and squeeze his head, and give his leg message like this.' He pretended to massage the baby then held it up to see if it would smile. But it just opened its eyes wide and dribbled. 'How this child so serious?' He asked Samdaye.

'Well, is your child, you know.'

'But it should be smilin' by now.' He turned to the baby, 'Eh? Aint you should be smilin'?' He laid the bundle in the hammock and stood up. 'I goin' to get grass for the cow.'

'The cow look like it callin'.'

'How you know?'

'It bawl whole day. And it pullin' at the rope and runnin' round the tree.'

Under the guava tree to which it was tied the animal was pawing the ground and moving about restlessly. Froth fell from its mouth. It let out a long moo and turned to look at Manu wild-eyed.

'Now look at trouble!' He had no money. His debts had increased because of the tonics he had bought for Samdaye and the few items for the baby.

'Ain't it callin'?'

His face took on a look of resignation. 'And where the hell you think I will get a bull?' Compai had said that there was a bull on the estate but he had not seen it. He had never been to the area at the back of the cocoa-drying houses where the animal pens were. He wondered if Gomez would permit its use. He enquired of Compai who informed him that Gomez charged two dollars each time a cow was brought. There was one other bull owned by a logger named Manuel but the bull had worked too hard pulling logs from the forest and was probably old and useless.

He discussed alternatives to paying with Prince and Compai. Maybe he could let the cow loose and say it was an accident if it found itself in the Yard.

'Gomez is just the man to take it to the Pound,' Prince said.

'All the way to Sangre Grande?'

'He crazy and wicked enough.'

Compai, whose duties included tending the animal, offered to leave the bull-pen open but tie the animal with a long rope to prevent it escaping. They could then loose the cow in the night and fetch it early in the morning.

'But you finish work for the day,' Manu said.

'Nobody would say anything if I go back to the animals.'

Late that night when the lights on the hill had gone out and the village was silent except for the shrill, unending 'zee-ing' of the cicadas and the occasional cry from the cow, Manu untied the cow which kicked out several times then scampered on to the road and up the hill. The cries of the cow continued intermittently seemingly getting louder instead of softer. He wanted to go and bring it back. The sound of its hooves pounding the gravel and its frantic cries must wake the overseer. For a long time they stood in the dark listening for the sound of voices on the hill.

'Don't worry,' Compai said. 'Everything will turn out right. Let us go to sleep. We will get up very early.'

There was just the faintest light in the eastern sky when Manu rose and hurried through the dewy grass. He soon came to the bull-pen but the calf was nowhere to be seen. Lighting a match in his cupped palm he searched the pens until he heard a single moo coming from the other side of the cocoa-drying houses.

A dog started single barks at long intervals. He waited behind a bougainvillea bush to see if the barking would stop but it increased as other dogs joined and the barking became furious and unending. He began moving stealthily forward. 'Moonie,' he called softly. 'Moonia.' But he could not see in the dark and he feared getting too close to the house. He kept still in the wet grass and cursed his luck. The barking was getting further away and he guessed that the cow was moving to the other side of the house. The light in the sky was swiftly increasing and he could now see the shape of the animals. The dogs were snarling at the cow. He hoped that the animal would head back for home but it had turned and was now coming towards him. He stopped in the deeper dark of the bush. As the animal passed he grabbed at the rope. The dogs now directed their fury at him. Boldly he stepped forward and began to lead the animal downhill.

'Who's that?' Gomez's voice came through the noise. 'Who's that?'

Manu kept walking. Only a few yards more and he would get behind the drying-houses.

'Stop!' Gomez shouted. 'I seein' you. If you move again I will shoot!'

Manu thought he heard a click. O Father! He shook his head in the dark. When things start to go bad for you even wet paper could cut you. 'Don't shoot, Mr Gomez, is Manu. Is me, Manu.' He began walking back towards the house with the dogs snapping at his heels. He could not see the overseer who was in the dark of the verandah. 'Is Manu from the barracks. Hold the dog, boss.' Gomez was saying something and he was shouting but the noise from the dogs drowned all other sounds.

'Stand right there. Don't move.'

'I ain't movin', boss.'

The yellow finger of a flashlight moved about until he stood in its glare.

The dogs stopped barking and Manu heard Gomez explaining to his wife. 'It look like a thief. Somebody thiefin' the cattle.'

'I ain't thiefin', boss. Is me, Manu. My cow get away and it come up here.'

Gomez laughed. 'How you manage to know about your cow gettin' away, Manu? And at this time in the mornin', too! You had a dream? You dream about the cow gettin' loose?' He emerged still holding the gun but he kept at a distance. He did not trust Indian labourers. They always carried their cutlasses and were only too eager to chop people. He observed that this one was without his cutlass. 'You sure that is your cow and is not one from the estate?' He did not know the animals except the horse which he rode occasionally.

Manu began searching his mind for excuses. He couldn't say that the cow had broken the rope the knot at the end was still there. 'Boss, I tie the cow up good good and I don't –'

'Tie the cow on that post,' he indicated the cocoa-drying house with the beam of light. 'No. No. Not the post,' he was not sure if these half-rotting posts could stand any pulling. 'Look for a tree,' he waited for Manu to move.

Gomez's wife stood at the door with a lamp. She asked what was going on.

'The cow get away, madam,' Manu explained. 'It was callin' since yesterday. And you know how they gettin' on wild when they callin'. Madam, in truth I tie the cow in the pen last night and I don't know how it get away.'

'Let the man go with his cow, Ignacio –'

'Let the man go? The damn beast wake me up all night bawlin' and now he comin' quiet quiet and sneak it away! You ain't see this man is a thief. Is only thief does behave so.'

'But nothing damage, Ignacio. Leave the man and the cow and come from the dew.'

'Nothing damage? Nothing damage? When day clear we will see if nothing damage.'

'Is true, madam, nothing ain't damage. If I could just go home now I will tie it up.'

'Ignacio –'

'Go home? I have a mind to shoot it right there. The animal trespassin'. And the man trespassin', too. You know I could shoot his tail right there.'

Manu knew that Prince and Compai must have been hearing the commotion. He hoped they would come and give him some kind of support. The man was behaving like he was mad, threatening to shoot and all. If only they would come he could say that they had been helping him search for the animal. He wondered where they were.

'You finish tying it?'

'Yes, boss.'

'All right. Leave it there. Tomorrow you could get it from the Sangre Grande Police Station. And I have a mind to make you take it there yourself!'

Manu stood shifting from one foot to the other. The wet sandals felt cold. The anger rose from the centre of his stomach. His neck was getting tight and his ears hot. He clenched and unclenched his fists regretting that he had left his cutlass behind. That was the only thing these people respected. They have a lot of mouth until you raise your cutlass.

'Sit down on the cocoa-house step and don't move until I tell you.' Gomez waited until Manu obeyed then he went inside.

A light breeze blew a fine drizzle in Manu's face and he shivered but he was so filled with rage that he refused to go under the drying-house for shelter. He felt his pockets for cigarettes. These he had also left at home. The brighter the eastern sky became the darker became his gloom. As in a dream he heard the approaching workers shuffling silently. They looked at him wordlessly.

While Gomez was still inside his wife came out and told Manu he should go quickly with the animal. Uncomprehendingly he stared at the woman. Prince urged him to leave. He untied the cow and began his descent of the hill pulling the unwilling animal. Halfway down the hill he heard Gomez shouting about thievery and dishonesty; about not having workers anymore but schemers; and about the last estate where he worked where the labourers were the most hard-working and polite. He said that he knew that they were all involved in this scheme of Manu's. 'And don't come out to work today. You hear? No work for you today. Go and tie your cow and think about how you try to make me a fool. But nobody could make Ignacio Gomez a fool. And don't forget to tell people how I nearly shoot your tail but I let you go this time . . .'

Manu could no longer tell what he was saying. As he neared the barrack Samdaye looked at him anxiously and asked him what had happened. Grimly he walked round the building and tied the animal out in the field. He cleaned out the pen, went for a bundle of grass, had his breakfast then went to the shop. He sat in the shop drinking alone. With every drink he became more angry. He felt he would have to move or he would certainly chop-up the blasted fool of an overseer.

In the afternoon when the workers returned home, Gomez, not satisfied with the outcome of the incident, marched down to the barracks his horse-whip in his hand. Calling out Manu, he demanded payment for the service of the bull.

'Stay inside,' Samdaye advised.

He sat on the back step listening to the ranting, until, feeling he could stand it no longer emerged red-eyed buckling his broad belt with the leather case from which the handle of the cutlass stuck out. Slung over his shoulder was his long 'devil-mask' whip. He walked over to the almond tree and leaned against the trunk.

'Don't do anything foolish,' Prince cautioned.

Samdaye had reached his side. 'That stupid cow!' she said. 'I don't know how the cow could get away. And the stupid thing was tied. I see when Manu bring the cow in and tie it in the pen.' She turned to Martina, 'And you see the cow tie in the pen, Miss Martina? Eh, Mr Prince, ain't you see the cow tie?' She looked at Gomez to see the effect. 'Animals could get you in so much trouble. I have a mind to beat the cow, yes. Beat it good for causin' all this trouble.' She looked around as if she was searching for something with which to beat the animal.

'You want to beat the cow?' Manu shouted suddenly and rushed to the pen with a stick. 'I will beat your tail for makin' all this trouble.' He began striking the creature which merely looked at him with its head lowered. It shifted only when struck. With every blow Manu shouted at the animal loud enough so that Gomez would hear. 'I will kill you.' Whack. 'I will murder your tail.' Whack. 'All-you animals too wicked.' Whack.

Samdaye encouraged her husband. 'Give it one for goin' in the overseer yard.' She waited for the whack. 'And one for disturbin' the people sleep.' His rage exhausted somewhat Manu came back to the front of the building but Gomez still continued his verbal attack.

'What happen, boy? I see you come out with cutlass and whip. Like you ready for me?'

Manu was looking at him directly in the eye. Gomez was still in the road about twenty feet away. After those hours of humiliation in the cold and the wet he was ready to take his revenge. He would wait for the man to come into the barrack-yard.

'You have the two dollars to pay me?'

'I don't owe you nothing, boss.'

'For the service.'

'I don't know about any service. You give any service, boss?'

'The service from the bull.'

'Service from bull? I ain't get no service from no bull.'

'Don't play games, boy. You know damn well what I mean. And you owe me two dollars.'

'I don't know what you mean. The cow get away and I went and bring it back. I ain't see no service and I ain't paying no two dollars for nothing.' Then he added slowly, 'You will have to beat me, boss.'

A crowd had gathered. Gopaul and his wife were urging the overseer to forget the whole matter. Samdaye, Prince and Compai were quietly advising Manu to get back into the house. Mangal, sensing the tension, began whimpering.

'I should have sent the animal to the Pound. I give you a chance and now you come out with cutlass and whip and threatening me. Like is **you** want to beat **me** and chop me up. Like you's some kind of badman.' Looking at the crowd, Gomez did not want to lose face. 'So you not paying the two dollars.'

'No, boss. I not payin'.'

Gomez began walking back and forth. His short neck thrust his head forward. He looked like a gamecock. 'I have a mind to give you a good cut-arse −'

'Try, boss. Try.'

'Try? **Try**? I will try your backside today. You just get me vex. All-you people come from where all-you come from and think all-you could walk all over anybody − walk over the overseer. Soon you will walk over the boss, himself. Since you come is only trouble you makin' like you is some kind of bad-john.'

'I don't take stupidness −'

'Hush,' Samdaye said. 'Don't say anything.' She advanced towards the overseer. 'And look, Mr Overseer, is you who leave your house and come quite here in front the man door to provoke him.' Her underlip trembled. Some moisture gathered on the tip of her nose and her face reddened. Her skin had begun to tighten after the baby and the extra fat of pregnancy was quickly disappearing. Her large black eyes opened larger. 'You don't know this man, eh. He is not any weak coolie you could shove about. You better have a care how you talk −'

'A-A. I don't believe this. The lady is a badjohn, too.' It was the first time he was really looking at her since she had arrived pale and pregnant. Her full body now swelled out the thin cotton dress and her skin looked as if it would burst with the firm flesh beneath it. Her eyes danced in anger.

'All you overseers think you could kick around everybody. But you meet your match here. You better don't get him blasted vex . . .'

Gomez was watching the woman's body jiggle under the dress. There was nothing under it. His eyes strained. Her teeth were good and made a white gash in her flushed reddish-brown face. The toes on her bare feet were not splayed and her calves were strong. This was a woman who took care of herself. She was just about his height.

'If the cow get full we will pay you the two dollars –'

'Is five now. It gone up for you.' He was enjoying this.

'But everybody . . . but . . .'

'No "buts". The price just gone up. Is not easy to get bull.' He looked at the whip in his hand. He was not going to provoke her too much. He did not want them to leave just yet. He had an idea how he was going to be paid. But because of the spectators he had to end on the upper note. 'I had a mind to fire you at once,' he told Manu, 'but I will give all-you a chance only because you just had a baby. Be careful from now. One bad move and I will throw your arse out in the road.' He turned away. 'And don't think I will forget about the cow. If it get pregnant you will have to pay . . .'

A car came round the corner and stopped in front of the barracks. Samdaye's mother had arrived.

Her mother never failed, Samdaye thought, to arrive at the most inopportune times. She embraced her and tried to lead her to the door but her mother was quick to sense what was going on. Samdaye shot a glance at Manu who dropped the whip at his feet then she wiped her face with the sleeve of her dress.

'What all-you quarrellin' for?'

'It wasn't a quarrel –'

'You can't fool me.'

'The cow get away last night,' Mangal explained. 'And that man,' he pointed to Gomez, 'come and makin' noise.'

Samdaye smiled. Her mother took up the boy and kissed him then enquired about her granddaughter. 'I come to take all-you away for a few days,' she announced to Samdaye.

'You stayin' tonight?'

'I ain't come to stay the night. I get a ride wit' Ramlal son and I come for you and the children to spend a few days home so you could catch yourself.'

'I ain't goin' nowhere, Ma. I feelin' well and everybody well . . . and . . . I can't leave Manu to see about himself. If you want you could stay tonight but we not goin'.'

'You not goin' for good. Is only for a few days. A little time by the sea is good for you.'

'Right now we can't go. Mangal just start school –'

'What you say, Manu?'

98

'They could go if they want,' Manu said.

'No, Ma, we ain't goin. Come, have some tea. I just goin' to cook dinner.'

Samdaye took her mother inside where she had tea but she did not stay. Failing in her attempts to get Samdaye and the children to leave with her, she handed Samdaye some pumpkin and carillee seeds then she left.

Chapter 10

It was the second reaping of the cocoa crop and from the trunks and branches hung red, yellow and green pods. They shone like waxen, artificial fruit. Many of the pods had turned black and become shrivelled and brittle. A few pods had holes where the soft shell had been chewed and the white pulp had become brown and discoloured. This was the work of squirrels. The pods turning black was blamed on the absence of rain or the lack of sufficient shade from the imortelle trees. The crop would not be as great as years gone by so only a few extra workers were hired.

Gomez, his pith helmet strapped beneath his drooping moustache, his gun in his hand, paired the workers: the men would be picking the pods and the women gathering. The men stood like lancers of old with their long bamboo rods topped by cocoa-knives, triangular-shaped with sharp, pointed, curving 'ears' for hooking the pods. The women stood near their large straw baskets that were crudely made with strong lianas.

Samdaye had hoped that she could go out into the field with Manu but once more he would have none of it.

They were soon in the cool damp of the field hooking and pulling, slicing and chopping at the short stems of the pods. The brush had been cleared so that it was easy to see the brightly-coloured fruit that was gathered into heaps. Near the end of the day the pods would be cracked open with cutlasses or machetes and the seeds covered with white juicy pulp would be filled in the baskets in which a layer of banana leaves would be put to reduce the leaking of the sticky juice. The fresh beans were taken to 'sweat-boxes' which were like small huts with roofs. There they would be left until the pulp had disappeared and they would be ready for drying.

Occasionally a shot was heard when Gomez saw a squirrel. Gabi hoped that Gomez would not shoot too frequently because he had come prepared with sling-shot and pebbles and would like to collect the ten cents for a squirrel tail. The estate encouraged the killing of the animal by paying for the tails which was accepted as evidence of a kill. He kept his eyes open for freshly chewed pods.

They worked like an advancing army through field after field. There was an occasional shout as someone saw a snake which was quickly killed whether it was dangerous or not. They regarded all snakes as dangerous. Manu and Gabi worked as a team and were moving ahead of the others. Gabi found that he had no time to look for squirrels so busy was he trying to keep up with Manu.

'Is day work, you know, Mister Manu.'

'Boy, I can't work slow.'

'But you don't have to run down the work as if you want to finish today. They not payin' by the basket like coffee.'

'I just like pickin' cocoa. I like the feel of the rod especially a nice straight rod like this with a sharp knife slicin' through the stems.'

'I don't like totin' the wet beans. The juice does drip all over you. And wet cocoa is too heavy. You have to jump drains and duck under branches with this heavy basket. When you reach the sweat box you feel like your head sink inside your shoulders and your neck vanish. For a few minutes you can't turn your head. Your neck get so stiff and you feel you will break it if you turn.'

'Whether I work slow or fast you still have to tote the basket.'

'But I wouldn't have to carry so much if you didn't work so fast.'

'You complainin' too much. And look . . . look over there. You didn't pick up all the pods.'

'You soundin' just like Gomez. And while we talkin' about Gomez you better pick out the black pods because he will quarrel like hell if he see black pods on the trees.'

Manu slowed down and began removing some of the black

101

pods. 'I not pickin' all the damn black pods. In any case they will rot and drop.'

'Who pickin' this field?' Gomez's voice came through the trees. He approached Manu with a pod in his hand. 'You leavin' out pods. You not pickin' it clean.'

Manu looked at the pod in the man's hand. He was sure that Gomez must have got it from somewhere else.

'I like my workers to do good work. You gettin' good money. I don't want to see sloppy work.' He continued through the field in his rubber boots that reached almost to his knees.

'We leave out any pods?' Manu asked Gabi.

'The man lie. We ain't leave out no pods.'

They had worked across a number of beds and the sun's rays no longer slanted but searched through the dark canopy of leaves overhead.

'Lunch-time,' Prince called. 'Nobody hungry today?'

They gathered at the foot of an imortelle tree with a carpet of faded orange blooms and unwrapped greasy brown-paper parcels, uncorked rum bottles with cocoa, took the covers off enamel pots revealing chunks of yam and swung the small mouths of calabash water-containers pouring the liquid into their cupped palms from which they drank. Manu opened his khaki bag which Samdaye had made and took out a thick 'sada roti' which had been cut in two and the pieces filled with curried potato. The inside had become orange with the curry. He drank cocoa from a bottle. It was neither hot nor cold.

'This is not a good crop,' Manu said. 'And too much black pods.'

'The estate only now gettin' back in some condition,' Prince said. 'But it will take a long time.' He looked around the field. 'When the Yankees come and open the base every man-jack left everything they doin' and rush for the Yankee dollar. Estate worker, mechanic, teacher, clerk . . . even policeman leave their job to work on the base. Trucks used to go all over the place to pick up workers and drop them off. From all over Trinidad people left their jobs for the base. When they couldn't get enough workers they bring thousands from Barbados, St. Vincent, St. Lucia, Grenada –'

'Grenadians comin' here since Adam was a boy,' Gabi said.

'You know when Adam was a boy?' Prince asked. 'Why you ain't hush your mouth when big man talkin'?'

'Say "old", not "big" because you old but you not big.' Gabi was perched on the low branch of a cocoa tree his enamel pot on his lap.

'Look a snake behind your head, Gabi!' Prince shouted then he laughed as the boy swung around in alarm. 'Boy, I should come back in my next life as a snake. I will run you all over the place.'

'You can't come back like a snake. You too short. You'll come back as a worm.' He laughed at his own joke. 'Or a "zandolie" lizard.'

'I myself work on the base. Compai, too. Everybody left the estate. The whole place was 'bandon until they raise the estate wages and some people come back. But it was not enough to do all the work.'

'I was still a young boy when the base open,' Manu said. 'But I know people quite from Manzanilla who used to travel every day to work with the Americans.'

'It was one big joke. People buy hammer and saw and say they was carpenter and get job as tradesman. Some buy brush and say they was painter to get more money. And if you see how they spend the money. Fellers used to light cigarette with five-dollar note when they get pay. Yankee dollar-note, too!'

'And what you do with your money?' Manu asked.

'How it come so it go. I don't know what happen to the money.'

'I suppose when you get plenty, you spend plenty.'

'True.'

'You should 'a see Prince,' Martina said. 'Wilson hat, brogue shoes, Miami shirts. He used to look like a new shilling. And we eatin' chicken regular. On Sunday was pork stew and crab calalloo. And not local rum but Barbadian "Mount Gay Eclipse". Boy, them was days!'

'I surprise that Compai didn't save something, eh, Gabi?' Manu asked.

'Compai didn't work long on the base. They say he was old.

103

But he always look older than he is,' Prince said. 'He was one of the few people who stay with the estate.'

'I don't think Compai liked the base,' Martina said. 'He is a strange man. He don't care about money. He do what he like to do. He like to make people feel that he got no education but every now and then the education does come out.'

'He don't like the Americans. I don't know what they do him,' Prince added. 'It look like he had some bad experience with them when he was on the sea.'

'What?' Gabi said. 'He don't like John Wayne and Tyrone Power . . . and Rod Cameron and . . .'

'That is not real American, stupid,' Prince cut in. 'That is flim star.'

'So –' Gabi was not allowed to finish.

'And what happen to all those small island people when the base close down?' Manu wanted to know.

'They all over Trinidad. But most of them went to Port of Spain to squat on the hills. Some went to Valencia to the forest to cut down the mora and burn coals. I don't think anybody went back,' Prince explained. 'You know George . . . the feller they call Vincey? A big, strong, black feller. He very quiet. Every fortnight from Friday to Sunday he and his other Vincentian pardner does be in the rumshop. They live in a ranch miles in the forest makin' coal-pit.'

'His pardner is a small feller who does stammer?' Manu asked.

Prince nodded. 'He starts every sentence with "loo-oo-k-ee". Everybody call him "Looks". Well, those fellers live in colonies in the forest . . . Grenada, St. Vincent, St. Lucia. And they work hard like hell.'

'Every now and then one will leave the bush and come to live in the village with a woman,' Martina said. 'It have one red St. Lucian whose pardner died. Well, he livin' with a Indian woman up the road from here. You must let Prince tell you about him. He is a real character!'

Gabi jumped down from the tree. 'Come on everybody, work time. It does have too much skylarkin' on this work.' He walked about like Gomez. 'And don't forget the black-pods, And don't leave half the pods on the tree or I will make everybody come back with flambeau tonight and finish the field.'

Prince looked at Gabi and shook his head from side to side.

Later, the picking of the day done, they gathered round the heaps of pods. Firstly they laid a bed of banana leaves on the ground then cracked open the pods with quick chops and scooped out the white, pulpy beans and heaped them on the leafy bed. From this heap baskets were filled and carried to the 'sweat boxes'.

For over two weeks the reaping continued.

Compai, too, became very busy. After a few days of 'sweating' the beans were removed to the drying houses. The dried coffee beans had been bagged, and the floors had been cleared for the new crop. Of the four drying houses still standing one had fallen into a very poor state; the floor had rotted and the roof-sheeting had rusted and decayed; the thin rails on which the sliding roof ran had worn so thin that some parts hung with just a rope-thin connection. One other house had also fallen into disuse. But the old man still had a lot of work moving between the two houses raking the beans over and over and spreading them in the sun as they became dry, brown and brittle. He also had to pick out the beans that were not fully formed and those that were bad.

Compai had to be there all day. Between raking sessions he would sit under a shady portion of half of the sliding roof and look anxiously at the sky for any sign of rain.

Occasionally he would take Mangal with him after school or on Saturday and Sunday. 'The old man can't run up and down these steps as he used to. You go over and rake this round,' he would tell the boy, who would accept the chore excitedly. But he was too small to use the wooden rake and the old man would be right at his heels taking over the work. 'In a little while you will be a big boy. Then you could do anything. Right now the rake bigger than you.'

Compai found it easier to relate to the child than to the others. In the bright and sparkling eyes he saw an entire future life. In the unending wonder of discovering the world he saw himself again where every bright colour and unexpected sound brought such excitement. At five years old life was filled with a sense of adventure and unbounded optimism. School was just beginning; there were all those games to be learnt and so many people to begin making attachments to. It was like stepping from a long, dark night into the fresh light of morning. All senses were intensified.

'So you like this place, Dorado?'

'Yeh.'

'And you like school?'

The boy nodded.

'And who you like?'

'Ma and Pa . . .'

'And . . .'

'Nani.'

'What about me? You like me?'

But the boy had become interested in a web in a corner of the roof in which a fly gave an occasional struggle. The spider was nowhere to be seen.

Compai took out a knot of guava wood from his pocket and with a worn knife, the blade of which had become thin and curved, he began to shape the piece of wood. 'I makin' a top for you,' he explained.

'And you will teach me to spin it?'

The old man nodded.

'Like how Gabi do it? With the nail pointing up to the sky?'

'Mmm hmm.'

'And you swing you hand in the air like this. And you hold one end of the string and the top come out with the nail on the ground?'

'And it will stay in one place spinnin' and swayin'. And it will "doh-doh" – sleep – like a baby.'

Mangal laughed excitedly. 'I don't want no top,' he said suddenly. 'Sometimes it get catch at the end of the line and could stick you in your foot. Or it could dig out your eye!'

'Not if you wind it good. I will show you how to wind it tight so that it will never happen.'

'Never?'

'Never, my "niño".'

'What is "niño"?'

'Little boy in Spanish. You want to learn Spanish?'

'Yeh.'

They could hear the boy's mother calling.

'Time to go,' Compai said. 'Mammy callin'.'

The boy sped away with the order that Compai should finish making the top that evening. The old man nodded and continued slicing and scraping at the hard knot of the guava wood.

Chapter 11

Darkness had risen from the land a long time ago but Samdaye had not seen Manu. He had left for the estate as usual 'to finish some work' and collect his pay. Normally he would have been home before noon. He would have given her a couple dollars 'to keep' and he would have collected the list of goods to be bought in the shop. The first thing he would do at the shop was to hand Japan the list then he would sit at one of the heavy wooden tables with a twelve-ounce 'flask' of rum. He would invite others to join him and when the bottle was finished someone else would replace it. A flask would last at least one hour and it would be a good half-hour before it was replaced. There was no hurry in the drinking and there was no tall glass with a long iced drink. On the table would be placed a bottle of water which had been kept in the tin-lined box in which would be a block of melting ice. By the time the flask was half empty the water, not very cold in the first place, would be slightly less than the temperature of the room. Each of the men would have a 'shot-glass', thick and heavy, and small, holding not more than one ounce of drink. There was no concerted action in the drinking. There were no toasts. A person would fill his glass whenever he pleased and toss it down his throat. He would then pour water in the glass and drink it. Anybody from the village walking into the shop could be invited to 'fire one' from the bottle. It was only on a special occasion that one would buy a whole twenty-six-ounce bottle of rum although on any Saturday afternoon they would drink more than that. But they felt that the large bottle would encourage too much drinking. Also more people would join the table.

On a few occasions Samdaye had gone to the shop to see what was keeping Manu back. Sometimes she had to fetch the box of goods herself, on her head, while he would wave her on cheerfully pouring himself another drink and delaying his departure so that it would not appear that she had hastened his leaving.

This evening she was worried. Prince had come home by noon and had announced that they had all been laid off, except Gopaul's wife and daughter. Prince was kept on for two days a week. Petit Pierre had arrived and had looked at the bags of dried beans, the mat of drying beans, and the sweat-boxes and had shaken his head. Looking at the list of names in the book a look of worry wrinkled his brow.

'What happen, Boss?' Prince had asked. 'Things bad?'

'Bad,' Pierre had said. 'You see for yourself. This is the worst crop I ever see.' With a look of regret he had announced that he could not afford to keep the estate running. After he had sold the crop he would see if he could rehire them. He could only deal with the few animals that he would sell and so get some immediate cash.

As if in reply to an unspoken question Prince had said that Manu went towards the junction. He had not said anything.

Later that day both Prince and Martina had gone towards the junction. Across the road, Gopaul swung slowly in his hammock humming and sometimes singing a few words in a whine, his child sunk on his belly. Gopaul's wife seemed to be calling her children more frequently and loudly.

Samdaye had nursed the baby, fed Mangal early, fetched a bundle of grass for the cow, brought two four-gallon tins of water from the well, swept the room and the kitchen, washed her feet, hands and face and sat on the kitchen steps looking down at the empty shelf and the box in which she put the groceries from the shop. There was almost nothing to cook: she had no rice, or flour, about two potatoes, some salt, half of a smoked herring, a few tablespoons of sugar, no onions and just about one inch of cooking oil in the bottle. She could have got a hand of bananas somewhere and a dry coconut to make 'chutney' but this evening she was not going to make any effort to cook. She did not bother to light the lamp but sat in the heavier dark of the enclosed room gazing into

109

the liquid dark outside, broken only by the blinking moving lights of the fireflies. Dozens of them would light at the same time then switch off almost immediately when another group would glow. The fireflies existed only at the edge of her consciousness. Her face and ears were burning with anger. She was hungry but she would not eat. She thought of going to the shop and confronting Manu. Scenes and dialogue flashed through her mind. She saw herself quarrelling with him and chasing him out of the rumshop, snatching the money from his hand and ordering the goods herself. She had seen other women drag their husbands from bars and give them good tongue-lashings and, as a girl in Manzanilla, she had witnessed a man being beaten by his wife with a length of the midrib of a coconut branch. He had just stood there while she had flogged him, screaming with rage and yelling incoherently. Her eyes began to burn and two tears rolled slowly down her cheek.

He had not even come home to tell her that he had lost the job. It was as if she and the children meant nothing; that they did not exist; that he could do whatever he wanted.

Prince had come back just as it was getting dark. Gabi was nowhere around and Compai seemed to have gone to sleep early. She could hear Martina softly singing a hymn.

'Ay, girl,' Martina called. 'You husband ain't come home yet?'

Choked with emotion, her voice came out cracked and hoarse and inaudible. She cleared her throat. 'Not yet. He must be get a job in Japan shop to sell rum.'

'Prince say he left him in the shop.'

'Japan must be give him a room to sleep.'

'You mustn't blame him too much. He get fired, you know.'

'But you get fire too. And Prince, and Compai. And I ain't see anybody gettin' drunk and sleepin' in rumshop.' She was rehearsing loudly what she would tell him. 'You have to be a man. If you lose you work, you lose you work. That is not the end of the world. You expect that. That is not government job where they can't fire you just like that.' Her voice was rising. 'This evenin' I will show him. I ain't givin' him one damn thing to eat. I ain't cookin'. If he think he could live on rum let him continue. Let Japan cook for him.'

'You have anything to cook?' Martina enquired.

'Yes,' she lied. 'But I ain't cookin'.'

'You want some "alu"? And rice . . . you want some rice?'

'No. I have food.'

'You could give me back Monday.'

'Thanks, but I want to show him a lesson.'

'You can't teach a drunk man nothing,' Prince said in a slurred voice. 'A drunk man got no reason.'

'Prince talkin' from experience,' Martina said. 'Drunk or sober he couldn't learn anything.' She approached from the kitchen. Seeing the room in darkness she said, 'You sittin' in the dark. You ain't have pitch-oil?' She sat on the lower rung of the steps. 'Girl, don't let man give you worries. All of them have the same madness. They like to do what they want, when they want. And it worse when they young.'

'This is the first time he do this,' Samdaye said in an emotion-choked voice. 'He come home drunk plenty time. You could always tell how much he drink by the amount of talkin' and laughin' he do. The more he drink, the more he does talk and make joke. Other than that he is a quiet man. Sometimes I prefer him if he got a few drinks.'

'I notice how quiet he is. I only start to hear his mouth since the baby born.'

'Is only two things does make him excited: carnival and drink . . . and now is the baby. But he can't afford to drink and play mas'. We can't afford that. We have to work hard and get a place. Now that he not workin' on the estate we will have to move soon.'

'Why? Nobody could put you out. Who will put you out?'

'But if they sell the estate . . .'

'That ain't changin' nothing. Let me tell you, I ain't movin'. They will have to carry me with a bulldozer. You know how much years I spend here? Me and Prince? And you think is so anybody could come and run me out? They must be crazy. Girl, you take it easy, eh, and don't let anybody fool you. They can't drive anybody out.'

'In Manzanilla we had our own house, yes. I mean, was no big house . . . no bungalow . . . but it was our own. Manu and his uncle and some friends build it in one week-end.

And we used to add a piece here and there. But we didn't stay in it long.'

'Why you leave?'

'Is Manu . . . he can't stay long in one place. That is what worryin' me. This will give him a excuse to move again, and to tell you the truth I ain't have the heart to move again. We already move twice in the five years we married. I not bringin' up my children how his father bring him up – runnin' from place to place . . . like crazy ants. The family growin' and a family must have a place.'

'You talkin' like if this is some kind of pig-pen –'

'Is not a pig-pen but I will not let anybody make him feel satisfied with this. I ain't satisfied with this and I ain't lettin' my children feel satisfied with this. I will stick in his tail until he could buy a piece of land somewhere and build a little house. I don't know when we could save the money but we will have to try.'

'Suppose he ain't get no job and he still drinkin' –'

'He will get work. He ain't a lazy man.'

'But if he gettin' drunk everyday you will have to leave him,' Martina said with some mischief.

'No, I ain't leavin' him. I will nhever leave him. He may leave me but I ain't leavin' him.' She shook her head slowly from side to side. 'It ain't have no reason to leave your husband.'

The fireflies continued their sudden, unexpected blinkings. From the cow-pen the acrid mix of urine and dung floated down-wind. Along the edge of the tiny stream and the cocoa field a thousand frogs made bell-like sounds while the occasional bullfrog rasped out a throaty bellow. Gopaul's dog began to bark with increasing frequency.

'Someone comin' up –'

Before Martina could complete her statement they heard Manu's order to the dog to be quiet followed by loud laughter as the dog became silent.

Samdaye rose quickly and lit the lamp and Martina went to her room.

'Prince! Tina! Compai,' Manu shouted. 'Wha' happen, all-you sleepin' already? Bu' how everybody quiet so? Everybody sleepin'? Everybody dead? Work dead so everybody dead.' He laughed long and loudly at his joke and he repeated it.

'Prince, I bring a drink, boy. Come out and fire a little one.'

Prince mumbled a reply and Manu repeated the call. When Prince did not appear Manu sucked the breath through his teeth and walked heavily up the steps pulling open the half-door. Slumping heavily at the small table he put the brown paperbag that he had brought on the floor. He belched loudly.

'Your belly full,' Samdaye observed.

He did not reply. The silence of the gloomy room was broken only by the sound of the frogs outside. He took the bag off the floor and placed it on the table. After some time he asked, 'Where the dinner?'

Samdaye did not reply.

When he saw that she had not moved he asked, 'You ain't hear? I ask where the dinner.'

She still had not moved. She felt her insides welling up with anger and feared to speak lest her voice break.

'Like you deaf of what. You ain't hear I askin' for food?'

'You bring food?' Her voice sounded clear.

'How you mean?'

'I ask if you bring food. You could only cook food if you have food to cook.'

'Don't talk stupidness. You ain't have food in the house?'

'If you used to mind your business you would know –'

'But what the hell is this! The woman ain't cook no dinner.'

'You see me, I stop frettin'. How the drum beat is so I dancin'. When you bring food I will cook. If you don't bring you ain't gettin' nothing.'

'But I buy goods this mornin'. You didn't go for the goods?'

'So is I who have to go for the goods? Like I don't have anything to do . . . like I don't have to see about the children and cut grass for the cow . . . and bring water . . . and see about the house . . . and ask everybody if they see my husband because he ain't come home since mornin' . . . since he get pay? I don't know if he drunk somewhere or somebody beat him and take away his money. I full of time to go and walk up and down the road with a box of goods.'

'But look at my damn crosses! I work whole damn fortnight. I buy the goods. I come home for food and it

113

ain't have nothing to eat! You mean to say you couldn't go for it? You couldn't just walk down the road to the shop before it close? And you do it one hundred times before.'

'Well I ain't doin' it again. I ain't sittin' down and worryin' about nothing. I have the children to see about and enough to do –'

He rose and brushed past her as he went down into the kitchen. There was no sign of food as he opened the few pots. Seeing that they were empty he knocked them one by one onto the ground. They clattered and clanged against each other shattering the stillness. The chickens fluttered in protest and Gopaul's dog started to bark.

'What happen, man?' Martina asked.

'The blasted woman ain't cook nothing.'

'Miss Tina,' Samdaye called, 'you know where this man go since mornin'? You think I know if he get pay or he ain't get pay? Since mornin' he gone without sayin' dog or cat I get pay and I goin' to buy goods or to drink rum. The whole day and half the night he gone. All decent people come home –'

'So now I not decent.'

'You call that decent? Look at you how you drunk and staggerin' – how you stink of rum.'

'But Tina,' he said, 'you know I buy goods before I go to Sangre Grande.'

'Oho, so is Sangre Grande you go. You have family in Sangre Grande? You tell anybody you goin' to Sangre Grande? What business you have there?' She then addressed Martina, 'You know why he go to Sangre Grande? Why he was in so much hurry? Clown costume. We will eat clown costume . . . "diable diable, pay the devil".' She went to the table and, taking up the bag, tore it open and spilled the contents on the earthen floor of the kitchen. The fragments of glass flashed a weak light as they fell.

Martina remained silent. She heard the rising of their voices and did not want to make matters worse.

'Look at the goods you bring to cook,' Samdaye continued. 'Put it in the pot and cook it.'

Manu rushed to her and slapped her hard across her face. She stumbled on one of the fallen pots and fell against the

114

low shelf in the kitchen scattering the remaining utensils. 'I will bust your damn mouth,' he shouted.

'Hit me,' she screamed. 'Beat me! Kill me!' She had risen off the floor and now she stood close to him defiantly. She had never done this before. But he had never hit her either, and though her eyes blazed and her lips trembled she did not cry. But she felt a pang of fear. She had seen him crack his whip and swung it swooshing through the air at other masqueraders, and knew that he was capable of violence. She knew his moods especially when he was angry.

'What the hell you take me for? You think I is some jackass you could ride?'

'You behavin' like one!'

'I have a mind to really bust-up your mouth.'

'Bust it! Bust it!' She went even closer to him. 'If you only touch me again I will lick you down tonight.' She picked up one of the fallen pots.

Martina looked over her half-door. 'Hush your mouth, Samdaye,' she advised.

'Hush my mouth? Hush my mouth?'

'You better warn her, yes. She don't know the devil she playin' with.'

'I know the devil — "diable, diable pay the devil",' she mocked.

'Quiet,' Martina said. 'All-you will wake up the children.'

'Wake up the children? If he don't care about feedin' the children I will care if I wake them up? Wake up, children, and see your father. See how he came home drunk and beatin' me up.'

'You ain't get enough that is why you workin' your mouth so. If I really give you a damn good cuff we will see who mouth will open.'

'Well I still here. Bust my mouth.'

'You think is right, Tina? A man come home and can't get something to eat. And the woman home whole day?' He turned to Samdaye. 'Unless you beat some woman they don't know how to behave.'

'Some man believe woman is animal. They could do what they want. They could treat them like dog. Well this is one woman who ain't takin' that anymore. I take enough.' She saw his fist clenching and expected another blow. Dropping the pot she grabbed a knife and raised her arm. 'You only hit me again.'

Swiftly he grasped her arm and wrenched the knife away cutting himself slightly. He threw the knife to the ground and strode into the night as Samdaye slumped on the steps and began sobbing.

Martina came and put her arm on her shoulder. 'You want some tea? Let me go and make some tea.'

Samdaye shook her head. She rose and went to the baby which had started to cry. Wiping her eyes, she picked it up and began to nurse it rocking gently. It quickly stopped feeding and fell asleep. From the front door she could see Manu sitting on the root of the almond tree leaning against the trunk. He was smoking a cigarette. For a long time she looked at him, at the glowing of the cigarette every time he pulled at it. He looked so sad. She began to feel sorry for him. The loss of the job must have been hard on him. He was never fully happy unless he was working, and she could imagine him looking very bleakly at the future. Her face still stung and she passed her hand over it feeling to see if there was any swelling but it was done absent-mindedly. His face looked almost old, and hung between his sagging shoulders.

She went into the kitchen and gathered the items on the floor. Lighting the fire she began to boil some water to make tea. Occasionally she shook her head regretting having threatened him with the knife. She wondered what could have come over her. When the tea was finished she went back to the front door. 'You want some tea?' She did not want to sound too subservient and it came out a bit gruff. 'I done make it already.' He seemed startled then he rose and came in the house. He drank the tea silently then washed his hands and feet and sloshed water over his head then he went to bed.

As he lay sleeping Samdaye listened to his breathing. It was so comforting to her. He was so trusting of her and she shook her head once more trying to shed the guilt of the incident with the knife. How like a child he looked with all the wrinkles smoothed in relaxation and the baby's tiny fist held in his palm.

Chapter 12

Samdaye woke early next morning with the grass wet with dew, and the sun glowing behind the hill. She greeted Compai who sat gloomily under the almond tree, then she cleaned out the kitchen and started breakfast. She had some flour, one smoked herring and two tomatoes. And she had half an ounce of coffee powder. She decided to roast the herring and the tomatoes and crush them together to eat with the 'roti'.

Manu was soon up. He took the cow across the field and tied it to a tuft of grass then cleaned out the pen. After washing his hands and face he chewed the end of a stick and began vigorously brushing his teeth, scraping his tongue, hawking loudly and spitting. 'Mangal, get up, boy,' he called. 'You want the sun catch you in bed?'

'Mangal,' Samdaye called.

'Come on, son. Time to wake up.'

'Mangal,' Samdaye called again.

The boy emerged slowly then sat on the step and began to nod.

'Come on, wake up,' Samdaye said, 'and go and help your father do something.'

The sounds and smells of the waking village multiplied: dogs barked, children shouted, mothers called, smoke rose from the kitchens and with the roasted smoked herring, fried salt-fish and coffee, the scent of coffee blooms added a subtle sweetness.

Prince emerged rubbing his belly and yawning widely. 'All-you people like to make noise, yes,' he said. 'Night and day all-you makin' noise so. Manu,' he called, 'you get anything to eat yet?'

'Why you don't hush your mouth, Prince?' Martina advised. 'You ain't smell Samdaye cookin'?'

'Compai,' Prince called. 'Gabi.' Hearing no reply he went to the front and saw the old man. He greeted him and asked for Gabi.

The old man looked up with a worried expression. 'I ain't see him since yesterday. He ain't come home last night. I don't know what happen. Something must be happen to him because he never do that before.'

'Manu,' Prince shouted, 'You see Gabi last night?'

'Not since mornin' when we get pay.'

'You ain't seen him in the shop?'

Manu came round the building. 'What happen, he ain't come home?'

Prince shook his head from side to side.

'He never do that before,' Compai repeated. 'Gabi don't do things like that. He always say where he goin'. I don't know what happen.' After a while he said, 'I must go and look for him.'

'Where you goin' to look?' Prince asked. 'Leave him. He must come home.'

'But suppose something happen to him – somebody hold him and rob him. He must be lying down in some drain –'

'Don't worry, Compai,' Prince said. 'Martina, hear this,' Prince called, 'Gabi didn't come home last night.'

Martina came, eyes bulging with surprise and some alarm. 'What you mean? And we see him yesterday at pay?'

'He tell you anything, Tina?' Compai asked. 'He tell anybody anything? He didn't say where he was goin'?'

'Gopaul,' Martina called, 'Gabi ain't come home last night. Ma Gopaul, you talk to Gabi yesterday?'

Gopaul and his wife quickly came over. The look of concern was on every face. No one had been told anything and none had any idea where the boy had gone. They wondered aloud if he had friends outside the village; if he knew any relatives where he could have gone. They tried to recall anything that could give a clue.

'A whole week ago he tell me that he fed up with estate labour,' Manu said.

'One day he tell me that he goin' to Port of Spain to play steelband.'

'He tell me he want to be a calypsonian.'

118

'I hear him say that he want to be a film star.'

'You think all the time he know where his mother livin'? Or his father? You think he gone to look for them?'

'Yesterday he say, "when you miss me I gone",' Mrs Gopual said. 'But people say that all the time.'

'That don't have to mean anything.'

It was finally decided that nobody should go to look for him just yet. He might have met with friends and spent the night.

'The boy promised to play "diable" with me this carnival,' Manu said. 'And he was serious, too.'

'You and your "diable"!' Samdaye said.

'No he really serious. Yesterday he was to go and get material for the costume.'

'You check in his room for his clothes?' Ma Gopaul asked.

'No clothes,' Compai said with a note of resignation. 'No clothes.'

'And why you didn't say so from the beginning?' Prince asked. 'The boy really gone, yes. And he ain't tell anybody. I wonder what could get in his head and make him do a thing like that – to just take up yourself and go like that.'

'Frustration,' Compai said.

'But he was a happy boy,' Martina said. 'You couldn't get a more happy boy.'

'Dasheen don't bear tannia,' Compai said. 'I feel the sea callin' him.'

'You must be tellin' him too much stories about the sea and about all the places you been to,' Gopaul said. 'You can't fill children head with all kind of things to get them restless. You coun say children is . . . is like . . . like little puppy dog: you could lead them astray easy easy. You can't make them feel that this place too small for them otherwise they will want to go in the big city and become loafer and crook. Parasite, I tell you, parasite.'

Gopaul's daughter was edging forward listening to the conversation. As she came nearer she said, 'He tell me he was goin'.'

They looked at her in surprise and she looked flustered.

'When?' Mrs Gopaul asked. She looked searchingly at the girl.

119

'Yesterday.'

'You talk to him yesterday?'

'Yes. When he was goin' for pay. He tell me he was goin' away from this place; that he ain't have no future here . . . that cocoa work is not for him. He can't take this one day work, one day no work.'

'But why he tell you?' Mrs Gopaul asked. 'Why he didn't tell anybody else?'

The girl looked away in confusion.

'You coun say, neighbour, that, maybe he feel he coun talk to the girl and she will understand.' Gopaul felt that he had to give an explanation. He did not want to ask any questions lest he unearth some relationship that was undesirable to him. He looked at her as if for the first time and saw that she was growing into a young woman. If indeed, the young man was confiding in her then, maybe, there was some kind of relationship that he knew nothing about. Maybe it was time that a husband was found for her. He became shifty-eyed and let his gaze fall on the ground.

They were all now looking at the girl.

'I don't know why he tell me. He just up and tell me.'

'He say where he goin'?' Prince asked.

She shook her head in a negative answer.

'Or how long he goin' for? Or where he goin' to stay?'

She kept shaking her head.

Samdaye went in and returned with a cup of coffee for the old man who sat as though there were no bones in his body, his dead eyes staring unfocused.

'Don't worry, Compai,' Martina said. 'Everything will go all right.'

'Let me tell you,' Prince said, 'Gabi is a smart fella, eh. I bet you he come back here lookin' like a million dollars. That boy is no fool. And he damn right to get away from this miserable estate.'

Samdaye looked at her husband. She did not like this talk about leaving the estate. All he wanted now was some little encouragement. Now that there was a cessation of work, it was easy to get him to move once more. 'The boy is young, eh,' she said. 'He ain't got chick nor child. He could just take up himself and move.' She tried to determine the effect of

120

her speech. 'I bet you he come back in a few days. Maybe he will come back this evenin'. Livin' in town ain't easy, nuh. My brother-in-law say how much people ain't have work, and how much vagrant they have and how much rent you have to pay for some little hole. I bet when he feel the pinch he will run back here fast fast. At least here you can't starve but I hear in town you have to buy everything, and you have to have money to buy, and you have to have job to get money. And they ain't have job.'

Samdaye went into the house and returned a short while later with an old paper bag in her hand. She thrust the bag at them. 'I think he leave this for Mangal,' she said. They crowded round the bag and began to pull out the items: a top with a few nail-holes and some places where it had chipped and where the wood had become mildewed, a few chipped marbles, a steel 'bullet' which had come from a large gear-wheel and was used for pitching marbles, some kite paper and a piece of stick with thread wound about it. There was also a corkball, the red coating of which had vanished long ago and was now a dingy grey. 'I find it in a corner in the kitchen.' She left them with the bag saying, 'I wonder if he left anything else.' She quickly came back with a bicycle rim and a curved piece of stick which was used to roll it along. A bicycle rim was a prized 'roller'. 'He left this behind the kitchen,' she explained. 'Mangal,' she called, 'Mangal come and see what your friend Gabi left for you.'

Looking at the boy running forward, Campai said, 'He will miss the child.'

'Mangal will miss him too,' Samdaye said. 'And me, too. I will miss him. He was plenty help for me takin' care of Mangal.'

'All-you talkin' as if the boy dead,' Prince said. 'The boy gone to see the world, you hear. You must know what is goin' on outside. Dorado, Arima and Sangre Grande is not the world. It have plenty places out there and a lot to see and do. The sky stretch way past them hills.'

'You know,' Compai said. The old man rose and went inside and one by one they drifted away leaving Prince and Manu sitting wordlessly under the tree.

A tiny black Austin rounded the bend dragging a lengthening cloud of dust. Its small rectangular windshield was pushed forward. In the car sat Ezekiel Mohammed and his three daughters who were on their way to the Presbyterian church which was what the school became on Sundays. The car stopped with squeaks and a final jerk and Mohammed greeted them with, 'When you fellas goin' to start comin' to church? All it will take is a hour of your time on a Sunday and it good for your soul.' He stuck his long bony face with an outsized hooked nose through the window. Red smiles stretched the heavily made-up faces of the daughters who all wore hats with wide bands and bits of black or white veils overhanging the rims in front of their faces. 'You must spare time to praise the Lord, eh, Mr Hanuman? Eh, Prince? When I passin' back I will pay a visit. About ten o'clock so.' The girls waved as the car seemed to drag itself forward.

'How the man know my name so?' Manu asked.

'What, you don't know Old Man Zeke! He make it his business to know everybody and everything about everybody. And when he say he goin' to pay visit, watch out, he ain't lyin', he comin' to pay visit.'

'What he want – to make me Pusbyterian?'

'He tried with me already,' Prince laughed. 'He try with everybody. He is a elder in the church and he always tryin' to increase the flock.'

'Well, I ain't know about me. I can't see what I have to praise the Lord about – especially now when I ain't have no work.'

'He is a good fella, though. And his daughter – the one in the front seat, Rachel – is a teacher in the school. They don't miss church and Sunday School.'

'She ain't married yet?'

'None of them married.'

'Something wrong with them?'

'What you mean something wrong with them, nothing ain't wrong with them. I don't know why they ain't married.'

'Ain't he got a estate up the road?'

'Yeh, he got a nice place about a mile from here.'

'The only thing I want from him is work. You think he want labourers?'

'Nah. He got two fellas who work with him all the time.'

'Well, Prince, we got to find something to do.' He fell silent lost in thought. He looked at the green hills' their distance cancelled in the bright light. Poui trees shot yellow flames against the green. The imortelle trees, leafless, seemed wintered against the sky and the one with the yellow-tails nests grew thick wild pines in the forks. The long, straw nests swung back and forth. 'You ever burn coals?' he asked suddenly.

'Boy it ain't have nothing I never do. I burn coals, yes.'

'What you know about burnin' coal?' Samdaye had over-heard. 'You want to get big foot or pneumonia from all that heat and cold?'

But Manu was rapidly becoming convinced that the quickest way to make some money without looking for a job was to burn a coal pit. In two weeks, he calculated, you could burn a pit and he had known of burners getting up to fifty bags of coal. At fifty cents a bag it came out to be almost one month's work on the estate. In a few months he could make a few hundred dollars. He could buy land and build a house . . .

'You know what it is to stand up in front of that fire rakin' coals whole day and then the rain come and wet you?' Samdaye asked. 'You want to make me widow?'

'Hush your mouth, eh, woman. You know how much people burn coals? You ever watch them trucks passin' loaded with coals? You know how much one truckload is worth?'

'I don't like it at all.'

'You shame that your mother might know I become coal-burner?'

'How my mother come in this story? No I ain't shame about that. But I don't want you to do something you ain't know about — and too-besides you could get sick.'

'Well the only thing left is makin' garden, and the quickest thing to grow is corn and ochro, and that ain't have no price. All I want is a pardner. Eh, what you say, Prince? We can't go and make a few pits?'

Prince waited until Samdaye had disappeared into the house before replying, 'She right, you know. You can't go just so in this thing. It very dangerous . . . very dangerous. Let me explain: first you have to find a good tree – a good mora tree, or a few smaller trees. It must be a mature tree to make good coals, then you have to cut it down. You ever use a axe? You ever try your hand on mora wood? Mora is like iron. The axe will bounce off that tree like nothing. You chop and chop and don't make a dent bigger than so,' he showed a space between thumb and forefinger. 'Whole mornin' you swing that axe before you get that tree to crack. And when you hear "crack . . . cr-a-a-ck" look out, that tree comin' down, then you have to know where the tree fallin' and which side to run. Man, you could get confused with all that noise. The biggest noise in the world is a big tree crashin' in that quiet high-woods. You never hear thing like that noise in that silence. And to see a big tree drag everything down as it come tearing to the ground, boy! And when it land it bounce back a few time then it shudder as if it now dead. And you alone in the high-wood? Boy, that ain't easy.'

'So you ain't comin'?'

'I ain't say no but I ain't say yes.'

'What kind of answer is that?'

'I have to think hard about this.' He had tried his hand once and had found it too hard and uncertain. It required a lot of experience to chop a large tree into logs then move logs and pack them one over the other filling the spaces with smaller branches then covering the whole with earth so that the wood burns slowly. Then you have to watch that pit like a sick child because the earth covering might crack if it is not thick enough and if the air gets in the wood could burn too fast and all your labour reduced literally to ashes.

'Well, I don't think a man could burn a pit alone.'

'You could do it alone but you must have help for the cuttin' and pilin'. A strong man could do it if he got a bull.'

Manu's eyes took a far-away expression. 'If we could only buy the estate bull . . .'

'You could see you ain't have experience. That bull never work hard; it will just lie down and sleep on the job. A bull must have trainin' to carry yoke and drag logs. Besides where you goin' to get the money to buy bull?'

'With two good pits you could buy a bull.'

124

'And you think about the loneliness? You could imagine you alone in the high-wood night and day wit' nobody but snake and monkey and all kind of strange noise; you sleepin' in a little ranch all by you'self?'

'For how long?'

'Two weeks at a time. Whole day strainin' to cut and move logs with lever, then in the evenin' you ain't have nobody to talk to. You could get crazy.'

Manu thought about Samdaye and the children. That was not too much of a problem. He needed to make some money before Carnival. 'Poor people does really catch their arse, yes,' he said suddenly.

'You see me, I don't care about gettin' rich.'

'I ain't talkin' about getting rich. I talkin' about gettin' out of this blasted place. My wife set on havin' our own place. Every time she get a chance she does say it. You know, I think I could enjoy livin' in the bush by myself for a little while.'

'You could try to join up with one of them St Lucian fellas.'

'I really miss Gabi. He would go.'

'I ain't sure. After how he run away. I don't think he wanted hard work again.'

Shepherd appeared walking slowly, his Bible in his hand.

'Look your man there,' Prince said. 'Ask him.'

'I hear Gabi gone,' Shepherd said.

'You hear that already?' Prince asked.

'In this village nothing don't hide. News travel fast.'

'Manu want a partner to burn coals,' Prince said.

'Not me, I ain't in that business. The Bible say that man should live by the sweat of his brow but that is too much sweat, boy. Burn coals!' He looked incredulously at Manu. 'So where the boy gone?' He had already dismissed the suggestion about burning coals. He opened his Bible and began reading a psalm. He said a loud 'amen' when he was finished. 'The Lord will provide,' he announced. 'You mustn't worry.' He said a short prayer and departed to a 'big meeting in Matura on the beach' where there was to be a few new Baptists being baptised at the mouth of the river.

Manu wondered about Gopaul but Prince laughed. Gopaul, he said suffered from piles, which he used as an excuse to escape working on the estate. Gopaul was lucky to have a hard-working wife who listened with sympathy as her husband complained incessantly about his fate. Most days he would sit pale and bloated, scratching himself and calling on Ram or some other deity to relieve him or take his miserable life. He always seemed to regain his good spirits and vigour on evenings when he would swing slowly in his hammock and sing 'bhajans'. Every morning, however, he would, with exaggerated grimaces of pain and loud groans, drag himself out of bed then walk round his house, alternately hugging and scratching himself. When he had a fever it was a wonder to see his actions: he would run around the house wrapped in a sheet making loud chatterings with his teeth: a-r-r-r-a-da-da a-r-r-r-a-da-da. 'That was the fastest you ever see Gopaul move: when he got fever and he feelin' cold. Nah,' Prince shook his head, 'You don't want to carry Gopaul. You could imagine him in the dark forest running around with that white sheet like some jumbie?' He laughed but Manu sat grim-faced.

'Come, Man, Prince,' Manu encouraged, 'come help me set up a pit. Only two-three days. Then you could come back.'

'When the hard work done? You too smart, boy. You think is stupid I stupid. So when we cut down the trees and pile up the wood and cover the pit you think I will just up and leave just when it ain't have nothing to do but lie down in a hammock and watch it burn?'

'I will watch the pit . . . and when it finished I will give you half the coals.'

'Nah, if we goin' half-and-half we goin' half-and-half. Is beginnin' to end.'

'So what you say?'

'You got a axe?'

Manu nodded. 'But it ain't sharpen.'

'Sharpen it. I got a old one somewhere.'

Manu slapped him on the back.

'I only hope all-you know what all-you doin',' Samdaye called out. 'Miss Tina, you hearin' what they plannin' to do?'

'I hearin', child. I only hope they don't go and kill theyself in the bush.'

'You better don't encourage Mr Prince in any foolishness,' Samdaye cautioned her husband. 'Miss Tina, you better tell your husband how dangerous this thing is. I hear him say so himself. I don't know what madness get in my husband head because he ain't know a from bull-foot about coal-pit.'

'I done make up my mind,' Manu said with finality. 'I ain't sittin' down here like a macajuel with a full belly to let moss grow over me. I got to get some money fast.'

'Don't think is buyin' food and clothes, eh Mr Prince. Is to make carnival costume. That is why he want money so fast. Carnival is two weeks away and he got to get his "diable" clothes in time. That is why he so want to make money. Is not food.' 'Talkin' about food,' she addressed her husband, 'wha' happen to the goods in the shop? You ain't goin for it?'

Manu rose wordlessly and went towards the junction.

From across the road at Gopaul's house came the incessant sound of Gopaul's wife screaming at one or another of her children; of the child crying; of Gopaul's monotonous and unintelligible droning combined with the creaking hammock in an effort to soothe it; of the dog's thin barking and the boys' occasional shouting.

Mangal, excited by the gift of the bicycle rim, kept trying to propel it with the curved stick fitted in the groove. Failing to do this he ran alongside it tapping it forward. Round and round the building he went with his arms and legs flailing. From the edge of Gopaul's yard Stalin watched.

Compai, who had been watching Mangal, came out and began giving the boy pointers on how he should first give a little push to the roller to get it moving before putting the stick in the groove at the right angle then letting it slide the wheel forward. The wheel kept rolling away, wobbling until it fell, making smaller and smaller circles. The boy kept trying until, tired with this, he abruptly left and began to run after a chicken with his stick. Looking at the boy Compai thought of how much he resembled Gabi who, not so very long ago, was the same age. There was an emptiness inside. It was not that he did not expect this. He had often thought about the time when the boy would leave and he felt that he was well prepared for it but he kept being filled with a variety of successive emotions: regret, anger, relief, even satisfaction when he felt that he had brought up the boy as best as he could, in fact it was so good that the boy thought that he could fly from the nest and make his way by himself. He smiled as he saw the same thing happen to Mangal. It was the way things were. This was the natural cycle: dependence, development, maturity then independence. He had been listening to Manu trying to get Prince to join him in a coal-burning enterprise and he understood Samdaye's reluctance to let him go. Compai would have welcomed the idea to go into the forest but he did not think that he would be of much help. First of all he had never burnt the pits though he had seen coal-burners at work because they sometimes made pits close to the road. He did not think it was any harder than working on the cocoa estate, in fact, it seemed much easier because you made your own hours; it was not the dawn to dusk labouring. The hardest thing was cutting down the trees, chopping the lengths of logs and piling them up. The rest was easy – just sitting there and looking out to see that nothing went wrong. And then it was just raking up the coals and toting the bags out to the roadside to be picked up. If Prince did not want to go, he would accompany Manu. It was not the money but the activity would give him time to get accustomed to Gabi's absence. Samdaye had looked at him with a tremendous amount of pity but she did not understand him; none of them understood him. He had been accustomed to the life of a single man, and for those who did not know, the single man is happiest being alone. Loneliness had nothing to do with being alone. A sailor on a small ship spent countless hours keeping watch with just the wide sky above and the stars and the wet wind whipping the spray. Even sitting in the cocoa-house drying the beans all day could be enjoyable. From the drying floor you could see the land westward for miles, and in the north, stretching almost from east to west, the mountains rolled with the green changing constantly, depending upon the time of the day and the extent of the clouds: it could go from a bright green to blue and purple. Few people had the joy of watching the day go by: from the early dawn when the air was wet and fresh and everything was soft and filmy; with the start of the morning sounds – the whistling and trilling and cheep-cheeping; the fast flitting and flashing past of red, blue or yellow, and the ordered formation-flying of the white cattle egrets heading east from their nesting places in the Caroni Swamp; to see how the light brought the colour out like developing film in a dark room; to have the sun arc overhead until it blazed its farewell in the western sky while you sit running your fingers over the strings of a cautro as the darkness rose again. But he will miss this boy, Carlos Pacheco, who was now called by everybody, including himself, Gabi. You don't bring up a child for almost twelve years having him as a constant companion and not miss him. Leaving silently like a thief was unpardonable. He could, at least, have told him what he intended to do. He felt very foolish having to know about Gabi's departure just about the same time as everybody else. It was humiliating. What did the boy mean by treating him like some everyday stranger? The anger was rising. One should not expect gratitude from anybody; the more you do for people the less you must expect to get in return. His eyes were following Mangal but his agitated thoughts were reflected by the movement of his jaws and the twitching in the temples. But maybe the boy was right. What was he doing with an old man in a village in which he had no future? It was better that he make a clean break and try to make something of himself: get a job on a ship and see the world. The ships these days were much better than those on which he worked, and Port of Spain was becoming a busy port. The boy had his whole life ahead of him while he was savouring each day because his time was limited. In his mind he wished him well and hoped that he did not get into bad company.

Gazing over the half-door her baby in her arms Samdaye observed the old man whose eyes followed her son as he ran with his arms and legs flailing after the squawking chicken. It must be difficult for him having no children, no relatives and now the boy running away. She could not imagine herself in such a position. He looked so shrunken and deserted. She wanted to ask him to dissuade Manu from going into the forest but it was the wrong time. Maybe it was a good time as it would take his mind off his troubles.

'Compai,' she called. 'You must not get worried. The boy will come back.'

'I not worried.'

'He must come back.'

'Well, if he come back he come back. I didn't chase him out.'

She did not like how he sounded. 'You know young people these days: their foot too hot. They can't stay one place.'

'All birds must leave their nests someday. I did expect this sometime so I not too surprised.'

'But is still a shock,' she said. 'For all of us,' she added.

He nodded silently.

'Compai,' she started down the steps. 'I want you to talk to my husband. About this coal-burnin'. I don't like it.'

'Is nothing wrong with that. Burnin' coal is work just like anything else.'

'But I don't like it. I think is dangerous.'

'Child, all work is dangerous if you don't know what you doin' or if you careless.' He held out the roller to Mangal who had given up chasing the chicken. 'You could dead from a accident in your kitchen, right here.'

'But I hear so much —'

'It ain't have nothing really dangerous about burnin' coals. It have disappointment, yes. You could lose your pit but, if you careful and know what you doin', is not too hard. If I wasn't too old I would go too.'

'You only sayin' so.'

She thought there was some truth in what the man was saying but she had many doubts. She did not like the idea of Manu being in the forest for weeks at a time. Who will cook for him? And what about snakes all around him in that little ranch? And the drinking: she had heard that the coal-burners moved in a group from area to area and that they had large stocks of rum. And women used to go and visit them in the bush and spend time. There was no reason for him to go just yet. They could survive for a few weeks on the little money he had left over from what he spent the day before, though she had no idea how much he spent in drinking and in materials for his costume. If he did not drink any more of the little money they could live for some time. Wrapped in her thoughts she did not see Gomez approaching until she heard the old man say, 'I wonder what he want comin' here Sunday mornin'.'

The overseer was striding forward making exaggerated long steps from his short legs, his head thrust forward and his arms swinging in long arcs. He called out loudly to Gopaul and his wife.

Compai greeted him coldly. Samdaye smiled and nodded.

He greeted them both and called out to Prince and Martina. 'I sorry about yesterday. I myself did not know this was goin' to happen. It was out o' the blue. Just so the man come and fire nearly everybody. He ain't give me no warnin'. He ain't ask me no advice.'

Compai shot a quick glance at Prince who winked secretly.

'But is so those big white people does do. They make up their mind to do something and they do it.'

'Well, is the man estate,' Compai said. 'He could do what he want, yes. If he want to fire everybody is his right. If the damn place ain't makin' money he can't run it for charity.'

'You right,' Gomez said. 'But them fellers don't think about poor people.'

Prince winked again. He wondered since when Gomez thought about poor people and what was the real purpose of his visit.

'You should see how them white people live in St. Clair. I been to his house a few times. Man, you should see the size of the house; is three stories tall with gables all round and the roof cover with tiles – not galvanize, you hear – but tiles they bring from England. The house is on about one acre of land facin' the Savannah. It set back from the road with a driveway going round from two big iron gates. You go in one and come out the other. It got a big saman tree in the middle of the half circle lawn. And flowers – if you see flowers – flowers of all kind: bougainvillea, lilies, buttercups, roses, ixoras hibiscus – man, any kind you could name.' His eyelids peeled back and his stubby fingers played the air. 'Grey stone pillars over the three wide doorways and a verandah running on three sides. The whole house resting on three feet of blue stone foundation.'

'He plant anything on the land?' Samdaye asked.

'Wha' you mean plant?' Compai laughed. 'They don't plant anything in town. Only grass, eh, Gomez? They does plant grass to make lawn.'

'What about inside the house?' Samdaye asked. 'You ever been inside?'

'Well . . . not upstairs. But I been on the verandah and one time I went in the study. The floor is patterned marble and the doors and windows have decorated glass with pictures make out of the glass. And all round the room is faced with wood for about four feet, polished so bright that you could see your face. Man, it have people polishing and cleaning whole day – maids and gardeners, and groom and chauffeur. I never see so much people to do so little bit of work. But they look busier than anybody.'

'So if he got so much people wastin' time in town why he don't fire them instead of comin' down here and firin' hard-workin' people left, right and centre,' Prince wanted to know.

'He didn't want to fire anybody here, you know,' Gomez said, 'he himself tell me so. He was really sorry but it had nothing he could do. At the end of this crop the estate ain't make any profit so he decide that instead of takin' money from his pocket to do maintenance work he will have to hold on the labour for a while. I tell you the man was really sorry.'

'Sorry my foot,' Compai said. 'Let me tell you, them white people live two lives, yes. One in town with the governor and them and all their big-shot friends, and the other as estate boss. They don't mix the two.'

'That is true,' Gomez agreed, 'I myself hear him talkin' to the Governor on the phone about some cocktail party.'

'What is a cocktail party?' Samdaye asked.

Gomez turned to her and she could feel his gaze stripping her. He looked at her oblivious of the question.

'They must be comin' to the party wearing cock-tail feathers in their heads,' Prince laughed.

'Cock-tail is a drink,' Compai said. 'On one boat I work we had cocktail party every evenin'. Is just a lot o' people standin' up drinkin' and talkin', and takin' little little bite on little little sandwich. They do that before dinner.'

132

'So what all-you goin' to do?'

'Live off me fat,' Compai laughed dryly.

Samdaye caught the overseer's eye and thought she should reply. 'Manu say he goin' to burn coals in the forest.'

'I might have something for you to do,' Gomez said to her.

At her astonished expression he continued, 'my wife want a little help and I lookin' for somebody.'

Prince glanced at Compai and smiled.

'Yes, is time I get somebody to give her a little help in the housework. With the children and all is too much.'

'I-I don't know.'

'Well you will think about it,' Gomez said. 'You don't have to start right away. You could let me know when you ready. The work not hard.'

A smile was playing round Prince's mouth. 'You lucky, girl,' he said. 'Not everybody does get invite for job. You very lucky. Anyway make sure you know exactly what the boss will want you to do.' He was looking at Compai in the eye.

Samdaye felt the hot breath of Gomez as he came closer to peer at the baby. 'He lookin' cute, eh?' he said.

'Is a girl,' Samdaye said.

'Doesn't matter. She still lookin' cute.' He attempted to take the baby and his hands pressed against her bosom. She felt that it stayed a while too long. 'She doesn't want to come by me.' He then made some baby noises then he left after telling them that the break in employment might not be too long.

As Samdaye left Prince said to Compai, 'I know it must have some reason for that damn kiss-ass to come here. He got his eye on Samdaye but, I tell you, he really lookin' for trouble.'

'I tell you.'

'The boss will have it real hard now,' Prince said loudly so that Gomez would hear. 'He will have too much work. The lady will have too much work too.'

Samdaye saw Gomez stop off at Gopaul's house then pick up the child. 'This child too cute,' he said as Gopaul struggled off the hammock and got to his feet and his wife and daughter gathered to welcome the overseer. She heard them invite him to stay for lunch which they had started to prepare. 'Dal-puri and chicken curry,' Mrs Gopaul said, 'and rice and dal. And I know how you like dal. And today Rosie cookin'.' She looked at her daughter.

Samdaye heard Gomez ask about when Rosie was going to be married. 'So when we goin' to have the "sohari" for this 'dulahin'?'

Prince shook his head. 'That man is goin' to be just like Benito Marin. He just can't help makin' move on woman.'

Manu was returning with the goods from the shop. On his head was a wooden box and on his shoulders a bag half-filled with flour. Perspiration ran down the sides of his face.

Samdaye made room for him as he came up the steps. 'Now you have food, woman, cook!' He laid down the goods and, taking his costume, and bits of material he had bought, he went under the almond tree to begin repairs. He said it good-naturedly and she was glad that he had almost obediently gone to the shop for the groceries. Absent-mindedly she felt her face where he had hit her and took a quick look into the small shaving mirror but it did not sting anymore neither did it show.

'And where you goin' with that old mas' foolishness,' she called over the half-door. 'You have time for that? And you have money?' He said nothing but began matching the various bits of cloth. Carefully he placed the small pieces of mirror over the torn pieces, and, where the holes were too large he placed fabric over them.

'Compai, why you don't tell him that is childishness; that he is a big man with wife and children and that he ain't have no work . . . and he can't go and put himself in danger. And ask him what profit he gettin' in that?'

'He is a big man, yes,' Compai said.

But Manu sat with his legs outstretched, cutting and matching and rearranging. He was so absorbed that he did not see when Ezekiel Mohammed drove up and he and his three daughters alighted. Mohammed, tall and gaunt, with his white shirt resting on his shoulders and curved back, and touching no other part of his body; his long, thin neck growing out of his collar like the eye of a crab, pushing back his hat, adjusted his tie and stroked his small white beard that hung from his chin. Rachel, the teacher spied Mangal and headed for him, who, when he saw her, stood frozen, his roller in his hand. The other daughters similar-hatted and veiled with similar short-cut hair went towards Samdaye who was still looking over the door which she opened to invite them in.

'What is that you doin', man, on this Sabbath mornin'?'

Manu raised his eyes and saw Mohammed with the sun making a halo round his silhouetted face.

'Eh, what you makin' – a mas'? You does play mas'?'

Manu nodded, 'Diable'.

'Diable diable?'

Manu nodded again.

Mohammed observed Manu whose finger worked none too deftly. 'You should let somebody who could sew help you. Why you don't ask your wife?'

'She wouldn't do it?'

'She wouldn't help?'

Manu shook his head.

'Oh ... I see ... she don't like you playing mas'.' He continued asking questions then suggested that Manu come to church next Sunday. He soon felt that he was getting nowhere in his effort to get the young man to respond with any interest. Nevertheless he continued trying to explain the life of Christ and the importance of his becoming a Christian; of living a life of piety and temperance; how Christianity is a religion for the modern man not like others which were more concerned with ritual and were primitive and backward. He did not call names.

Samdaye examined the two girls. They were about her own age yet they seemed to belong to some other country. She looked at their shaved legs, the painted toe-nails visible through the cuts at the tips of their shoes, the painted faces – the rouge and lip-stick, the hats at slight angles on their heads, their smiles of confidence and, it seemed, a knowledge of some shared secret. She became aware of her bare feet and her shabby dress stained with banana milk. But she did not really envy them with their pale skin and bony frames. They ignored her open door and stood near the steps under the shade of the almond. They, too, were impressing on her the importance of becoming a Presbyterian between playing with the baby which had a smell of stale milk.

The eldest girl, Rachel, the teacher, offered Mangal a Christmas card which he took. It had a picture of a Christmas tree gaily decorated and with snow hanging from the branches and beneath it was stacked beribboned boxes. Inside, in addition to the printed wishes, was the inscription in a flowing hand, 'Our fondest wishes to you, John and Margaret. Hope the winter in Moose Jaw is better than ours in Redwater.' Mangal nodded a promise to be in Sunday School the coming Sunday.

Samdaye watched her husband silently mending. She did not remark on the smaller quantity of groceries he brought, he had used some of the money on his costume. If, indeed, he decided to leave for the forest in the morning she would give him most of what he had brought and would have to make do with what was left.

She listened as the girls called the names of the members of the church and said how the membership was growing; how the Canadians had come to help the East Indians and that it was left to them to avail themselves of the help so that they could advance themselves. They were all employed – one as a clerk in a bank in Arima and the other in the Warden's office in Sangre Grande. The eldest one was about to enter a Teachers Training College in Port of Spain. It was all due, she implied, to their being Presbyterians. 'You get to know a lot of people,' one of them said, 'and make a lot of contacts.'

She waved to them as they left and felt pleased that they came to visit her and promised to return. They, at least, showed an interest in her and her family. She would have to learn more about their religion.

Manu was restless all day. He took out his axe and sharpened it, and examined the handle closely. Prince did the same saying that his axe had become rusty. She heard Prince and Martina arguing. Martina was telling Prince that he was too old to spend weeks in the forest and to do such difficult work. Compai walked about aimlessly occasionally making a gesture expressing something that went on in his mind. Samdaye went about her day hoping that Manu would change his mind when the morning came but when, late in the evening he asked her to put some groceries in a box and he rolled up a pair of trousers and a shirt in a paper bag, she knew that he had made up his mind and that he would be off in the morning.

Chapter 13 when James

Chapter 13

A fine drizzle merged with the dark of the early morning
as Manu left. He did not kiss the children or say goodbye.
He merely said, 'I gone, eh.' To Samdaye's query about when
he would return he replied that he would try to be back by
Friday. Samdaye, not seeing Prince join him, asked if he was
not waiting for Prince but he did not reply; he just kept
walking away briskly into the damp darkness. 'Take care,'
she said. A feeling of fear created a hollow in her stomach.
'Prince,' she called. 'Mr Prince. You not goin' too? Look
Manu leavin, you know.' But there was no reply from the
room next door. After a while Martina said, 'Prince not goin',
girl. I tell him he too old to get himself in that business.'

Manu had vanished in the darkness. He stirred a trail of
thin barks that gave evidence of how far he had reached.
Several cocks crowed. 'You could tell me where he goin' in
this weather, Miss Tina?' The fear had thinned her voice.
'And he ain't know not one damn thing about what he goin'
to do. If I know Mr Prince was not goin' I wouldn't let him go
alone. What he will do in the bush alone?' She kept expressing
her fears aloud but she elicited no further communication
from Martina.

She could see no other light in the village. Nothing stood
out except a few pale stars near the horizon. She blew the
lamp out and lay on the bed but she felt guilty that she
was lying down while Manu was out in the rain and the
dark. She felt her eyes welling. It was more from frustration
than from anything else. And helplessness. Working on the
estate was the problem. They just hire you and fire you as
they pleased. And if you complained they could just as easy
throw you out from the barracks. If only he could get a job

like Shepherd who worked with the road gang, weeding the grass verge and the clumps that grew in the centre of the gravelled road or sometimes wheeling loads of gravel to fill the potholes. The small gang even had a water-carrier who brought cups of water from her bucket which stood in the cool shade of some tree. By one o'clock every day Shepherd could be seen heading home his hoe on his shoulder or his 'swiper', crook-stick and file stuck in his back-pocket. It was a government job and you got paid even when you took sick. She did not know how you went about getting a job 'on the road'. If only she could get a job as a water-carrier to sit in the shade with her bucket and just occasionally have to take a cup of water to a worker. It is true that people said things about water-carriers: how they were easy women and how the road overseers had affairs with them. Also they were the subject of many rude jokes by the workers. She had never seen an Indian woman as a water-carrier.

The rosy haze of dawn was faintly spreading as she went to the pen and untied the animal from the post and took it to the field. She returned and cleaned the pen. She threw some crushed grains of corn to the hen and the few chicks, and busied herself round the house. As the first rays of sunlight shot through the trees she woke Mangal. Soon she was finished with her chores and found that she had about two more hours before Mangal could be sent out to school. The time just seemed to drag on. Taking the four-gallon can that originally contained coconut oil and still bore the fading mark of the Coconut Growers' Association, she went to the well in the cocoa field and fetched two trips of water. With the second trip she took Mangal along and bathed him. She had him bring his one-gallon tin in which he too, fetched water on his head.

She began to plan what she would do now that Manu was away. First of all she would not have to get up around four o'clock to cook both his breakfast and lunch. But knowing that he was out there in the woods she knew that she would not be able to stay in bed. Also, she had never let the sun catch her in bed. But there was no way Manu would stay long in the forest. She was sure that he would be back before Friday disgruntled and disappointed. That, however, would be better than the uncertainty of his existence. He had never spent a night away from her although she had been away at her mother's not more than once a year. But not Manu. There was nowhere for him to go. He had an aunt somewhere in Tamana but he had never been to see her. He had cousins there, he said, but he did not know them. No matter how much he had drunk or how late it had become he always returned home. And he always rose before sunrise. As if sensing something was not right Mangal asked, 'Where Pa gone?' 'To burn coals,' she replied. 'Your father gone in the high-wood to burn coals.'

'Why we want coals?'

'To make money. You sell the coals and make money.'

'What time he comin' back?'

'He not comin' back today.'

'He spendin' the night in the bush?'

'Whole week.'

'We can't go with him in the bush? Eh, Ma. We can't go?'

'And where we will stay?'

'We will build a house.'

She smiled. The idea did not sound too bad. She could help with the pit and when the pit was empty she could plant a vegetable garden on the site of the pit. Nothing grows so green as when it is planted in the ash of a coal-pit. And where a trench had formed round the pit where the earth had been taken to cover the wood dasheen and tannia could be planted. There was nothing to better working for one's self: get a few acres of cocoa and coffee, and plant bananas and citrus; make a vegetable garden to supplement sales; build a little house with your own yard and field where the children could play and where you could mind a cow and goats. That is all she wanted from life. So many people had land that they did not work. Estates were being abandoned if not entirely at least large sections were just left to be reclaimed by the bush. Coming along the road from Manzanilla she had seen a few examples of this where bird vine and wild-pine smothered the cocoa trees. In some places orange and grapefruit trees struggled fruitlessly for space with black sage and wild heliconia. There was so much land about. In the now defunct American base there were thousands of acres and thousands of building sites where the buildings had been removed – the walls, floors and roofs, and all the fittings – and now all that remained were the concrete foundations and the red-clay pillars sticking out in contrast against the green increasing bush intersected by well-paved roads. Why didn't the government give the land to people who wanted to work it? Although she had heard that the land had been graded and all the topsoil used to fill the hollows and to build foundation for the miles of roads and the huge runway. She had heard about people who squatted far from the main road. They covered a section of the foundation of some of the buildings by putting a straw roof over the pillars. But the government sent out warnings against squatters and some of them had been chased out. Some rumour went around that the Americans still had ammunition stored in the bush and MPs still roamed the area. It was also reputed to be a haven for criminals who could not be caught in that deserted maze. In any case it was too far from the school.

Maybe that is what she should do: get a place near the school and open a small shop in which she could sell sugar-cakes and sweet-drinks to the school children. The land there belonged to the estate and there was a large open space across from the school. If they went and squatted maybe no one would object. She could start with putting up a very small shack and still live in the barracks. She would have to talk to the overseer.

She thought about the overseer and the offer of a job in his house. Maybe that was the answer. With Manu away she could give it a try. She remembered the way Gomez had looked through her thin dress and the length of time he had spent pressing his hand on her bosom as he prolonged the act of taking her child in his arms. But nothing could happen if you don't want it to. The only problem was if Manu became provoked over some real or imagined incident. She smiled to herself. She realized that she was experiencing a feeling of independence and Manu not gone but a couple of hours.

Up to then there had not been a sound from Martina's room. She wondered how they could sleep in a time like that. On any normal Monday morning they would have been up and out to work. Gopaul's wife and daughter had already left. Compai had been moving around silently since daybreak. But Prince and Martina were behaving as though they had independent means and not a single care in the world. 'Wha' happen, Compai, like Mr Prince and Miss Tina on honeymoon o' what? They ain't gettin' up today?'

'They ain't have nowhere to go.'

'Like you think my bed wet or what,' Prince called.

Samdaye felt slightly embarrassed. She had never engaged in such banter but she continued bravely, 'But Mr Prince, how you could lie down in your warm bed and let my husband go out alone in this kind of weather?'

'Is not I married to your husband, child.'

'But I think you was goin' to go with him.'

'You think so but I change my mind.'

'Just so?'

'Just so.'

She heard him yawn loudly then saw him emerge scratching himself like Gopaul and leaving long white fingernail marks. Slowly and carefully he came down the few steps, his feet encased in motor-car tyre sandals.

'Girl, you ain't see that I too old for that foolishness? What I doin' sleepin' in that bush like I don't have bed. You see me, I don't intend to kill myself for money. I ain't want to come millionaire.'

He really looked old with his tightly-curled white hair making a horseshoe around his shining bald area which went over to the back of his head. There was a long white smear at the corner of his mouth and rheumy residue at the corners of his eyes.

'I was only goin' to give him a start and keep him company,' he explained. 'But I decide to let him go by himself to see if he really serious. If he come back on Friday to go back then I might go with him.'

'He ain't goin' nowhere,' Martina said with finality. 'I ain't lettin' him go in the bush and play young boy to burn no coals and get sick and dead on my hands.' She watched him walk outside on to the bare, grassless yard. 'He ain't the best-lookin' man in the world but he is all I got.' Some

142

bangs and clangs came from her kitchen as she moved empty utensils about. 'Prince,' she called, 'you better go down in the cocoa field and look for a bunch of fig and a breadfruit. I see a few on the tree by the well.'

'If you get bring a breadfruit for me too,' Samdaye said. 'But make sure that they full.'

'So what you think, I will pick young breadfruit?' Prince said. 'You think I don't know a full bull?' He laughed at his joke. 'But I not goin' before I get something to eat. Martina, wha' you got to eat?'

A low, dark cloud started to spread like an inkstain. A strong wind whipped it from behind. In less than half an hour it was overhead sending down large isolated drops which soon became a shower that raced across the sky leaving ragged grey shreds stuck motionless on the pale blue sky.

'It look like we goin' to get some rain,' Samdaye said but no one replied. 'Mangal,' she called, 'you better get ready for school.'

'So soon, Ma?' He was trying to wind the top Compai had made for him but the string kept slipping down as it was not wound tightly enough.

'And put away that top! You like to play too much.'

'All play and no work make Jack a fool,' Compai said. 'Go to school, Mangal boy and you not goin' to be a fool.' He looked at Prince. 'How you like my poetry, eh, Prince?' After a while he said, 'Gabi used to like poetry.'

'You talkin' as though the boy dead,' Martina said. 'The boy must be enjoyin' himself in town, somewhere.'

After a while the voices of children came around the corner and Mangal joined the band on the way to school. Coconut oil ran behind his ears. His thin, khaki bag had a long strap that hung from his shoulder across his chest. Like most of the other children he was barefooted and, like the other boys, he wore a blue shirt and khaki trousers made from the same material as his bag.

The school was about a mile and a half away from the junction and stood at the top of a hill round which the road wound. A ragged fence of teak sticks, bound with wire, hung unevenly along the top of a high bank at the edge of the road, which levelled off at the entrance to the school. Children from the junction end, finding it a waste of effort and time to walk past the school to the top of the hill in order to enter through the gateless entrance, had cut a hole in the fence and created their own pathway where the bare earth had been eroded by the beds of tiny rivulets. In the rainy season the pathway became very slippery. This morning the few children who had shoes could not chance walking up the gluey, slippery clay because of the early morning rain. They wiped their muddied feet on the edge of the concrete steps or on small tufts of grass because the water level in the cistern was low and the water was restricted to drinking and not for washing feet. In any case the worn, brass tap had a sort of hasp and staple that was secured with a lock and was only opened at intermission times.

The Principal was standing at the doorway looking to see who would enter the school with dirty feet. He had a length of dry sapling from a guava tree in his hand. His eyes glinted through rolls of fat under a threatening brow. He went to his desk and shook a hand-bell which was the signal for a number of boys to run toward the bell hanging between two poles near the front steps. The winner used a short piece of iron and beat it against the bell for half a minute. This was the first bell. Five minutes later it was tolled again and this was the signal for the children to form lines in the schoolyard. The Infants were lined up in a separate section of the yard. The Standards formed rows according to their 'Houses': Shakespeare, Milton and Dickens. Mr Jeremiah Jaglal, the Principal, was a lover of literature. He had the names changed from 'Hollis', 'Fletcher' and 'Young', past governors of Trinidad and Tobago.

When they had lined themselves according to height and House, the Principal gave a signal for them to mark time. He brought them to a halt when he saw bits of wet clay flying off their feet. But he was a man who believed in exercise so he had them raise their hands above their heads, bring them out in front and put them down at their sides. A dozen times he ordered: 'up', 'out' and 'down'. Then he shouted 'roll' at which they brought their fists with elbows bent in front of them and rolled them round and round each other. They stopped at his signal then stood still. Sandflies buzzed around their bare legs but they dared not more. Mr Jaglal was known as a strict disciplinarian.

'By labour and intent study' was his theme for this morning and he spent several minutes speaking on this line from Milton while they longed to scratch the sandfly bites and move from the damp earth. On dry mornings he would walk down the lines, stick in hand, looking for dirty fingernails, shirts out of trousers or any of his infrangible rules. Then they would have to run the gauntlet of going past him at the top of the stairs. Their bottoms would contract and their backs would arch for they expected the whip to descend for some infraction real or imagined. Their eyes would be slanted towards the whip hand, the girls as vigilant as the boys for they would be examined with no less severity.

Mangal stood in the Infant lines where his teacher, Miss Mohammed, did everything in imitation of the Principal. As soon as she saw the lines of the bigger students moving, she marched the little ones inside.

The muffled sounds of the marching on the earth would resound on the wooden floor as some of the bigger boys would stamp their feet with exaggerated movement. They would march to their positions behind their desks and keep marking time until the Principal rang the bell to signal them to stop.

Miss Mohammed called out the title of a hymn and gave them the note with a hum. They sang three hymns then Teacher Laloo said a short prayer which he read from a piece of paper. The bell was then rung signalling them to sit, which they did with a great shuffling and scraping of desks.

The Principal reminded them of Milton's lines of 'labour and intent study' then he thanked Miss Mohammed whom he referred to as Miss Ravisham, which he had changed from Havisham because she was ravishing, he said; and he thanked Laloo whom he called Cratchit because he thought Laloo was crotchety, his seven children before he was forty making him short-tempered.

As he continued speaking Mangal gazed round the walls, which on two sides had wooden windows that were hinged at the top and were pushed out with sticks. At both ends of the building there were three Demerara windows that were also pushed out. On a green board with a red border was painted 'Our Motto, Labour Conquers All'. The board hung directly over the head of the Principal. On one side of the motto was hung a coloured photograph of Queen Elizabeth and on the other side a picture of Jesus with a crown of thorns, with the word 'PAX' underneath. Mangal recalled Prince's account of Gabi catching chickens – pax pax. Queen Elizabeth II was pink and smiling with her shining crown of gold and pearls. The picture of Jesus was a reproduction of a black-and-white pen and ink drawing, and was very sad. He did not like it and preferred the young and glowing face of the Queen. There was no space for any more pictures on the walls but the wooden screens that separated the classrooms were all covered with coloured chalk drawings. The screens were free-standing and were shifted aside whenever the Principal spoke to the entire school. They were now put back in place. Only one eight-foot-wide screen separated the two rows of the First and Second Years of the Infant Section from the rest of the school. On the board were four sections bordered in red chalk: a numbers chart in which the numbers from one to ten were written in yellow and against each number was put a corresponding number of white dots. Mangal counted each one to see if it was correct. In another section of the board was 'Word Building' with two columns of words – one with three-letter words built on 'an' and the other with three-letter words build on 'at'. The 'ans' and 'ats' were all in blue chalk. The third one was about the weather. There was a drawing of a smiling sun and one of a white cloud with raindrops, with 'sunny' and 'rainy' written under them and the words 'Today is' standing large and yellow.

While Mangal gazed around the room Miss Mohammed was calling the roll from a very large book that had been brought from the Principal's desk by a senior pupil. From all over the school came the echo of names and calls of 'Present'. As from a distance Mangal heard his name and felt a nudge at his side and he answered. The books were all taken back to the Principal who examined them and added the numbers.

He then rose and marked '105' against the words 'Present Today' that were written in red paint on a black square just below the picture of the Queen. Above were the words 'No. on Roll' and '112'. Smiling he called over the low rumble of voices and movement, 'Today, we have crossed the hundred again' and the children applauded.

Miss Mohammed wrote the numbers '5' and '6' on the small blackboard against white dots. She also wrote 'Arithmetic' and the date. She then distributed beans – large donkey-eyes. Busily craning his neck to see the colourful pictures on the other boards Mangal absent-mindedly joined the choruses of 'Five, Miss' and 'Six, Miss' to the repeated questions of what the numbers were.

'You, boy, what number is this?'

Mangal did not see the finger pointing at him.

'You paying attention, boy?'

He felt a nudge, turned and saw the long finger with the painted nail stretched accusingly at him. Another nudge at his side was accompanied by the advice to stand up. He kept still.

'You sleeping, boy? Stand up!' She took a step towards him. 'What number is it?'

He had no idea what she was talking about.

'We just did it ten times . . . ten times. What is this number?' She pointed to the number but the boy's eyes were welling and his lips trembled. He could neither see the number nor speak. 'Stretch out your hand,' she ordered and he felt the sting of the ruler twice. It had all happened so suddenly that the tears that rolled down his cheeks were from shock rather than pain. 'Tell him, Stalin. Tell him, children.'

'They all, including Stalin, chorussed 'Five, Miss.'

'Say it, boy.'

'Five.'

Another nudge was accompanied by 'Miss'.

'Five, Miss.' But he still did not know what the question was.

He was still rubbing the tingling from his hand and wiping the tears from his face, trying to hide his embarrassment, he did not realise that they had all finished taking out their five donkey-eyes. Looking up he saw the teacher with arms folded gazing fixedly at him. So were the other children.

'So you can't count up to five and you don't pay attention!' Her brows knitted. 'Stand up when I talk to you!'

He stood up slowly.

'Let me hear you count from one to five.'

His lips shook and there were cobwebs in his throat. She appeared like a red blur, her dress spreading all over the front of the class. The entire school swam before him.

'Sit down!'

He sat down only when he was told a second time. He was then advised that the boy sitting next to him, Stalin, would teach him the figure five.

Stalin, imitating what the teacher had done, wrote the figure on the slate then asked Mangal to write it with his finger on the desk, then write it in the air repeatedly. He then had to trace his pencil over Stalin's figure. By then he was entirely bored and irritated. He could write from one to twenty and count from one to a hundred. He could add figures up to twenty and could 'share' and 'times'.

'Come on, boy, write the thing,' Stalin said loudly.

Miss Mohammed, who had the children writing figures in the air, heard the order. 'What is wrong, now?' she asked.

'He not obeyin', Miss. I askin' him to do it and he not doin' it.'

'Boy, how you so harden?' Miss Mohammed asked.

'Yes, Miss, he too harden,' Stalin said. 'He want some more licks.' He said it with some satisfaction and gazed around the class. 'He really harden, yes, Miss.'

'All right, leave him alone, Stalin. Some people like to remain duncey. Eh, boy, you like to remain duncey all your life? You think is nice to be duncey?' Everybody was now looking at him again and he sat staring at his slate. He felt like scratching his pencil all over his slate or throwing his slate at his teacher. He bent as if to scrape a bit of caked mud on his foot and stuck his elbow in Stalin's ribs.

'Miss,' Stalin appealed, 'look he hoonch me, Miss. He just stop so and hoonch me in me ribs. Miss . . .'

But the teacher was no longer interested. She was busy checking the number of beans against the number on each slate. As she passed she glanced at Mangal's slate which was still empty of beans.

Arithmetic was soon followed by Reading which, today, consisted of calling out ten words of two and three letters, in one column in their Reading Books. She had them read individually then made two red ticks including another column of ten words, then she put the date on each and initialled them.

Mangal was called up to the teacher's table to read but he was still confused and did not perform well so he had not been 'changed'. His red marks remained where they were. He was told to learn his Reading for the next day.

Intermission finally came with the sound of a hand-bell and the children spilled out of the building running and shouting all over the schoolyard. Mangal found himself carried along and for a few minutes he also ran aimlessly round the building. A vegetable garden overgrown with weeds lay at the back. Drying yam vines with a few green leaves hung from bamboo poles and in one corner a clump of banana plants huddled together. On the dozen or so beds a few ragged plants, left over from the previous year's planting, jostled with the weeds. Overshadowing a corner of the garden was a large mango tree with an impenetrable mass of leaves. Very little grass grew among the bed of dry leaves under the tree because, in the dry season, on hot afternoons it was used as an outdoor classroom competed for by teachers. On the opposite side of the garden from the mango tree stood two latrines one for the boys and one for the girls.

Beyond the garden the land sloped sharply down to the cocoa plantation. Erosion had dug into the roots of the trees on the slope making them look like gnarled fingers grabbing desperately into the earth.

It was only a ten-minute intermission but some boys had started a game of marbles. Mangal stood at the edge of the few children who looked on. He looked at their faces but no one recognised his presence.

The intermission over, they all marched back into the building. Miss Mohammed had them chorally echoing syllables and words in her 'Word-building' exercise. The luncheon interval seemed to arrive more quickly and Mangal walked back home for lunch. He heard Stalin telling the other children about his inability to read and how he was a dunce. They all laughed loudly. After lunch he had to be urged by his mother to return to school.

Later in the afternoon with the smell of sweat filling the building the buzzing of the voices rose in volume. The Principal rang the silence bell a number of times then threatened to flog anyone he found talking. He walked up and down between the two rows of classes his guava whip in hand. Suddenly he was heard to bark out, 'You boy . . . yes . . . you . . . stand up!'

Mangal craned his neck round the board.

'I know I would catch you. If there is anybody to talk it was going to be you. What you talking about? The weather? Eh?' The Principal's anger was rising with his voice. 'What you come here to do, eh, talk or learn? Eh, Mr Oliver Twist?' By now the boy had come close to the Principal who grabbed him by the side of his pants pulling it tight across his bottom. 'Now we will see you twist.' Whap! The whip fell. The boy stiffened and he remained in that position waiting for the rest of the blows. The Principal kept talking loudly before every stroke making jokes about Oliver Twist. The school had now become very quiet and all work had stopped. The Principal then took the opportunity to admonish them all over talking in class. 'God gave us two eyes and two ears . . . two eyes and two ears . . . but only one mouth. Now why you think He gave us only one mouth – so we will only say half as much as we see or hear. When we talk we can't listen. When we can't listen we can't learn.'

'Why he call the boy Oliver Twist?' Mangal whispered to Stalin.

Stalin sat quietly.

'Eh? Why Oliver Twist?'

'Hush, boy,' Miss Mohammed said loudly.

The Principal approached the class and saw all eyes on Mangal. His small eyes glinted and bored into the little boy. 'You talking, boy?'

Mangal felt himself shrinking before the bulk of the man.

'Miss, this boy was talking?'

She nodded.

'What you saying, boy?' He looked at Stalin. 'What he was talking about?'

Stalin did not reply.

'Come, boy, stand up. What you was talking about?'

Mangal rose, his mind a complete blank. The corners of his mouth starting to curl downwards and his face turned to a grimace of impending crying. But the Principal had begun to lose his anger. Nevertheless he hit the desk in front of the boy a few times and warned him not to talk in class. By this time Mangal was almost doubled with fear and the tears streamed down his face.

'You have to learn from early that you must not talk in class. Only when someone ask you something you must open your mouth. Sit down!'

Mangal kept standing. He had not heard the order.

The Principal turned and walked away.

'Boy, you really stubborn, you know,' the teacher said. 'You didn't hear Schoolmaster say to sit down?'

Mangal slumped in his seat. He spent the next hour in a sort of daze. He did not know what was wrong and what was right but he began to regain his composure when the teacher brought out crayons and paper and asked them to 'take a line for a walk'. She explained that they were to start at a point and draw a line all over the paper then they should fill the spaces with any kind of marks of any colour. He made a blue line meandering and crossing itself over and over then he made dots and circles and dashes and 'x's'. Then he made a parallel orange line to his long blue line. Having finished filling in his shapes he began to shade some of the areas with different colours rubbing in the crayon stubs almost angrily. The teacher was pleased and pinned his piece on the wall. Her attitude softened and she told him how he must try to be a bright boy.

On his way home he trailed the small groups of children.

Samdaye was quick to notice the traces of tears and she hugged him.

'He get licks again, today,' someone said.

'For talkin',' another added.

'And not payin' attention.'

'He very harden.'

151

'Ma, they beat you for nothing in that school.'

'Wha' happen, Mangal, you behavin' bad again?' Compai asked.

'The Schoolmaster is a fat bully. And he like to shout and beat too much.'

Samdaye gave him a banana and told him to take care of his sister while she went for a bundle of grass for the cow.

When she returned he started towards the bridge. A blackbird buzzed him then sat on a low branch nearby and chirped defiantly, its head cocked to one side and its white-ringed eyes gazing at him. On a guava tree some small birds hopped from branch to branch and pecked at the worms in the over-ripe fruits. He picked up a stone and threw it in the direction of the blackbird but it was way off the mark and almost hit Poland who was sitting quietly with his brother, German, some distance from the guava tree. The boys glared at him and shoo-ed him away with violent gestures. It was then that Mangal saw the cage hanging from a bamboo rod concealed among the leaves of the guava tree. In the cage was a small bird with black wings and a bright yellow chest. Jutting out from the top of the cage were two sticks from a coconut frond that were covered with coagulated sap that had been chewed to a sticky paste. At the end of each stick was a small 'chiquito' banana. A bird, trying to eat the banana would have to alight on the 'laglee' which would entangle its tiny legs in this glue. Occasionally the caged bird emitted a long, shrill whistle which it varied in tone, length and complexity. A similar sound was heard coming from somewhere in the bushes. The boys, who had been whispering, stopped suddenly and an electric silence descended. The bird in the cage whistled again and there was a clear reply from the green bush. It came from an olive-green bird that was approaching the cage cautiously.

Mangal stepped closer and the boys frantically signalled for him to go away but he was fascinated by the two birds and waited to see when it would get stuck. He had never seen that. The olive-green bird was now about two feet away its head cocked with one eye on the prisoner. It hopped to the top of the cage. Mangal moved nearer and the bird retreated to the top of the tree.

BETWEEN TWO SEASONS

The scowls directed at Mangal became more threatening but the boys remained quietly crouching hoping that the caged bird that had become silent, would continue. They tried to imitate its call but the olive-green bird would not be enticed. It remained at the top of the tree.

After a while a bananaquit alighted on the stick and in its frenetic attempts to free itself became more and more ensnared. In a rage the boys began throwing guavas at Mangal who backed away but stayed at a distance watching the attempt to free the bird and clean its feathers with oil. The approaching bird had fled. Suddenly German came darting at Mangal who began to run but he was not fast enough and was caught by the pants. German gave him two taps behind his head and promised to kill him the next time Mangal got in his way. He shoved the little boy away.

Mangal rubbed the stinging area behind his head and half-ran until he reached the small bridge that stood across the silent slow-moving brook. The sides of the bridge were wooden and painted black and white. He leaned over it and looked at his reflection indistinct and greenish. Picking up a pebble he dropped it and watched the radiating ripples. There was a movement on the grassy edge below and Stalin's pale, round face peered up like a reflection.

'You mad or what?' Stalin asked angrily.

'What I do now?'

'You nearly kill me!'

'I didn't know –'

'You never know! You didn't see me fishin'?'

It was then that Mangal noticed the cork bobbing up and down over the ripples his pebble had made.

'Now I don't know if fish muddin' or not with the cork goin' up and down,' Stalin stared at him accusingly. 'Now I have to wait until the water settle . . . and move your shadow from the water.'

Mangal moved to the side of the bridge and began to climb down to the edge of the water. Five minutes passed and nothing seemed to be happening. Stalin just sat there shaking the rod occasionally then he lifted the rod and examined the piece of washed-out worm on the hook. 'A cascarob was bitin' the bait and you come and drive it away. Look how it eat out the worm.' He spat on the worm and dropped the hook into the water. 'Don't make any noise, eh. Don't move.'

'I can't sit down?'

'Sit down but don't shake.'

Sandflies started to bite at his leg and he found difficulty in staying still. 'You catch any yet?'

'Hush, don't open your mouth. You will frighten the fish.'

Mangal saw the small empty basket at the boy's side. 'You ever catch any?'

'You think I foolish? So I will come here everyday if I don't catch any?'

'You come every day?'

'Every day.'

'You like fishin'?'

'Naw.'

'Why you fishin' for then?'

'Is my father. He send me fishin' every day. He must have a fish or a crab or something fresh in the evenin'.'

'And if you don't catch?'

'I always get something. Today I might have to find a river conch or a red crab.'

Mangal could see the house where the boy lived. His father was slowly rocking in the hammock. 'What happen to your father – he doesn't go to work? How I always see him home?'

'He ain't well, you know.'

'What he sick with?'

'Dunno.'

'How long now he sick?'

'Forever.' He raised his head. 'What happen, you is a lawyer or what? How you like to ask so much question? You like to talk too much. Is the same thing in class – you talk too much.'

The cork began to dance and Stalin's eyes brightened. He jerked the line a few times then gave a swift pull and the rod swished past Mangal's head. Stalin looked at the hook and saw that the bait was gone. 'I feel is a sardine,' he said. 'Sardine too troublesome.'

'Why we don't go higher up the river? I will go with you.'

Stalin looked at him as if he was seeing Mangal for the first time. 'You ever fish?'

'No. I don't have a hook.'

'I have a extra one.'

'Here?'

'Home. But I don't want to go back for it.' He jerked his head towards his father.

'Let's go, nah. The sun still high.'

Glad to play the leading role, the boy rose and gestured Mangal to follow him. At home, being the youngest, he was always pushed around by his brothers. He was one year older than Mangal and was in the Second Stage in the Infant class while Mangal was in the First. 'All right, but you mustn't talk too much.'

They were about to step into the road when they saw Stalin's mother coming round the corner. Stalin quickly jumped back on the bank started running along the edge of the brook with Mangal trying to keep close to him.

'Why you runnin' for?'

'She will start a quarrelin'.'

'Why?'

'I dunno. Maybe because I ain't catch anything yet. Maybe . . .'

Mangal stooped behind some low coffee branches and looked closely at the boy's mother. She was a thin woman with protrusions at her elbows, knees, collarbone and upper gum from which her teeth stuck out like guns on a battleship. Two of her front teeth were missing and he wondered whether she had blown them out with her frequent shouting and screaming. Maybe that was what caused her gum to stick out so. The skin was stretched tightly over her bony face from which her thin, hooked nose stood out between small, sunken eyes that darted about in piercing glances as if searching constantly for errors and misdemeanours.

'Germa-a-n! Pola-a-nd,' she shouted. 'Look the goat loose. All-you ain't see the goat loose? Eh, Shanti?' The girl, baby astride her hip, was sweeping the bare earth in front of the house raising small clouds of dust. 'Shanti, where them devils gone?'

'They in the bush catchin' bird,' she said mischievously.

'Pola-a-an! Germa-a-an! Why all-you so damn harden? All-you help all-you sister do the housework? All-you ain't do

155

anything and all-you gone to catch bird? What happen – all-you will eat the bird? One o' these days I will cook the damn bird and make all-you eat it, you hear? Eat it!' She continued walking in her brisk, short steps.

Mangal could feel her eyes looking directly at him and he dropped his head lower. Stalin was nowhere to be seen. He saw German and Poland emerge from the clump of guava trees with the cage and rod.

'And you, Mister Man,' she addressed Gopaul, 'You mean you can't keep a eye on the children and see that they do something around the house? If I don't watch out them children will come out just like you – lazy and sweet-skin.'

Gopaul mumbled a weak protest.

'Put down the stupid cage and go and catch the goat and tie it. You want some car to knock it down or you want it to go in somebody yard and let them carry it in the Pound?' She continued her quarrelling into the yard and round the back of her house.

Not knowing where Stalin went Mangal emerged from the field and passed close to the cage which had been placed on a guava stump. A thin, brown-and-white cat with bony haunches stared unblinking at the fluttering bird. He shooed the cat away.

Chapter 14

The leaves of the poui trees had been replaced by clusters of yellow flowers. In the distance the trees looked solidly rounded like gold coins on the green carpet of the hills. The imortelles had dropped their rooster blooms and looked strangely lifeless against the clear sky. Day after day the sun rose and blazed across, passing directly overhead with not a cloud to provide respite. The clouds hung at the edge of the horizon as if they, themselves, sought shelter.

The small vegetable gardens were failing for lack of moisture and Compai had abandoned his to the weeds which, he said, would help to conserve what little water there was in the soil. Samdaye kept her few plants – string beans, peas and carailli – watered with buckets from the well. Prince and Martina lived off wild 'devil' yams and whatever they could get from the estate. There was no chance that anyone would starve but the little money they had could barely purchase a pound of fresh fish from the vendor who came around every Saturday on his bicycle, selling herring or snapper.

Martina's source of meat was Japan's shop. She bought pickled pig parts: snout and tail, and saltfish. Every day she stewed one or another of these items. Sometimes Prince would go out late in the night to look for manicou or opossum. He would take his flambeau of kerosene oil and a cloth wick in a rum bottle, and his lance that was made from a straightened bucket handle sharpened to a point and tied securely to a long bamboo pole. He would shake the light behind his head to attract the manicou's attention then he would try to get close enough to stick it with the lance. Once on the ground he would chop at it with his machete. But getting a manicou was becoming more and more rare.

'Is that damn American base that cause it, yes. They drive away all the wild animals from the area with their noise and their light. And the little that was left, well the small islanders eat it out. This damn place really get hard. Was a time when you could go just at the edge of the village – not even in the highwoods – at any time night or day and catch something. Eh, Compai? You remember the time when we hold a deer right under that mango tree? It was a Saturday and the height of the dry season and the sun was hot like hell and the deer stand up under that tree with his tongue hangin' out . . .'

'Them days gone, Prince, and they ain't comin' back.'

'Man, you used to catch manicou on that mango tree. Soon as it get dark you could hear them movin'.'

'No sense worryin' about what gone. It done gone.'

'But that was a time, eh? You don't think that things could come back so again? Look what happen to the Base: the whole thing gone back in bush. You ain't think them beast will come back? Eh?'

'An what about when the first rains come and the flood water rush down to this little bridge, you remember the size of guabin we used to hold right under that little bridge?'

'Big so!' Prince extended his arm and marked from his bent elbow.

'Is that what give me the habit to have something fresh every day.' Gopaul had been listening and he joined in. 'You coun say them was time, neighbour.'

'Man, the whole country get hard. Like old cassava bread, dry and hard. Like the country gettin' old just like me.'

'You didn't need no gun; just a dog and a cutlass and you could track down a tatou or a 'gouti in some hole and dig it out. Now you can't see a tatou for medicine.' Prince stabbed his stubby fingers towards the hills. 'Even up in the bush the animals disappear.'

'Mus' be the war, neighbour. Them white people throw all kinda things in the air. You never know what kinda poison it have floatin' round all about. I see in the Base they spray something on the bush and it dead. I see big tree get poison by them 'Merican. They used to spray poison at everything: bush, tree, grass, cockroach, mosquito . . . everything.'

'Is something causin' this kind of weather – when it rain it rainin' non-stop and when the sun come out it ain't have no end. It didn't used to be so. We used to have more sun than rain in the dry season and more rain than sun in the rainy season. It must have something interferin' with the weather. Something happenin' that ain't pleasin' God.' Prince looked up at the sky. 'Too much damn sin, man, too much sin.'

'The world must change,' Compai said. 'Nothing don't stay still. And let me tell all-you something,' his raised hand shook weakly, 'all-you ain't see nothing yet. I see two war – the first one with the Kaiser and this one with Hitler that just gone. The first one I see real action. I see ship loaded with food sink by other ship. Loaded with food, I tell you.'

'And what about the last war?' Prince asked. 'You think is little bit of destruction take place? You ain't hear 'bout the millions of people who get killed and the billions and billions in property blow up. Is all them damn destructive thing still floatin' in the air. Is that damn 'tomic bomb they blow up Japan with and now they droppin' it all about and testin' bigger and bigger ones. Boy is one set of mad-ass people rulin' this world, yes. I really don't know what could get in people head to kill each other so by the million. You know, one bomb that they throw down on Japan kill about half the people livin' in Trinidad. I hear that bomb does blind you if you only look at it and it does melt iron like ice in the sun.'

'Neighbour, the Hindu scripture say this is the Dark Age. The whole world will get full of sin before it get back good again. We ain't have no say in nothing. We just like little ants or jigger-flea. Them big countries have all the power.'

'And they gettin' more and more powerful,' Prince said. 'Now the 'Mericans and Russians want to fight. Is one set of threatenin' they threatenin' each other.'

'And durin' the war they was friends, yes,' Compai said. 'They fight side by side.'

'Neighbour, white people is one kind of animal nobody could understand. They will fight each other for anything.'

'Not for anything,' Compai said. 'For land . . . for property. For power. They have this thing inside them they must have more than the next man. They must have the biggest estate, the biggest house, the most money. I don't know why they don't bomb each other out of this world. They too damn greedy and covetous. For the whole of history they only killin' one another.'

'The amount of money and energy they put in war, that amount of waste in people and property, that amount of material they put in battleship and plane and bomb could make this whole world a paradise. Man, the cost of one bomb could make a garden of La Louise, it could replant all the cocoa, dig all the drain, fix up the road, bring pipe water and lights, and build over this rickety barracks. One old bomb. And a bomb don't fall down and make rose grow, it just blow up every damn thing.' Prince rose from the box under the almond tree. 'Just thinkin' about all them thing does make a man feel for a drink. Eh, Compai? Let we forget about all this war talk and go down to Jap. I mean, is Saturday, you know, and we ain't take one for the week.'

'You right, yes,' Compai said.

'Come on, Gopaul,' Prince called, 'let we go to the shop.'

'Naw, neighbour, I ain't feelin' too good today,' he injected a little whine in his voice.

Compai and Prince sat at one of the three heavy wooden tables in Japan's bar. They sat on crude, heavy stools which, like the tables, were made to withstand any kind of treatment by drunks including throwing them at each other out in the road. Crudely written signs announced various prohibitions: NO OBSCENE LANGUAGE, NO SPITTING ON THE FLOOR, PAY FIRST, NO CREDIT. One sign announced ROOM No 1. A large coloured calendar with a full-length picture of an angelic round-faced Chinese girl with a small, red mouth and large, black eyes looked at them with a Mona Lisa smile. The writing was in Chinese. The counter ran the length of the shop but the customer section was divided by a partition of wooden laths separating the rumshop from the grocery.

Prince ordered a 'nip' of White Star rum which was poured into a small square bottle. Two thick shot-glasses were put out with about half a bottle of water taken from a tin-lined box in which the ice, put since morning, had melted into a cool, slippery, milky appearance in which beer and stout labels floated.

They did not drink immediately but sat in silence. There was no hurry. Japan clip-clopped on his wooden sandals attending to the few customers in the dry-goods section. His wife stood in the doorway leading to the dark interior. Occasionally a pale, young face with bright, slanting eyes materialised from the gloom. The faces came at different heights, peered about, then vanished as quickly as a dream. The woman emerged, looked about the shelves and repacked a few items. She then went and attended to two customers, nodding and smiling all the while. Her long, black blouse protruded in front.

'How much this one will make in all?' someone asked her. She lifted five fingers.

'Lord, Jap, you don't make joke. Every year, so?'

She could not understand all of what they were saying but she had an idea and continued nodding and smiling. She had come from China about six years before and spoke very little English. No one knew her name. She visited no one in the village and no one visited her. She had appeared mysteriously one Monday morning and the word went around that Jap had got married over the weekend.

A muscular Spanish-looking man with a shaggy head and an unshaven face walked up to the counter. 'One for me, Jap, and one for Amelia.' He tossed the first drink down then drank some water. After a minute or so he emptied the other glass. 'Boy, she needed that drink,' he said. Smacking his lips he greeted Prince and Compai. 'So the estate close down again?'

'It ain't close down,' Prince said. 'They just lay off almost everybody.'

'All-you must do like me, boy. Make work for you'self. I can't take this one day on one day off business. Is me and Amelia.'

Prince and Compai looked at each other. They had been told once that Amelia was the man's mother who was long dead. It was also said that she was his wife who had died. But no one asked him why he always took a drink for her and why he went about as though she was always at his side. He now had a wife, an Indian woman, who never went into the forest with him. He would arrive every two weeks with

161

his bull, Kaiser William, which he would tether on a post in a small shed at the back of the house, then, after briefly greeting his wife, he would head for Japan's shop. He would not buy a bottle but about every hour he would call for two drinks – one for him and one for Amelia. Sometimes he called for only one drink saying that he did not want any but Amelia needed hers. His name was Antonio Garcia but everyone called him Columbus; except his wife who alone called him Tony.

'So, Columbus, where Kaiser William?' Prince asked just to make conversation.

'By your mother,' came the instant reply.

'Don't be rude, Columbus.'

'Ask a foolish question –' Compai said.

'Tell him, Compai,' Columbus said.

'I just want to ask how the bull is.'

'Like a bull, nuh. How you think the bull is, dumb. Dumb and strong. And damn hard-workin'. Not like some of all-you.' He called out to the shopkeeper, 'You have oats, Jap? I want a bag of oats and twelve bottles of stout. I have to feed the Kaiser well this weekend. He work too hard this past two weeks.'

'And what about the wife?' Prince asked. 'She ain't need stout, too?'

'For what?' Columbus launched into a verbal assault on women on the whole.

Prince liked to provoke him about his wife and his bull. Twice he had put her out of the house and had burnt her clothes in a heap. Once she had been left only with a cotton night-gown. Several times, in his drunkenness, he had taken the bull into the bedroom and tied it to the bedpost telling her that the bull was of more use to him than her so he ought to treat it better. Nobody could understand the relationship: how the woman could absorb the beatings and abuse. And she was such a small woman. Her name was Happy and she really was a pleasant person and seemingly happy. 'All-you don't know Tony,' she would say. 'He does make all that noise when he drink and behave foolish but he is a very nice man when he sober. It ain't have nothing I want he doesn't give me. After he burn the clothes he take me to town – not

Arima, you know, to town, Port of Spain – and he buy back everything new. Then we eat in a Chinee restaurant and he beg me to stay with him.'

Prince was not sure that he could believe the last line but she really did sport new clothes after the incident.

'And about Amelia, I myself not so sure who she is. He never tell me but I think is his grandmother. She used to put him on her knee and give him a small sip every time she take a drink. She used to tell him is good for worms. He grow up with her and he like her very much. Up to now he does cry for her.'

Columbus always cried when he got drunk. He would lie anywhere and sob himself loudly to sleep. Almost every Saturday when he returned from the forest he would sleep under the eaves at the front of the shop or at the side of the road on the grass which would be wet with dew on mornings. He would swear at the top of his voice calling names no one knew alternating this with sobbing. Then he would invite Amelia for a drink which he would pour from the bottle into a small enamel cup. He always bought a bottle when the shop was about to close. Very often he would be accompanied by his coal-burning partner, La Veau, who spoke in grumbles and ground his teeth so much that they had been worn down almost to the gums. He was always grumbling about Ram Dayal and money. Sometimes he called other names but it always had to do with money. People thought that La Veau had been taken advantage of by various employers because he was not altogether sane. He had no wife but showed interest in women by sliding quietly along the counter in the shop towards any woman until he was leaning against her. They would push him away and he would look surprised and grind his teeth and mumble.

Both of them, Columbus and La Veau, working alone in the forest amazed everyone. They would not sit and talk together nor share a drink, nor show any indication of friendship except on a couple of occasions Columbus had taken La Veau to sleep on his bed nudging his wife out.

How could they work all these years in the high woods without communicating with each other? It was not as if

Columbus did not get angry with La Veau. Very often Columbus included his partner in his swearing and would threaten him with violence.

'One day those two will have some real trouble,' people said. 'One day either Columbus will kill La Veau or La Veau will kill Columbus. But something bad will happen one day. You will see.'

But both men seemed to do well burning coals. At least, Columbus did. Nobody knew what La Veau did with his money. It was said that Columbus kept it and would give some to La Veau when he needed it.

Compai toyed with his glass which still had the first drink that he had poured. He looked at a small pool of water on the table. With the bottom of the glass he made a pattern of rings dipping it in the water and resting it lightly on the unpainted wood of the table. He paid no attention to the half-humorous half-serious raillery between Prince and Columbus. He found that nothing affected him anymore and wondered whether it was another sign of old age. Everything around him seemed to be happening on a screen with him unconnected and uninvolved. He thought of Gabi and how quickly he had dismissed the boy's absence. There was not even a feeling of guilt that he had not seemed too troubled and had not made any effort to discover where the boy had gone. Even the cessation of work at the estate did not make much of an impression on him. Maybe this was the way the mind prepared itself for death becoming more and more detached, loosening bit by bit the bonds to life and earthly things and the mesh of emotional involvement.

Through the small window on the left which opened in two wooden sections he could see, between the leaves of a clump of bananas, Happy, Columbus's wife, washing clothes in a tub, her elbow and body moving rhythmically as she rubbed the items on the scrubbing board. Flecks of foam flew like moths around her head. Every now and then she would take a quick glance at the shop especially whenever she heard her husband roar out some obscenity. Her long hair, when she turned her head, left strands plastered to her wet face. After this had happened a few times she stood up and with her soapy hands tied it in a bun.

Kaiser William, big and dirty grey, with one sawed-off horn, nuzzled and munched at a bundle of grass.

'Wha' happen, Compai, you ain't drinkin'? You dreamin' again?' Prince asked as he threw the contents of the shot-glass down his throat, swallowed it contentedly, paused a bit then filled the glass with water and chased the drink. 'Life is short, you know, and you got to enjoy it.'

'A man does stay dead longer than he does stay alive,' Columbus said, laughing loudly at his own joke. 'When you alive is just for a while, but when you dead is for ever.' He turned to the customers in the shop, 'Eh? how I talk?' He smiled and nodded sagely as they mumbled approval. 'I always tell La Veau that we could dead anytime in the bush. Snake, scorpion, spider – anything could bite you and kill you – a tree could fall on you . . . man, anything could happen. And, you ain't goin' to believe this but La Veau does say that he ain't goin' to live long.'

They wondered how La Veau told him. Prince looked at Compai and lifted an eyebrow.

'I tell La Veau that livin' is not for long . . . that we got to enjoy it now.'

La Veau, hearing his name, came through the narrow gateway in the partition of laths that separated the grocery from the rum-shop. Columbus clamped a heavy hand on La Veau's shoulder. 'Eat, drink and be merry, eh Pardner?' La Veau ground his teeth and mumbled then he bared his stumps of teeth with his head cocked to one side in his usual attempt at a smile. No one had ever heard him laugh. 'Tomorrow, we die.' Columbus continued as he hung over the much smaller La Veau.

'Ram Deen . . . dollars . . . two thousand . . . Ram Dayal . . . wouldn't give . . . thousand . . . Ram Singh . . .'

'Who owin' you all this money, La Veau?' Prince asked.

'Ram Jis-een?'

'Ram Deen with all them trucks?'

He skinned his teeth, 'Ram 'Een . . . one thousand.'

Columbus ordered a drink for La Veau who drank it in one gulp then went back into the grocery section.

'You really think anybody owe La Veau any money?' Columbus asked nobody in particular. 'And where the hell he goin' to make two thousand dollars?' He tapped one finger on the side of his head. 'One day he might even say that I owe him a lot of money.'

'Well –' Prince raised his eyebrows.

'What you mean "well"? Where he will make so much money?'

'And he burnin coals all this years?'

'I don't know where he keep his money.' Columbus shrugged. 'You ever see him eat? The man does eat more than Kaiser William. And drink ... by himself he could knock out a bottle. I hear that Indian boy up the road gone in the bush to burn coals,' he changed the subject. 'He know anything about coals? Take care he ain't kill himself in the bush.'

'You ain't see him in there?' Prince asked.

'One day I was scoutin' for another site for a pit and I hear cuttin' but I didn't go to see who it was. Must be him. He don't know you can't do this work alone? You ain't tell him that, Prince?'

'He is his own man, yes.'

'He will learn.'

Compai drank his shot wordlessly then looked up to see Manu enter the bar.

Chapter 15

Samdaye felt the blood rising up her face. Her eyes burned and her lips trembled. She looked at Manu who was completely absorbed with attaching the small mirrors on to his clown outfit. Mangal sat on a box next to him peering at the morning sun through the various pieces of coloured cloth. Occasionally he would place the cloth over his father's eyes and comment on the effect of seeing the sun through the red, yellow, purple and blue fabric.

'Mangal, you ain't have anything better to do?' She called roughly.

The boy looked at her with a mixture of surprise and hurt. 'Come and see how the sun lookin'.' He held up the red piece of cloth to his eyes. 'It lookin' red red red.' He rose and started towards her but his father ordered him to put the material down.

'Put down the stupid old cloth and come and do your home-lesson.'

'But, Ma, is Sunday and I done do my lesson already.'

'Well, come and read for me, then.'

'I don't want to read.'

'You don't want to read? You playin' harden? You ain't see you botherin' the man from his hard work? You ain't see makin' clown costume is the most important thing? You ain't see how hard he concentratin' and you humbuggin' him. Boy, come here eh, and don't make me come down there for you.'

The boy rose tentatively.

'Go to your mother before . . . before I eat you.'

'Some people does eat their children without knowin'. Some people don't care if their wife and family live or die.

167

Some people so jokey they have to make clothes for all the world to see how they jokey. They have to dress like a joker and look foolish and make everybody shame. But they ain't have no shame.'

Manu sucked his teeth loud and long but said nothing.

'Some people don't even tell their wife and children, "Dog or cat I miss all-you" even after a whole week. Not one word about what happen in the high-wood whether coal burn or coal ain't burn or if coal will ever burn. Nothing, I tell you, nothing about if their wife and children starve or if they eat or if all they had was wind-pie. Without sayin' "boo" they go to the rum-shop because their wife and children livin' like genii in bottle on top shelf swimmin' in rum and so they drink them and eat them with love.'

The boy stood half-way between his mother and father. He could hear the pots and pans loudly clanging as his mother shouted from the kitchen.

'I never thought they had people so in the world, who don't study nobody but theyself, people so foolish that they play man all the time but they could sit like woman and sew clothes in front the house for everybody to see. And they ain't feel no shame. Eh, Mister Prince? Eh. Miss Tina? You ever thought they had people so?'

But there was no reply.

'You think the man would ask if his son go to school for the week; if his daughter is well; if they get sick. You think the man would buy a sweetie for them before he full his belly with rum comin' home smellin' like Japan shop.'

The boy walked round the house to the rose-mango tree where one red fruit shone brilliantly on the green grass. Two blue birds hopped warily around the fallen fruit getting closer and closer until one of them pecked at the fruit, and seeing that it was safe, continued to peck at it. The other jumped on the fruit and his mate retreated. The boy threw a stick at the birds and went and picked up the fruit, and when he saw that it had been pecked on both sides, flung it at a ripe fruit that swung on a long stem. Surprisingly he struck it and it fell. He did not like rose-mango but he bit into it nevertheless then used it to pelt at another fruit. He preferred it when it was half-ripe. His mother liked it green and ate it with salt and pepper after cutting it in small strips. Stalin's sister liked it in the same way also and his teeth would get on edge whenever he saw her with her bowl of green mango 'chow'. It was a feeling of discomfort almost as bad as hearing his parents quarrel which could still be heard above the chirping of the birds, the crying of Gopaul's child and the shouting of Mrs Gopaul. It was not his father though, it was his mother and he could not understand why his mother liked to quarrel with his father who was doing nothing but mending his costume in which he looked so nice on carnival days. He wished he could get a costume like that too but he remembered how sharp was his mother's slap when he mentioned it. His sister had started crying now and he headed towards the edge of the field to get away from the sounds coming from the barracks. He reached the small stream which had become swollen with pale brown water from rain that must have fallen on the mountains sometime the night before. The gurgle of the stream added to the sounds but he could still hear his mother's voice above all the rest. He wished he could drown it out. If he got under the water maybe he would not be able to hear her.

For a long time he stood on the slippery bank mesmerised by the curling flow, then, on a low-hanging branch of a coffee tree just above the water he saw a yellow-breasted bird hopping about and making its quick 'chip chip' sounds. Finding a stone nearby he took aim and flung it at the bird, which on the impact, fell heavily into the water and made only a feeble flutter with one wing then floated slowly past, its tiny feet stuck in the air. He was rooted with shock. He had not intended to kill the bird. Maybe it was not dead. Maybe if he could only get it he might revive it by sapping its head with water. He felt tears running down his face, and with his vision blurred, stepped forward, lost his footing and slipped into the water. He tried to reach for a tuft of grass on the bank but he could not touch the bottom. Frantically, he thrashed about but he could not stay above the surface. He tried to call but the water kept getting into his mouth as soon as he opened it. All he wanted to do was to make a sound and to get out of this sinking. There was no thought in his mind about drowning; there was no idea of time. He only felt that this struggle was interminable and hopeless then there was a tugging at his hair, then his shirt, then he was being hauled up the bank.

'Wha' happen, Mangal, you crazy or what?'

He tried to cough to clear this choking in his throat and vomited. He could not breathe. He could see Stalin but he could not speak.

'How you so foolish, man? How you stop so and fall down in the water?'

He was lying on his belly with water flowing from his mouth, nose and eyes which were wide and staring.

'Talk, nah, man. Say something.'

The breath came in two quick short intakes and then he breathed deeply.

'You want to drown you'self? How you fall in the water so?'

'I-I slip.'

'You stop just so and slip?'

'I kill a bird – one of them coconut bird.'

'I was watchin'. You didn't see me?'

He got up unsteadily. He shook his head.

'I was right under that cocoa tree,' he indicated with his head. 'Right there. Fishin'. I see when you come but I didn't say anything. A fish was muddin' – a cascarob. The cork was just goin' down when I hear this crash in the water and see you drownin'. You can't swim?'

He shook his head again.

'Man, you ain't know nothin'. All of us could swim. We learn right here. We learn to swim from there to there,' Stalin pointed out two spots about twenty feet apart.

Mangal's mind was a chaos of thoughts and feelings. Everything seemed to be happening to someone other than himself. Was he really drowning? If he should drown maybe his mother would cry and then the quarrelling would end.

'. . . quarrellin' . . . quarrellin',' he heard himself muttering.

'What you mean "quarrellin"? You think you hear quarrellin'? You ever hear the noise by me? Is whole day my mother screamin', the baby cryin', my sister shoutin' for me to do something, my brothers tappin' me behind my head, my father groanin'. The only time I have quiet is when I come by this river to fishin'. Man, I too glad my father like fish.' He glanced to where his rod was. He saw the bamboo rod floating slowly downstream. 'Shit, look what you cause.' He ran along the bank and retrieved it.

Mangal started unsteadily towards the barracks.

'Where you goin'? You want to get your tail cut with your clothes wet and muddy? Come, take off your clothes and wash out the muddy part, then hang it out on that branch in the sun. It will dry in no time.'

He did as he was told, then, suddenly, he began to tremble.

'Go and stand up in that patch of sun.'

Stalin examined the worm at the end of the hook. It had become bleached and frayed. He replaced it and continued fishing.

Mangal broke two cocoa leaves and sat on them. The trembling was decreasing but occasionally his body would shudder. Around the bend the spot of yellow caught his eye where the bird had become stuck among some dead leaves. He was engulfed in sadness and wished he had drowned. He had heard the teacher during morning prayers say that when you sinned you died. 'The wages of sin is death,' she had said. He had sinned by killing the bird and he almost died. He would never again throw a stone at a bird nor would he ever put one in a cage. And he would not think evil thoughts about his mother or his father. Maybe quarrelling is normal with big people. 'You ever go to Sunday School, Stalin?'

'Shh-hh. Talk quiet, man. Sunday School?' he whispered. 'Nah, I is Hindu.'

'And Hindu don't go to Sunday School?'

'Nah. That is for them Pestbyterian. That is how my father call them.'

'And you does go to the school?'

'Yeh, but that is different. In Sunday School they teach 'bout Jesus and . . . and they make you Pestbyterian and we is Hindu. None of my family go to Sunday School. You not Hindu?'

'I don't know. Maybe. The pundit did come home by us after the prayers by you, and Pa called him "Baba" and Ma bent down to touch his foot and hit me when I say he dress funny. But we never had prayers or put up flag and thing.'

'But when you go to school the first day they does ask what is your religion. You don't know what religion they write for you?'

Mangal shook his head.

'You must be Hindu.'

'So I can't go to Sunday School?'

'Only if your mother say so.' He stopped talking and concentrated on the dipping cork. Swiftly he pulled and the line swished over his head and wrapped itself around a cocoa branch. 'That damn fish givin' me hell whole mornin'. But I will hold your tail,' he shouted at the fish. After untangling the line and spitting on the washed worm he asked, 'Why you want to go to Sunday School?'

'I like the hymns . . . and the Christmas cards . . . and I think Miss Mohammed nice.'

'Not you alone think Miss Mohammed nice. You ain't see how the schoolmaster does watch her and Teacher Willy . . . and all the big boys. And you see how she does shake she behind when she walk? So that is why you want to go Sunday School — to watch at Miss Mohammed.' He shook with laughter.

'Not only that — I will get away from home.'

'Man, get a rod and hook and come and fishin'. It quiet and you will get away from them Sunday School teacher tellin' you how you goin' to dead and singin' them dead hymn with sad sad face. You must be crazy.'

Mangal rose and felt his clothes. He sat down again.

'Why you in a hurry? You hurry to go and see Miss Rachel little bottom — to see if she wearin' blue panty again.'

'How you know what panty she wearin'?'

'Zander and Mora could tell you every day.'

'How?'

'They have a small mirror and they does throw it down on the ground when she passin'.'

'I don't know how they could enjoy that,' Mangal wrinkled his nose.

'Me, too. I find that foolish.'

'What you want to see somebody panty for? Ugh!'

'Shh. I will catch this one. Don't talk.' Stalin bent over the rod and watched the cork as it dipped low beneath the

172

surface. He gave a short quick pull then swung it out of the water with a small black squirming fish. 'Aha! You think you could get away this time.' He pulled the hook from the mouth of the fish and stuck a thin stick through its gill.

Mangal saw the excitement and pleasure on the boy's face. 'I don't think my mother would let me come out to fishin' on a Sunday mornin'.' He reached for his clothes and finding that they were almost dry put them on. 'I goin',' he said.

'You goin' to Sunday School to see Miss Rachel panty. Pant-ee pant-ee. Maybe she will give you a hug and a kiss.'

'Ugh!'

'Well, stay and help me catch something.' He proffered the rod.

'Nah. I goin'.' As he walked away he listened to see if his mother was still quarrelling but he heard nothing.

Chapter 16

Behind the top of the rose-mango tree, high above the leafless imortelles, between the overhanging eave and the wattle-and-daub wall, Samdaye could see a dark cloud spreading like an inkstain. It was going to rain. She knew this when early in the morning she saw a line of ants snaking up the wall. Other lines were coming from the direction of the road seeking higher ground. Also a few corbeaux floated lazily in circles. She smiled. A black, rainy day might solve her problems; at least it would fill the barrel, but, best of all, it might just prevent Manu from going to the carnival. She quickly dismissed that thought as she knew it was childish. Nothing would prevent him from going. Not after he had spent the entire morning mending and re-designing the costume. Nothing, not even the deepest flood would hold him.

She was surprised when Mangal asked to go to Sunday School and gave him permission without asking Manu. She thought that he would object but so absorbed was he that he only looked absent-mindedly at the boy as he joined some other children. Miss Mohammed was passing at the same time and, dismounting from her bicycle, patted him on the head in approval and said a loud 'good morning' to Manu. Samdaye had some doubts and felt that both her father and mother would have objected. She, herself, was not too pleased but there was nothing really wrong about his going to Sunday School. At least he would be occupied learning something and would not be hanging around his father filling his head with silly ideas of getting his own costume. She still wondered what could have prompted the boy to want to go especially since he had not mentioned anything about this before. It would also keep him from wasting his time hanging about with those no-good Gopaul children who were always taking advantage of him. Also, she admired the parents of the Sunday School children. They would follow about an hour later on their way to church with clean, starched shirts and smoothly-ironed dresses. Some of the women wore hats and held their heads at stylish angles but some of them retained their traditional 'orhni' and looked just as if they were going to a 'puja'. They even greeted each other with palms joined and sometimes said 'Sita Ram' just as any Hindu. She had heard them sing hymns in Hindi and called them 'bhajans' just like any Hindu. So there did not seem to be any real difference. She also liked the way they went with their Bibles and hymn-books under their arms which proclaimed their literacy. Even the priest, the Reverend Buchanan, with his handlebar moustache and his thick snowy hair, would stop his car and get out when he was passing them and shake their hands, rocking on his feet as they said he did in church. They said that he had been a soldier in the war and had been awarded the Military Cross.

So she watched her son with his oiled, bare feet and his oily, plastered hair disappear with other children just like him round the corner.

She took the baby and bathed her then powdered her sparingly. She could see that Manu had tied the cow out in the field and had cleaned the pen. He must have done this before daybreak. He had also made a cup of coffee which was very unusual. The week in the forest had certainly done some good.

'So tomorrow is the big day?' Prince called to him. 'You goin' to carnival or you goin' to the coal pit?'

She heard him chuckle.

'Why you don't let Gopaul help you with the costume?'

'It ain't have much to do again.'

'You have to put it on for us to see . . . to see how it fit and thing . . . to see how you lookin'. Eh, Compai? You ain't want to see how Manu lookin' in the costume?'

'He will look like a maypole with mirror,' Samdaye said.

'Nah, man. The fellah will look nice. And we want to hear you crack the whip.'

175

BETWEEN TWO SEASONS

From the side of the building, the baby held to her bosom, she looked at her husband who did not lift his head. She tried not to get angry. It was not that she did not know of this hobby or pastime or whatever it was. Madness, more likely. She knew it and in the early part of the courtship and marriage she admired him for his courage and bravery, and for his toughness and good nature; for his swaggering walk and loudness, always poking fun at others. People always talked to her about him. When others wrapped goatskin around their torsos to protect themselves from lashes with the whip he would unbutton the top of his costume and let it hang about his waist to show that he was wearing no protection and was not afraid of any man. On Carnival days he would sometimes walk up to her and, putting his arm around her, would take her down the street for a few yards while she protested half bashfully but her eyes shone. She would see the perspiration gleaming on his lean body as he swept past leading the chorus in the band.

But it had all changed. It was not that he had changed so much. He was almost the same. The drinking had been there when they got married. It seemed fun then. But it had grown imperceptibly – from a few drinks on a Friday afternoon and only on the pay fortnight to every Friday, then Friday and Saturday, then almost every day. And with the increase in drinking came the decrease in liveliness with a corresponding growth of sullenness. He became less talkative except when he had some drinks and then it would only be evident in the shop where he still made people laugh. But he was less and less communicative at home.

She did not think that she had changed. She still admired his strength and his capacity for hard work. But circumstances had changed. Two children had been born and that coloured everything. They could not go on as if only two of them mattered. When that was so the horizon lay just about their feet but the horizon had lifted with each child and if another came . . .

What had become more disturbing to her was the needless exposure to danger. She did not know how to discuss this with him and all her attempts resulted in her nagging and whining which made him angry and, it seemed, more determined to

176

continue in his old ways. She had asked Martina for advice but Martina had counselled her to let him be. He would soon come to his senses. But he had not. Gopaul's wife told her that he was a damn no-good drunk and if she had a husband like that she would kick his arse out of the house. That she had a sister with a husband like that and her brothers had given him a good cut-arse which taught him a lesson he never forgot. Samdaye often thought that this was probably the best measure whenever frustration and anger overcame her.

'So what you goin' to do now that you break away from your band?' Prince asked. 'You goin' out alone?'

'I ain't break away from the band.'

'But you did not practise with them.'

'No.'

'You don't have to practise?'

'No.'

'I thought that all bands used to have to practise.'

He did not reply.

'When he concentratin' so, Mr Prince, you have to let him alone. He ain't got time for anybody.'

Prince said nothing.

Samdaye noticed how they now avoided taking her side. In fact they seemed to avoid speaking to her. But she continued relentlessly, 'Tomorrow is the big day. Tomorrow he will look like a million dollars flashin' and shinin' and walkin' down the centre of the street as if he is the mayor or the governor.'

Martina said something to Prince and he went inside.

'Well, I have nobody to take up for me so I better shut up my mouth.'

Compai who had come outside now looked hard at her and put his index finger to his lips.

'But I will not shut my mouth. No matter people want me to stay quiet. Is because I have nobody to complain to he does do me that.'

'You could complain to the Reverence,' Manu said. 'I see you send the boy to come Christian. The Reverence will help you. Go tell him.'

'I send the boy to learn something more than what you will teach him.'

'He will learn to jump up with cross in his hand.'

177

'That is better than jumpin' up with mas' on his face. Too-besides I don't care if he come Roman Catholic, Baptis' or Seven Day Adventist since he don't play mas'.'

Manu rose and held the costume to his chest.

Samdaye clapped mockingly. 'You lookin' nice yes. You lookin' too nice. Miss Tina,' she called, 'come and see how the man lookin' nice.'

Prince and Martina joined Compai and they beamed in appreciation.

Gopaul, his wife and his children gazed from their house. 'Neighbour, you coun say you is a artis',' Gopaul said. 'The costume really good. You have a nice touch.'

'Go and put in on,' Martina said.

'Is bad luck,' Manu said. 'I'll put it on tomorrow.' He went inside and brought out the whip and a bottle with some cooking oil in it.

'And where you goin' with the cookin' oil?' Samdaye asked. 'That is my oil to cook with. I take my time and grate coconut, bruisin' my fingers to make that oil and you not goin' to waste it on that stupid whip.'

But Manu paid no notice. He calmly poured some oil in a tin, and sinking back down on the almond root began to apply the oil with a rag.

'Gi'me the oil,' she ordered as she walked up to him. She took up the bottle and walked back to the kitchen. 'One of these days I will chop up that whip, I tell you . . . chop up that old rotten whip. I will chop it up today. If you only put it down I will take it and cut it in one hundred pieces. And then you will stop this mas' business. Compai,' she called, 'Mr Prince, lend me a cutlass.' When nobody moved she said, 'If allyou don't want to help me I will get his own cutlass and chop the thing.' She went into the kitchen and returned with his cutlass in one hand and the child held against her chest with the other. The child had begun to whimper. Samdaye advanced to Manu and tried to get to the whip but both her hands were full.

'This woman crazy, yes.' Manu continued to rub oil on parts of the whip that had become stiff.

'Even if I don't cut up the whip I will see that you ain't play any stupid mas' this year.'

'And who will stop me?'

178

'Who will stop you? Who will stop you?' Her voice rose with her rage. 'You feel you is so much man nobody could stop you. I will stop you.' The baby began to scream. 'You see how you frightenin' the child!'

Prince had retreated to his step but Compai looked on anxiously.

Throwing down the cutlass she stood with her lips trembling and tears of frustration filling her eyes. 'If you don't put a end to this foolishness I will – I will kill myself. As God hearin' I will go by the river and – and drown myself.'

'Look the rain comin'. You will get enough water to drown you'self,' he said with a chuckle.

'My mother warn me about this man, yes. She say the man is a mas' man and he wouldn't grow up to shoulder responsibility.'

'Him shoulder responsibility . . . you better take the child inside before it catch a cold wit' the rain.'

He got up and went to the back of the house and she followed.

The cloud, which had spread overhead suddenly opened and the rain, in large drips, came hurtling straight down. The yellow-tails which had been chattering moments before became silent but somewhere a parrot screeched, breaking into the washing sound of the falling water.

In less than an hour the cloud had drained itself out and all that was left of the big black cloud was a few ragged remnants of grey cotton-wool moving very slowly against the cerulean sky.

Mangal returned from the Sunday School with the inevitable Christmas card given out as reward for attendance regardless of the time of the year.

'You make the sign of the cross, boy?' Manu asked.

'Is not a Cat'olic church, Pa.'

'Tell him, son,' Samdaye said. 'Now even your son start to teach you.'

The boy realised that the argument still hung in the air and wondered if Stalin had ended his fishing. He changed his clothes and was about to go out when his mother warned him about the wet grass and mud. He took out his Reading book and sat quietly in a corner on the floor.

'Ma, when Gabi comin' back?'

'Gabi? I don't know anything about Gabi?' The voice came out harsher than she intended. 'You reading your lesson?'

The boy grumbled a reply.

'Come let me see where you reach in Reading.' She sat on the edge of the bed and waited while he rose slowly and came to her. Running her fingers through his hair she looked at the book and noticed that his portion had been changed progressively every day. The teacher had ticked it and put the date. She hugged him and said what a bright boy he was and asked if he could read the new assignment which he did with little help. She took him through the next page a few times and then asked about his Arithmetic. When he began to fidget she hugged him again and allowed him to put away his books. 'You remember what I tell you about what you should be when you grow up?' When he nodded she coaxed him to tell her and when he said 'doctor' she smiled and warned him that he should tell no one else. That was their secret. 'Don't let anybody know our secret. And you know how you will come a doctor? You have to learn your lesson every day and always do more than everybody else in the class so you will know more than them. Then, when you get a big boy, you will pass the College Exhibition Examination and you will go free to Queen's Royal College in town. And I will feel proud.' She poked his belly. 'And baby Phulo will feel proud.' She poked again. 'And Pa will feel proud. And the whole village will feel proud. And Miss Mohammed . . .' Each time she mentioned someone she poked until he was really laughing and trying to get away from her grasp.

'Why I must be a doctor?'

'Why? That is he best thing anybody could be.'

'It ain't have anything else?'

'Yes. It have lawyer, engineer and all kinds of things.'

'Teacher, too.'

'Yeh, but it have plenty teacher already. And too besides, you want to be something better than teacher.'

'I like to be teacher to beat all the dunce children in the class. I will cut a good guava whip and dry it for one week then, when they dunce, I will give it to them pai-patai.'

'That ain't no reason to want to be a teacher.'

'And if I come a doctor I could chook everybody with needle and make them cry. Chook chook,' he thrust his arm with his forefinger outstretched and made stabbing motions.

'I want you come out from this hole.'

'Which hole?'

'This place, monkey. I want you to have a nice house with concrete wall and glass window, and Morris set inside. With livin' room and dinin' room, and bedroom. And garden outside wit' flowers growin'. You like that?'

He nodded.

She ran her fingers through his hair and the oil shone on them. She saw that her nails were broken and there was no longer any trace of the nail polish which she had put on many months ago. She felt her abdomen which had almost become flat again, she had lost a great deal of the weight she had put on during her pregnancy. Peering at the small shaving mirror which hung on a nail beside the door, her red-rimmed eyes looked back over darkened rings. She cocked her head and looked at the thick, black hair with a few curls framing her face. She must get a hold on herself. A creeping anger came over her as she thought how foolish she must look and how carping she must seem. She could not understand how she could lose her temper so easily. Her jaws clamped she promised that she would not let it happen again. She would get out of this situation.

The few times she had been to the school, she had seen a piece of land just opposite the building. In her mind she could see a small parlour selling drinks and sugar-cakes and sweets to the children. She had enquired and was told that the land was owned by the estate and she knew that the estate was not selling out small portions although it had done so to many people in the village years ago, and had donated the portion on which the school was built. She would ask Gomez about renting a lot on which she could put up a shack temporarily until she could build something substantial. She did not know how much she could depend on Manu who did not seem to worry about the next day.

She remembered the advice given by Mrs Gopaul about throwing Manu out but that was out of the question. So was leaving him. Such a thing had never happened with any member of her family or even relatives. Women who left their husbands were looked down upon. And where would she go – back to her mother's? And let her sisters laugh at her? Her mother would say, 'I told you so' but would certainly take her back. But leaving was not an option. She had chosen and she would abide, and if she had to eat salt and 'roti' she would rise out of the barracks. She would not become a woman who left her husband and who would be looked upon as easy prey for any marauding male. It was not that she had not seen it happen. Many an African woman had children and was living alone. Some had children by different fathers. But things were different for an Indian woman – especially Hindu. You had to bear out your portion in life however hard.

But it had not always been hard. She recalled how dashing he would look before Mangal was born. With his red hand-kerchief tied round his neck and his shirt open to halfway down his chest, and his hair, no matter how much he greased and combed it, would in a few minutes fall over his eyes. His body was lean and hard, and he could toss drinks or exchange blows with any man.

Now she could hear him talking with Compai about how he got in the mas'-playing business. Carnival was an African thing but he had grown up in Manzanilla with Africans. All his friends were Africans. He would walk with them for miles to go to some dance and this easily led to playing with some band dressed as sailors with long sugar-cane stalks and tins of powder. But this was neither colourful nor exciting. 'Diable diable' – devil mask was the thing. He could make the most elaborate clown costume and with a long whip in his hand he could prove something. In very little time he was classed with the toughest. 'Man Man' they called him; not 'Manu'.

'Man Man?' Prince called out, 'You?' There was disbelief in his voice. 'Don't tell me you is Man Man, boy. I hear Man Man is a big black man but I never see him. You know how much time I go to Carnival in Sangre Grande just to see this Man Man play 'diable'? But I never lucky to see him without the mas' over his face. In fact, now that I think about it maybe I never know who to look for. Boy, I must be see you a hundred time and I didn't know. You did know he is Man Man, Compai?'

'How the hell I woulda know that?'

'Tina, you hear who this is? The is the great Man Man we used to hear about.'

'Don't lie, man. Is years I hearin' about Man Man. You too young.'

'The man wouldn't lie just so, dry dry, Tina. Boy, I wish Gabi was here. He would get real excited.'

'If this is true it have a lot a fellers out to get you,' Compai said. 'What about Tasso? They say he is the best.'

'True,' Manu said.

'You never fight him?' Compai asked.

'No.'

'But you will have to face him.'

'Sometime.'

'But why you never fight him?'

'He was the leader in the band I play with.'

'And now you not with the band anymore?'

'I don't know. I ain't see anybody in the band for a long time. Not since last year.'

'But they can't stop you just so. And you been with the band long?'

'About eight years.'

'Well.'

'That don't mean anything. I feel Tasso want to challenge me long time now. I feel he got doubts about if he still better than me.'

'And he want to prove he is still the best,' Prince asked.

'Mm hmm.'

'That is dangerous business, yes,' Compai said. 'I can't imagine what could get in fellers head to beat each other with big whip just to show who better than who. Better in what?'

'Ask him, Compai,' Samdaye could not refrain from speaking. 'Let the brave man say what they fightin' each other for. Ask him if is just to see who could take more licks.' She had noticed how talkative he got as soon as they started talking about Carnival.

The conversation died.

The yellow flood of morning light had been replaced with a clean white wash and the grass glistened. Drops of water still fell from the tips of the leaves and the edge of the roof. The birds resumed their whistling. Samdaye could hear Manu's whip swishing through the air as he flexed it.

'Some people soak their whip in pee,' Prince said. 'I don't know what that does – if it make it more heavy, or if the whip could cut you more.'

'I don't know about that,' Manu said.

'I hear some people does 'range their whip. They take it to some obeahman and get them to pray over it,' Compai said. 'They say that does make you bad. Nobody could beat you.'

'You better check with Shepherd,' Prince said.

'Shepherd ain't no obeahman,' Martina poked her head through the door. 'The man does just preach a little. You want somebody who could do a little "jingay" so he wouldn't get cut.'

'You ever get cut?' Compai asked.

'Cut?' Samdaye interjected. 'You should see him when he come back. His body does be black and blue with long weals. You ever see the scar by his neck. Let him show you the long mark. Is the tip of the whip that catch him there. It could have cut the vein in his throat and he could have bleed to death.'

'Bad business,' Compai shook his head. 'Bad business.'

'I hear some people does weave wire at the end of the whip,' Prince said. 'And some does stick razor blade in it.'

'I know about the wire,' Manu said.

'That could give you blood-poison, man. That is bad business. Sport is sport but wire and razor blade is bad, man. Too bad.'

'Let him tell you about Lalman, Phulwa son,' Samdaye called from the kitchen from where she listened. 'Let him say how the boy was playin' man in a diable diable band. How it was the first time he decided to play mas' and how he lost his eye. And now he goin' about with one eye. And a good-lookin' boy.'

'You could get injured real bad with the end of the whip,' Compai said. 'Especially if it got wire and whatever.' Compai

184

approached Manu. 'You bound to do this, boy? I mean, what you really gettin' from it?'

'Food and clothes. Food and clothes,' Samdaye called out.

'You' wife don't like it and now that I hearin' more I don't like it either,' Compai said. 'You' wife right, you know. You should stop this thing now before you get damage. And you have two nice children to see about.' Compai had lowered his voice so that he would not add fuel to Samdaye's fire. 'This is wild thing – jungle thing . . . for savages.'

'Mr Compai, ask him who throw the whip that cause Lalman to lost his eye.'

A flash of pain crossed Manu's face. 'Is the last time I playin', yes. After this I givin' it up.'

'Is you fire the whip that damage the boy eye?' Prince asked.

Manu shook his head slowly. 'Is not me. Is Tasso. And for a big man with experience – a old man in the business – he should never take on the boy. And it was the first time the boy was playin'. The boy had a few drinks and he was gettin' on like he was some big-time whip-man. And he challenge Tasso. I sure it was just a joke he was makin'. But Tasso force him in the ring and start to chant and circle him. All of us round the ring thought Tasso was makin' joke too. And we start to sing. But then I see Tasso eye as he rush the boy and hit him bam bam bam – three lashes – fast like lightnin'. And then we see blood from Lalman face. And you think Tasso look at the boy. He just walk away – just walk away like he do something great. All of us in the band see him but he went and tell everybody is me who do it. He make up a long story.'

'So you goin' this time to take Tasso?' Prince asked.

He said nothing for a while then he said, 'Is the last time I in this thing.'

Chapter 17

'Roo-a-roo-roo.' The voices broke into the pale light of the early morning amid the flapping of alarmed chickens, the excited barking and yelping of dogs, and the screeching of roused yellow-tails. 'Roo-roo-a-roo-aah. One cent to see the Devil.' Each syllable was accompanied by a bang on a can. 'One-cent-to-see-the-devil.' Bang bang bang badangbang. A dragging chain rang against the gravel.

Mangal rushed to the window but he could see nothing at first until the fierce barking drew his attention to three shadowy figures running in a zig-zag. He had been waiting – interminably, it seemed – for this morning. He had watched his father work at his clown's costume and had begged for one to be made for him but his mother had roughly ordered him to keep his mouth shut. Compai had been secretly making one for him and gave it to him the evening before. It was made from the sheath of a cocorite palm and had been decorated with paint. He had put it on and everyone had remarked how frightening he looked and how no one would recognise him. Even his mother, who initially had frowned in disapproval, had patted him on the head and had said how nice he looked.

Through the space between the boards he followed the dark figures as they leaped and danced and made their noisy way across the bridge. 'Ma! Ma! Look, is mas'.' He ran to her and shook her. 'Pa! Come and see. They playin' Ol' Mas' already.' He raced for his mask and placed it in front of his face. 'I could put on my mas', Ma?'

His mother got up and tied the mask at the back of his head then she took flour and whitened his skin. She got a pair of torn trousers and tied bits of an old jute bag on it. She

186

gave him a broom and told him that he could go outside. 'Go and play mas' just like your father. They always say "dasheen don't bear tannia" so I ain't see why I frettin' for.' She said loudly so that her husband could hear.

Another clanging and banging reached the barracks and raced round the bend. Mangal peered but did not go outside.

'Wha' happen, Mangal, you ain't comin out?' Compai called. 'Look everybody playin' mas' already.'

'He 'fraid,' Samdaye said.

'Mas' 'fraid mas'?' Martina said. 'Come and let me see how you look.'

'Gwan,' his mother urged.

His father chuckled.

'Come, man,' Martina coaxed.

Haltingly, Mangal went outside where a mist still hung and words came out with light puffs of smoke. He held the mask in his hand.

'Come', Martina said, 'we will fix you up good. Prince, get your old hat. And bring a broom. He will play sweeper.' She held his hand.' You want to play sweeper? You will just pretend to sweep somebody yard and tell them to give you one pound.'

'A pound o' what?'

'A pound, boy, money. You don't know what is a pound? That is just a sayin'.'

He held the broom limply.

'Nah, that is too ordinary. Eh, Compai?'

The old man had emerged and was looking with interest.

'Prince,' she called again, 'you ain't comin' out to see Mangal? Wake up, man, wake up. Prince, you hearin'?' When he grumbled a reply she asked, 'Ain't you have a old shoe box?'

'Yeh.'

'Bring it out. He will play "See-the-Devil".'

'Them boys playin' that already,' Mangal said.

'If he had a friend he could play "doctor",' Samdaye said. 'I wonder if Stalin wake up.'

'Is Stalin playin' "See-the-Devil",' the boy said.

'I wish Gabi was here,' Compai said.

'He will play "doctor". He don't need anybody else. Eh,

Mangal? All you want is a "sound".' She went inside and came out with a piece of string and a 'crown cork' which she proceeded to flatten. Compai took the flattened metal and made a hole through which he passed the string in a loop and placed it around the boy's neck.

'You must say, "One pound to see the doctor",' his mother advised. 'And hold out the "sound" like this. Tell them "One pound to see the doctor" and put this on their chest.'

The boy was made to repeat the words and action then he went out, his legs heavy with apprehension.

'Make them pay you,' Martina called. 'Be brave and don't leave until you get money for soundin' them.'

Concealed behind the mask, he began to gather courage. 'Roo-a-roo.' His voice sounded strange. 'Roo-a-roo-roo. One cent – one pound to see the doctor.' The more he repeated it the braver he became. It was a good feeling to be in disguise. Nobody knew who you were. He began to jump around in imitation of the boys who went before and turned and saw his mother and the rest watching with satisfaction. The bashfulness came again and he stopped.

'Gwan, gwan,' his mother urged.

He decided not to go to the Gopal house in case the boys had got back home so he scampered past. At the corner, past the bridge, he heard the distant banging of an approaching group. He waited until he could see three young men, white eyes flashing from soot-blackened faces and greased bodies gyrating. When they saw him they increased their speed. He turned and ran back but before long they were surrounding him. The lead player with horns and a tail and a chain around his waist, which was held by another, looked fearsome but he quickly noticed the bandaged toes and knew that it was Popo, a boy in the fifth standard in school. Popo's toes were always in bandages. He quickly lost his fear and even joined them in jumping up and down and shouting with them, 'Pay the devil. Diable diable. Pay the devil. Diable diable.' He thought that it was more fun than playing 'doctor' and followed them until they chased him away. He stood and watched as they went to the barracks.

'Wha' happen, Mangal? You playin' mas' or you watchin' mas'?' Martina called.

Much braver now, he continued up the road. Soon he came upon the Gopaul boys who also tried to scare him but he was no longer afraid. In any case he was sure they could not recognise him behind his mask and other disguises. But Stalin approached and offered to be his partner and he marvelled at the boy's ability to recognise him. At first he was reluctant but he thought it would be great fun to have a partner.

'German and Poland don't let me do nothing. I just runnin' behind them. And they won't give me any money that we make.'

Mangal felt good at having been asked a favour and he agreed after some hesitation which he exaggerated for effect. 'But you not dressed for "doctor",' he said.

'You don't worry. You is the doctor. I will just collect the money.'

Mangal began to have doubts about the idea. 'Wha' you mean you will collect the money? Nobody ain't collectin' money for me. I collectin' for myself.'

'Doctor don't collect money.'

'Who say?'

'You ever been to doctor?'

'No, but –'

'You see? You ain't know. I been to doctor and I see my mother pay a girl in front.'

'Well I ain't no real doctor so I could take money.' He was glad that the sun had now risen and it was no longer dark. He had become less afraid especially now that Stalin was with him and the feeling of sounding silly saying "one pound to see the doctor" had dissipated.

At one house the woman gave them two bananas: at another they got one cent. Frequently other children would come close and giggle trying to discover their identities. Occasionally one of them would call out their names and peer into the box to see what they had for medicines. Sometimes he actually had to pretend to 'sound' some bared chest before getting a marble for his pains.

Stalin stuck close to him and made a lot of noise with his tin and shouting out his invitation to see the doctor which sounded increasingly like the call to see the Devil. But the banging of the tin increased the excitement.

189

They walked a long way past the school; past the Principal's house where nobody went for fear that they may be punished for something when school reopened on Wednesday; past Teacher Willy's house with the windows and doorway crowded with his children, and Teacher Willy pointing out the masqueraders to the small ones. He did not give them any money.

The heat was rising and so was their hunger. Removing their masks they hid between some coffee trees and ate the bananas.

'How much money we make?' Mangal asked.

'We ain't make nothing. Only one cent.'

'This business ain't have no money, nah.'

'We will turn back when we reach by Elton. That is the last house before the forest.'

'Nah, we ain't goin' so far. We will go quite up by Elton and we won't get anything. We turning back when we reach the next bridge.'

'We could go and fishen,' Stalin said.

In the yard of the house near the bridge a small group of men and women were spreading blue colouring over their faces and bodies. On a crude workbench were several feathered headpieces. A tall man who was topped by a mass of thick, white hair in tight curls, his mouth a red cavern in the blue, was rehearsing some members of the group. He made long, slow, stylized movements and they followed.

'Blue Indians,' Stalin said. 'Let's go closer.'

'Nah,' Mangal said. He was always afraid of masqueraders playing Indians.

'That is Mr Nelson – the old man, and Ma Nelson and – and they won't mind.'

They edged closer.

The old man was rehearsing the chant: 'hey-toe-mamu-mamu-sagua-jagua-wey-bin-ay-koraa.'

'What they sayin'?'

'Don't know. Sound like something they make up.'

'Die-see-kay-Monte Christo . . .' Shrieks and shouts punctuated the chanting. They really looked wild.

'Me ain't goin' no closer,' Mangal said and he started backing away. But the headpieces of coloured feathers and the very large structure that would go to the chief's head looked so attractive with its hundreds of feathers of various lengths and colours that he wanted to touch it. With that length it would surely touch the ground even though it was placed on the head of a man as tall as Mr Nelson.

'San Antonio wey-bin-ey-koraa . . .'

'They look well serious saying that,' Mangal said, 'you don't think is some magic words?'

'Don't be stupid, boy. They ain't know what they sayin'. Is one heap o' mumble jumble.'

'Like the pundit?'

'Nah, the pundit know what he sayin'.'

'How you know?'

'I hear my father say how he sayin' true things and how he preach well.'

'I don't understand a lot o' things.'

'A-a-a-ay-ya-ya-ai. E-ee-ee-hoo.' It was a hair-raising scream and Mangal shrank involuntarily and backed away.

Not far from them sitting on the front steps a woman was sewing beads along the side of the legs of a pair of trousers; a young girl was painting a headband with anatto juice. Her lips and fingers were red. Two men were putting the last touches on an enormous structure that would fit over the long headpiece of the chief and into which he would have to stand. The structure stood on four small wheels that would roll along as the chief moved.

'Come on. Is either we move close or we turn back from here.' Stalin was not sure he wanted to get too close.

'You 'fraid, too, nah?'

'I ain't 'fraid. I could go and touch the head-piece.' He screwed up his face behind the mask but, realising that Mangal would not see the effect of his determination, he stepped forward and was about to touch the costume when someone yelled at him and he ran back into the road and in the direction in which they had come. Mangal followed close behind.

Some distance away a woman emerged from a house and called out to Mangal to take something for his mother. She brought about a pound of tomatoes and two cucumbers. 'Mangal, tell you' mother I will send some pepper next week.'

191

He felt so humiliated. Not only was he recognized but he was given all this weight to carry. Now he could no longer play 'doctor'.

Back at the barracks Martina laughed at his being given vegetables to bring for his mother. 'And I thought you had such a good disguise.'

'Look,' Compai said. 'Look I givin' you one cent for playin' mas'. Come,' he coaxed, 'come for it before I change my mind, yes.'

He went slowly forward and took the coin.

'What happen? You all not goin' down this side to the junction? You sure to make some money down that side,' Martina said.

'You must be hungry, son,' Samdaye said. 'You had anything to eat, Stalin?'

They both declined. The excitement had not yet died completely.

'I ain't playin' no more,' Mangal whispered to Stalin and took off his mask.

Manu came from the back of the barracks where he had gone to fetch grass for the cow. 'Who say dasheen don't bear tannia?' He looked at Compai. 'This fella ain't no mas' man for sure. Eh, son? You ain't like this playin' mas'. I could see that.' He put his hand on the boy's shoulder. 'How much money all-you make?'

The boy related how all they got was two cents, two cucumbers and some tomatoes for his mother.

'Is a waste of time,' Stalin said.

'Boy, you really preach, there,' Samdaye said. 'Tell that to the big mas' man. He still think is a great thing to dress up and pretend. Miss Tina,' she called, 'they really say from the mouth of children you will hear wisdom.'

Stalin felt that he had got into some argument as he could sense a rise in the pitch of the woman's voice.

'Waste of time? Waste of time, yes,' Samdaye continued.

A heavy silence descended. Distant sounds of shouts and banging and an occasional shriek punctuated the quiet. To this was added the fluttering and an occasional caw from the yellow-tails.

'Don't worry with your mother, son,' Manu said, 'sometimes

192

a man got to do something what nobody could do for him. He just have to do it. He got no escape. And . . . and sometimes a man got to have some enjoyment in life. You can't spend your life working . . . You know, I see my father work day after day, in the rain and in the sun, from January to December. I watch that man dry up like a coconut getting dry and wrinkle and crack-up. And the man never complain until he dead at forty-five. He say a man got to live his life. I know the times when he had fever. He used to shiver and his teeth used to rattle but he would get up in the dark before the sun raise and make his coffee and food to carry to work. And sometimes it would be raining and he would be trembling and his teeth chatterin' and only sometimes he will let out a groan but he will try to cover it with clearin' his throat. I watch him continue after my mother – your ajee – dead. The day after the funeral he go back to work keepin' everything inside. Not complainin', just workin' workin' workin'. Only once or twice he ask if I miss my mother and then he say never mind she wouldn't want you to mourn and hang down your head like any sick dog.'

Mangal had never heard his father talk for so long and he was not listening to the words but it was the droning sound and the tone that reminded him of when he would be begging his mother for some favour. It was as if his father was begging him for something. He was holding his father's hand and they were walking across the field where the grass, wet from an early morning drizzle, had dried. They sat on the roots of the rose-mango tree. A white egret, snowy in the green, alighted and stood frozen for several minutes as if, surprised by encountering anyone, it waited to observe for signs of threat. Although Manu's voice was low the bird seemed to hear and laboriously flapped its way off the ground then smoothly accelerated as it went over the clump of guava trees.

'I remember my mother with one cotton dress, with little red flowers, and one white shinin' dress with little blue flowers, and an orhni of fine white cloth you could see through, with a border of little raised white flowers, and one pair of leather slippers. She didn't have stockings and high-heel shoes. She used to tie her head with a piece of cloth and get up earlier than my father to cook breakfast and lunch, and then both of them would go together to some cocoa estate and come back when it is again dark. She would cook again then sit with him and have a cigarette. That go on so day after day from Monday to Saturday. And when they get fed-up on one estate they go to the next one. Always doin' the same thing.'

'They didn't have no sport. Nothing to pass the time – only work and more work. On Saturdays, though, they would sit down with a half-bottle and drink that. And that is after work. My mother dead at thirty-two, when I was twelve, and my father take me with him to work every mornin'. I think he just wanted company. I didn't mind. I didn't like school anyhow and I didn't learn anything in the three years I go to school. Most of the time I didn't go to school because it was too far.' He lit a cigarette and leaned against the tree. The smoke was briskly whisked away by the wind.

Mangal tried to hold the smoke in his hands.

'That is what life is,' Manu said, 'like smoke. You see it; you smell it; but you can't hold on to it. It come from where it come from and go just so, easy easy.'

Compai came across the field and joined them. 'Fatherly advice, or counsel from the son?' he asked.

'We just talkin',' Manu said.

Mangal looked up at him. He had not said anything.

'I was tellin' him about my young days.'

'Young days? You still a little boy, yes. Well, what about your young days?'

'Just how my father and mother work hard.'

'Everybody work hard.'

'And how they never had anything.'

'Nobody still don't have nothing.'

'Well that is it, that is it. I intend to enjoy myself a little. I not goin' to kill myself wit' work and don't enjoy myself.'

Compai did not want to give any advice about how Manu should not let his enjoyment bring grief to his family. He had heard enough bickering over the issue of his mas' playing. 'So you not goin' to Carnival today?'

'I only goin' to see what happenin'. I will go later this evenin'.'

'You not wearin' your costume?'

'Not today. I just goin' to see if the band come out and if they will let me play wit' them. I have a feelin' that they don't want me back. I feel they want to gang up on me. I feel, too, that Tasso want to show me that he is still the best and he want to challenge me. Since last year I gettin' that feelin'.'

'That bad,' Compai said, 'and dangerous too.'

'I ain't 'fraid none of them.'

'Suppose they attack you this evenin'.'

'I ain't takin' my whip. They wouldn't challenge me if I ain't got my whip.'

'I know those fellahs, yes. They will throw a whip for you.'

'I ain't takin' bait. I don't want to fight the band but I not goin' to back off. I will go back for them tomorrow if they show me any bad face.'

Compai looked at the young man for a long time; at the jaws tightening; at the ash growing at the end of the cigarette; at the wisp of smoke flowing through his nostrils; at his unseeing eyes. Ah, the fire of youth, he thought. What seems of such great importance in early years becomes so insignificant in the long backward glance. But no counselling could change such fixed attitudes. The man would have to learn for himself. He edged closer to the tree, pulled up his legs, rested his head on his knees and closed his eyes. The air was warm, clean and dry, and that was enough for him. Overhead, the yellow-tails slipped in and out of their long swinging nests through holes near the top, they chattered and shrieked. A few pecked mangoes lay on the ground, the pecks being enlarged by an army of black ants.

By mid-afternoon the village was almost deserted. Samdaye busied herself in the kitchen and saw Manu leave without his costume or whip. He had gone by himself. Mangal, after crying to go with Stalin and his brothers, and then again, when his father did not take him, was now trying to fly his brown-paper kite with his few yards of thread. Not long after she saw Gomez with his quick, cocky walk, his neck invisible as his head seemed stuck on his shoulders. He walked briskly onto the verandah at Gopaul's house where Shanti came out to see him standing at the door. She seemed surprised and stepped outside the house. Gomez followed her with the dog running around him and wagging its tail. He seemed to be examining the marigold flowers but Samdaye could see the white at the bottom of his pupils. Realizing that he had seen her she looked in his direction and saw him walk out into the road and continue towards the junction. She thought that he left in too much of a hurry. But he often went there and she gave no further thought to the matter. After about a minute she saw Gopaul emerge from inside the house scratching himself as usual. Samdaye heard him ask who had come and heard her reply that it was the overseer. She watched Gomez until he went around the bend where he swung his head sharply and looked back.

'You coun say is a nice day for carnival, neighbour.'
Samdaye heard him but did not reply.

Chapter 18

One small, dark cloud grazed the hills as it crept in with a powdery, floating mist of rain. The morning sky beneath the distant edge showed that it was a passing cloud but it wrinkled many an eyebrow in expressions of apprehension for this was Carnival Tuesday — the real day of festivities when all the masqueraders would come out and the streets would be thronged with people.

From early, as though it was an ordinary working day, smoke curled from the wooden fires in the earthen stoves and the smell of pelau, roti and curry mingled in the wet air. As though sensing the excitement dogs barked, birds fluttered and children shrieked cries that they had heard the previous day, and sang or called out first lines of calypsoes composed for the season.

'You get up, Compai?' Prince called. 'Look, the sun come up.'

'Yeh. Long time.'

'You goin'?'

'Yeh.'

'What time?'

'About nine.'

'You tell Chicken to pass for we?'

'I ain't go out nowhere yesterday. Why you didn't tell him?'

'I tell him,' Martina said.

'You tell him what time?'

'About nine.'

'Aye neighbour, you coun say it goin' to be a good day.'

'The little drizzle will start it cool,' Prince said.

'But it goin' to be hot like hell, today. That rain will only raise the heat.' He walked lazily, yawned widely and scratched. 'Wha' happen to the mas'man?'

197

Prince indicated with his head that Manu was still inside.

'I ain't goin' out. I stayin' home. Only Shanti say she want to go. My wife like to go on a Monday. She say it have less people. She can't take the pushin' and the jammin'. But Shanti say she will go if Samdaye goin'. To tell you the truth, neighbour, we ain't too like this carnival business. Too much nakedness and them calypso songs too rude. The whole thing is foolishness.'

'Is not for any right-thinkin' Hindu or Muslim,' Mrs Gopaul added from her kitchen. She was going to say that it was for a lower class but she remembered Manu. 'Is for a different kind of people. Some people like it . . .'

'One man meat is another man poison,' Shepherd said. He was starting out early Bible in hand. He had to round up his group and collect the flowers. He also had to hurry them in their dressing, for today they would wear long gowns and tie their heads with turbans and long head-dresses before they would walk the four miles to the town ringing their bells and singing hymns.

'You ain't goin' to preach today!' Prince said.

'This is the day to preach, Prince. Not Sunday. This is the day when the sin come burstin' out; when the whole place does smell of wickedness.' He raised his finger in his usual preaching pose. 'You know who is the real King of Carnival? You think is the man with the best costume? Nah. Is the Devil – the Devil himself. That is the real King today.'

'All right, Sheppy, you go give it to them today.' Martina stuck her head out from the back of the building. 'But don't start from now. Save it for the real sinners.'

'All of us is sinners, Tina. All of us need the message.'

'Hallelujah!' Prince exclaimed with a tinge of derision.

'You ain't mockin' me, Prince?'

'Nah. How you expect me to mock you? You really talkin' the truth. But Carnival is the fête of the people. Is time when all could dress up and play anything – from king to clown.'

'Is a waste of time, neighbour,' Gopaul said. 'All that expensive cloth and all that time spend in makin' and decoratin' the costume. And all that energy – after makin' it to jump up with it two whole days. You coun say is too much waste.' He shook his head. 'Eh, Shep?'

'Great waste. Great waste. Man must sing praises to the
Lord not obscene calypsoes about shakin' your waist and
windin' and what they goin' to do with their "Mopsy".'

Mohammed's car came around the corner and ground to a
halt in front of them. His wife sat beside him and his three
daughters heavily made-up were squeezed in the back seat.
'I goin' to Port of Spain,' he said. 'I like to go early to get
parkin' near the Savannah to see the nice mas'.' He stuck his
head out. 'All-you ain't goin'?'

'We goin' to Grande,' Prince said.

'The girls like Carnival in town with the big bands playin'
Romans and pirates and Arabian Nights.'

'I like all the colour,' one of the girls said. 'Is a lot of white
people playing Carnival.'

'And the huge bands playing American soldiers invading,
and sailors from American battleships,' another said.

'It is very educational,' the teacher said. 'A lot of reading
and research is done to make the costumes authentic.'

Mohammed waved his hat and drove on.

'That Teacher Rachel really educated, you know,' Martina
said. 'She know so much big words.'

'Education is a great thing,' Prince agreed.

'I goin',' Shepherd announced.

'What happen, Manu, you ain't comin' out?' Prince called.

Manu mumbled something. All morning Samdaye had
been quietly pleading with him not to go. Especially since
he would be alone. An owl had hooted directly over the
barracks last night and that was not a good sign. Somebody
would die. She had also dreamt that she was at a wedding
where the bridegroom was dressed in white. The identities
of the couple were not clear. Sometimes she thought that it
was her wedding and sometimes the faces were hidden. White
flowers: lilies, petunias and roses were being scattered about.
But he was wordlessly dressing making final adjustments to
the small mirrors and clipping the ends of thread. He tied
a strip of red cloth to the back of the wire mask and
pulled it snugly over his face. He tied another strip of
the same cloth to his forehead as he slipped the mask
to the top of his head. His unruly hair stuck out on the
sides. He pinched Mangal's cheek and looked at Samdaye

but her eyes were lowered. The baby looked alarmed as he bent down to kiss her. Then he walked out into the sun.

Mangal sneezed.

Manu, on hearing the sound, stopped and turned to the boy in the doorway. He walked back a few paces before he faced the road. A sneeze on departing was not good luck.

'Jeezan-ages!' Prince exclaimed. 'The man come out!'

'Boy, you lookin' nice for so,' Martina said. 'The costume look real nice.'

Gopaul and his wife came out and the children ran on to the road. Mangal started down the steps but his mother ordered him back.

Manu had pushed his mask back over his head and its unseeing eyes and reddened cheeks took on a bizarre and grotesque look as it faced the sky. The large multi-coloured satin heart covering his chest and fringed with white fluff flashed its many mirrors.

'I goin', Prince. Tina, Compai, I goin',' he said.

'Alone?' Compai asked. 'You foolish, yes. You better wait for us. We will go just now.'

'Compai is right,' Martina said. 'You shouldn't go alone.' She turned to Prince, 'Why you ain't go with him. The boy can't go alone.'

'Don't worry, Prince, is only one day for a man to dead.' Manu's eyes became slits and reflected with a metallic glint. 'Is only once a man could dead.' He started a slow, stylized dance. 'Mooma Mooma, you son in the grave already. You' son in the grave a'ready, take a cloth and tie up you' belly,' he sang.

They had never heard him sing nor seen him dance.

'Tell him don't sing for his mother, sing for his wife and children,' Samdaye called.

Manu continued singing then he cracked his whip a few times.

'You goin', Prince?' Martina asked.

'Yeh,' Prince said as he rose from his seat on the step.

'You don't have to go,' Manu said. 'I ain't 'fraid.'

'Nah, gi'me a minute.'

BETWEEN TWO SEASONS

Soon Prince emerged and the two of them left.

Samdaye peered through the window and watched them leave, then she shut her eyes and prayed silently. Mangal was whimpering and mumbling how he would like to go with his father and she shut him up.

After a while the band of blue Indians passed making wild war cries and brandishing spears. Their feathered head-dresses bobbed gracefully. They walked to the Junction where they hoped to get a ride on a truck since, with their bodies smeared with blue paint, no taxi or bus would take them. Chicken, the only taxi-driver who regularly plied that road, passed twice. He promised to take Martina and her group within the hour.

An hour later with the sun in a blue bowl of a sky they were all dressed and waiting. Samdaye would not have gone but Gopaul's wife insisted that she leave the baby with her. She had already brought up six babies. Furthermore, she wanted Shanti to go out and enjoy herself and would not send her unless she went with Samdaye. The Gopaul children shifted from foot to foot sullenly looking on at the people getting dressed and leaving. To their constant pleading to be allowed to go Gopaul's wife screamed, 'All-you think money does grow on tree? And all-you have a good time yesterday buyin' ice cream and ridin' the merry-go-round? I know how all-you wicked, if I don't go all-you will get lost. In any case I not sendin' all-you with Shanti so shut all-you mouth! Is time the girl go out and have a good time without havin' to spend the day lookin' all about for all-you.' Every now and again she screamed at one of them asking if they had nothing to do and suggesting various chores.

Mangal jumped up excitedly at every imagined sound of an engine.

Martina stood stiffly with a new flowered dress and a large straw hat. She had huge circles of rouge on her cheeks and the white powder lay like a layer of dust on her black skin. Mangal wore a domino of cardboard from an old carton made and decorated by Compai. Shanti looked very attractive with rouge and lipstick and a shiny red dress with puffed sleeves and a bow around the neck. Only Samdaye did not wear a new dress.

The sound of an engine began to get louder and the children ran to the edge of the road. The car pulled a low cloud of dust as it crunched along.

'Petit Pierre,' Compai said. 'I wonder what he doin' here today. Like he don't go to Carnival or what.'

'Them fellers like money too much,' Martina said.

'He had that Indian fellah in the back seat with him. The same one who was walking round the place the last time he come. I think he intend to buy the estate.'

'You know who he is?'

'Nah. Better ask Gopaul. Gomez always go by him. Maybe he get the news already.'

'Gopaul,' Martina called, 'who is that strange man that come with Pierre?'

'Ali Khan. You hear about T. Ali Khan and Company in Port of Spain?'

'The dry-goods people?'

'He self. That is the man who lookin' at the estate to buy it.'

'He makin' a bad mistake,' Compai said. 'This land ain't worth one damn now. Cocoa and coffee done dead and the land get hard.'

'You coun say, neighbour, citrus will pay. This is good citrus land.'

'But it will take five years before you could prepare, plant and get your first fruit. Is plenty investment.'

'No Indian man does spend money bad, neighbour. If that man buy this land he know what he goin' to do.'

'I hope so. The only thing is citrus don't need much labour after you clear the land, dig the drains, and plant. All you do after that is cutlass the grass and pick fruit when it ripe.'

'Neighbour, I really don't know if the man will buy but I know he interested in the land.'

'Strange how the white man gettin' out of the land and is more strange how the other people buyin' it up.'

'It ain't strange. My father used to say how you must put your money in the land because land doesn't get rotten. He used to say that God ain't makin' more land so you should aim to get your hand on a piece because the price will never go down.'

202

'How you ain't have a few acres you'self?'

'Neighbour, is not that I ain't have hope but with the sickness and all the children and me dependin' on makin' a crown here and a weddin' gown there I can't see how I could ever afford it.'

A heavy rumble increased in volume and an old Vauxhall sped into view and rattled to a halt. The car backed into the Barrack-yard in a cloud of smoke.

'Chicken, how you take so long, man?' Martina asked.

'That ain't long. All-you ready?'

'You can't take everybody,' Martina said.

'Come on, get in and don't waste my time.' He started to pack them in. 'Big people lean back, small ones lean forward. I have more people to take up in the Junction.'

'Samdaye,' Martina called, 'You ain't goin' or what.'

Samdaye came out reluctantly. She took the baby over to Mrs Gopaul and Shanti accompanied her back. 'Don't worry,' Gopaul's wife said, 'You' baby safe. Enjoy yourself.' She saw the worried expression on Samdaye's face. She came to the car surrounded by her children who gazed at their distorted reflections on the chrome strips around the lights. One of them tried to get in. 'Ramkallia!' she shouted.

'You only licensed for five passengers, Chicken,' Gopaul said. 'You ain't 'fraid the police hold you.'

'Nobody obey the law for carnival. I see Man Man reach Grande already,' he said to Samdaye. 'I hear Tasso and the boys waitin' for him. He shouldn't go out today.'

'Prince is with him,' Martina said as she squeezed herself in the far corner against the door.

'I don't know what old Prince could do,' Chicken said. 'He just lookin' for licks. Them fellers will make him pee his pants.'

The vehicle groaned forward and strained to increase speed. 'Keep a look-out for the police,' Chicken said. 'When I say "duck" all of you on the edge of the seat go down low. I only want five heads to show.'

'And you just say the police won't bother you,' Martina said.

'I ain't say that. I say nobody obey the law but the police still watchin'.' He squeezed the horn outside the window –

a-roo-ca-a-roo-ca – then, fumbling among the tangle of legs, he found the lever and changed the gears. He picked up three more passengers and the inside of the car became dark and heavy with breath and the smell of powder and cheap perfume.

After about fifteen minutes he looked anxiously at the dashboard and pounded it a few times then he pulled aside on the narrow grass verge. He ran to the back and returned with a can of water which he poured into the steaming radiator. 'Damn thing over-heatin'.'

'Why you don't sell this thing and buy a car?' Martina said.

'Car cost money, plenty money.'

'Well take off the tyres and run it on the track. It done steamin' like a train.'

Chicken laughed. 'This car could give me five . . . six more years. All it want is a little water sometimes.' He peered ahead. 'As soon as I tell you "duck" I want you to go down.' He had seen a policeman. They ducked as he had advised and Chicken waved to the officer, who shook his finger at him as he leaned helplessly on his bicycle.

They stopped at the edge of the town. Watching them get out Chicken said that they were coming out like worms from a ripe guava.

'Don't laugh,' Martina said. 'You should pay me, Chicken. I pay to get ride not to give one. I don't know how much people was on top of me.'

The policeman on the cycle had caught up with them unnoticed. 'You bring all these people, Mr Boodram?'

'Who me, constable?' Chicken, stuffing his shirt around his hanging belly, put on an innocent expression. 'You crazy? All these people can't fit in this car. They just gather round admirin' it.'

'The policeman laughed and rode off. 'Don't over-do it, Boodram, not because is Carnival.'

Throughout the journey Samdaye had sat quietly with Mangal on her lap. For more than four years she had not been to the town for the Carnival. The last time she was pregnant with Mangal. It was then that she had started to become concerned about Manu playing devil-mask and battling with whips. Before that it had been exciting, even glamorous. But the heaviness of her pregnancy and the oppressive heat and the noise had overwhelmed her, and soon it all seemed so pointless. She had leaned against the wall of the Red Store and saw him prancing down the street with his unruly hair flying and the mask upturned to the sky, his whip cracking like gunfire and his mirrors glinting. Now all the thrill she used to feel had turned sour. The laughter, the loud greetings, the back-slapping and the recognition of her as his wife no longer meant anything. What she considered important then was trivial now.

'You want to go and look for Manu?' Martina asked.

Samdaye shrugged.

'Is not easy in this crowd. Anyhow, it too early for Diable to be fightin'.' Her big feet encased in thick rubber sandals Martina waved expansively to the people she knew, and identified them to Samdaye as they progressed weaving their way on the crowded pavement where every few yards a vendor hawked his wares. Rosie, who sold vegetables in the market at the corner, now stood before a pile of boxes with a few peeled oranges; Vincey, who burnt coal pits on the Toco Road stirred a large enamel pot with souse, his wife turned slices of black-pudding in a black iron pot; Prengay, a red band on his forehead and a thick poui stick across his shoulders walked down the middle of the street. 'Samdaye, look at that man. That is Prengay, the best stickman. You don't want him catch you in a ring with a stick in you' hand.'

'Aye, Martina, come and taste a good souse, girl. Pig-feet, cucumber and hot pepper. You can't make souse like this. Sweet, sweet souse,' she called, 'come and get you' souse! Hot souse.'

'A-A Buttah, since when you could make souse. You better don't take your stand by the Police Station.'

Bertha sucked her teeth. 'Here, taste a piece and you will bite you' tongue.' She bent to two children sitting on a soap box, 'Is your Auntie Tina.' There was no sign of recognition on the children's faces. 'You can't remember Tantie Tina and Uncle Prince, how they used to come and visit?' She raised her eyes to the sky. 'Children these days have chicken-shit in their head. I don't know why they goin' to school. Everything goin' in one side of their head and comin' out the other.'

'You ain't see Prince?'

'He didn't come with you?'

'He come with this girl husband – a fellah who does play diable.'

'Wha' happen, Prince playin' mas' now?'

'Don't be dotish, Buttah, he come as company for the fellah. This is Samdaye, my neighbour.'

'You talkin' 'bout Man Man?'

'You know him?'

'I see Man Man, yes. But I ain't see Prince in the crowd that was followin' Man Man.' She turned to Samdaye, 'That man in plenty trouble today, eh, Vince?'

Vincey nodded. 'Them Manzanilla fellahs out for Man Man, today. That will be fight father!'

Martina's face reflected the anxiety she saw in Samdaye's eyes. 'She don't like her husband in this business. We warned him not to come out today.'

'What you goin' to do, child?' Bertha spoke to Samdaye. 'Man is a strange animal. I tell you, is eighteen years I married to Vincey and I really don't understand him. Is beg I beg him to help me out. If you pass in the next ten minutes you ain't goin' to see him here. He gone with friends in the rumshop. Is only when he hungry he will come for some souse and pudden. And he will bring friends too and give them my stuff free!'

'I hear they givin' a big prize to the best man with a whip – one hundred dollars.'

'Is more than that. Some of the rumshop owners addin' to the prize money. Is nearer two hundred dollars!'

Martina nudged Samdaye. 'I hope he could win.'

Three black young men, their bodies greased with black paint, cardboard horns on their heads and wire tails stiffly bobbing, clad in black bath trunks which made them appear naked, dragged chains and beat empty tins and threatened the clothes of spectators until they were given a few cents.

'How long since he pass?' Samdaye asked.

'Long time, now. Must be a hour, eh Vincey? They went so,' she pointed in the direction of the Police Station.

206

BETWEEN TWO SEASONS

Samdaye felt Mangal's grip tighten as the devils passed. She led the way to the other side of this small town that sprung along the Eastern Main Road for about two hundred yards on either side and spread out at the Toco Road Junction, where, within the fork of the "Y", the Police Station stood two stories high and a few feet off the ground, boldly looking down the main street.

At the corner of the market street the vendors bunched. The smell of roast corn, and corn boiled in salted beef stock, of fish frying and 'accra' or salt-fish cakes mingled with the scent of powder and cheap perfume in unidentified bottles. In boxes with wire mesh sides were heaped currant rolls, sugar cakes and home-baked bread, dark brown and decorated with plaits of dough. Flies hung around the mesh.

A rhythmic beating of a brake-drum rang over the rumbling sound of a steel band playing the most popular calypso – the road march. At intervals voices would join in a refrain: 'Mary Ann Mary Ann how you leave for some damn yankee man?' The crowd pushed to the edge of the pavement to see the band which was identified by a cloth banner with the title 'USS Iwo Jima'. About fifty men and women were dressed as sailors – in white, with white caps jauntily set – with cans of powder in their hands. They were led by a row of beribboned 'admirals' with pipes in their mouths and canes in their hands. They were all chipping to the rhythm of the steel band. Following the band was a crowd of stragglers.

Samdaye waited until the band passed before attempting to cross the street. But another group was approaching from the market street and the crowd closed in once more. This was a band of some two dozen players all dressed in white flannel suits and red bow ties. On their heads were panama hats. With canes in the crooks of arms that ended in gloved hands they danced to the strumming of guitars.

'They playin' English tourists,' Martina explained to Mangal.

Seeing how difficult it was for her to tug the boy through the crowd Samdaye took Shanti's hand and placed her son's in it. 'Stay here,' she said, 'Miss Tina and I goin' to look for him.' She put six cents in Mangal's hand. 'And don't run away from Shanti, you hear?' She pointed to a weathered wooden sign which creaked on its rusty hinges. 'Remain under this sign.' She patted him on the head and disappeared.

Mangal looked at the coins in his wet palm. He had never had money to do as he wanted and he thought of things he could buy. A few feet away a man held a pole on which were hundreds of tin-foil pinwheels whirring away in the breeze their many colours blurred. Mangal edged closer and saw a girl buy one for five cents. He realised that he could buy one but then he saw a woman over an ice-cream tub pasting the top of a cone. It looked so juicy. That must be five cents, he thought. 'I want a ice-cream,' he told Shanti. But she told him to wait. He saw a man wheeling a bicycle with a large tray in front. A wet jute bag wrapped a block of ice. On a shelf above the tray were bottles of different coloured syrup and a tin of condensed milk.

'Snow ball,' the man said and looked at Mangal straight in the eye. 'Press.'

Mangal swallowed. The heat from the sun and the air-lessness standing down deep into the crowd combined with the dust and the noise made him thirsty. And there was so much to eat and drink. Across the street a woman fanned a coal-pot driving the smoke in gusts. Bits of ash and sparks flew. Perspiration gathered on her brow and she wiped it with the short sleeve of her dress. On her left two pretty girls with brown eyes kneaded dough and broke them swiftly into small round lumps. The one nearest the mother squeezed the lumps and flattened them then she deftly rolled it into almost transparent thinness sprinkling flour over it before throwing it on the hot griddle smoking with coconut oil. The woman patted the rolled dough with a wooden spatula and turned it round and round. The dough swelled. She flicked it over and greased it with a rag tied to a stick. She turned it once more and greased the other side, then she lifted it with the spatula and placed it on the top of several others in a cardboard carton marked 'Gossages Soap. Stow away from boilers.' Her husband immediately took it out and, pouring a large spoonful of chicken curry on it, folded it over the curry and wrapped it in a piece of brown paper. He handed it to a young man who paid him and bit into it. Olive green gravy ran down the side of his mouth.

'Roti!' the man said, 'Get your hot roti. Hot with pepper, hot with heat. Is the bes' roti you will eat!' He looked at every passerby, 'Roti, mister? Roti, friend?'

Mangal saw that his eyes were the same colour as his daughters. He had crossed the road and was looking up at the man. 'Roti, boy?' the man asked. At his silence the man said sharply, 'If you don't want nothing, boy, go and look at mas'.'

A drop of perspiration fell with a hiss from the woman's brow. The drop immediately disappeared from the hot griddle. He found his arm being firmly held and he raised his head to see Shanti pulling him back under the shop-sign.

'If you was my brother I would give you one good box.'

He had seen her box her brothers and sometimes whip them. She would come out just like her mother. He tried to peep between the arms and legs that hemmed him in from the street. 'I can't see nothing,' he whined. 'We could go a little bit up that street and we could see from there. Is not far. Ma must see me when she come back. And – and you could leave me if you want and go and see mas'.'

She thought it was a good idea and started to steer him in front of her. They had been standing near the entrance to a rumshop and the stench of the liquor assailed her nostrils. Also there was loud talking and obscene language that competed in volume with the noise on the street. The market was closed and, although very few bands passed in front of it on the southern edge of the town, the pavement was wide and from there she could catch glimpses of bands that passed on the main street. She was not too concerned about her not being able to see. Like her parents she thought carnival was a waste of time unless, of course, you were playing.

In front of the market some children under the guidance of a man in a suit with a top-hat were dancing and singing, weaving a maypole. About ten of them held long, coloured ribbons that stretched from the top of the pole. They weaved in and out as they skipped to the rhythm and, magically, to Mangal, the design grew. A small music group provided the rhythm with 'cuatros' and maracas. A few of the children were just about his age and the rest were older and he imagined himself gliding round, brightly dressed weaving those flashing colours with lightness and grace.

'You stay here,' Shanti said. 'I goin' round the corner a little. Don't move from here, eh? You hear?'

He nodded absent-mindedly. He wouldn't move from such a lovely sight.

He did not know how long he must have been standing when he thought he saw his father at the head of a group of people moving away from him. 'Pa!' he called. 'Pa!' But he could not be heard so he ran after the group but when he reached the junction he could not see the direction they had gone. He thought that they had gone in the rum-shop so he went in but was quickly chased out. His father was not in there. He decided to walk up the street and had difficulty as the crowd seem to be coming in the opposite direction. He ducked and side-stepped and weaved until, finding that it was impossible to go further, and hearing the sound of an approaching band, he stepped on the sidewalk and found himself pressed against a wall. He had no idea how long he stood but it seemed like hours, then he stepped into the street that now held few people. At one end moved the retreating band and at the other end, in the distance, another one was coming. It looked like the blue Indians from Dorado. They had no music and no following so it was easy for him to pass by.

Near the entrance to a rum-shop he saw a red cap and bells above the head of a small crowd and he ran towards them. 'Pa,' he said and grabbed his hand but a stranger turned round and someone laughingly asked the man to introduce his son.

Mangal found himself in front of the police station, a point where five streets converged. Suddenly he was filled with panic. He had no idea from which direction he had come and he started up several roads only to return disappointed. He peered into every face but there was no one familiar. From a distance almost every woman looked like his mother. Sitting down on the pavement, he began to cry. A young man stooped down and asked him if he was lost and, when he nodded, held him by the hand and led him towards the police station. As soon as he saw the first policeman he wrung his arm away and started to run in the opposite direction. No policeman was going to lock him up.

The cap and bells again flashed above the heads. He went slowly this time and discovered that it was the same man he had mistaken for his father. He now knew the direction from which he had come and he proceeded along the street. Two blackened bodies gyrated a few yards away and he slunk to the wall until they went by. He began to look for Shanti's red dress but she also was nowhere to be seen. At the junction above the crowd he saw the rusty sign UNCLE SAM BAR and went under it but his mother was not there.

Up the street near the market there was emptiness where the maypole had stood and Shanti was nowhere. He went and leaned against the gatepost of the market. The gate was closed and a short chain with a large lock held the two halves together. The slanting shadow of the roof fell across the pavement and now reached the road. The sun was where it would be when school was over for the afternoon. It was late and he had eaten nothing.

The smell of food was overpowering. Obliquely across from him wafted the smell of fish being fried and he could see a woman biting into a round, crusty hops bread which left flakes round her mouth; a boy about his age shelled nuts from a brown paper-bag and popped them into his mouth; down by the corner a man was biting into a roti after peeling back the paper wrapping. He was opening his mouth wide and sucking in air after every bite because it was hot; a little girl crunched into the top of her ice-cream cone. Behind him on the stalls of the market peeping under the cover of jute bags were ripe bananas, and in the glass box on the counter of the cafe he could see currant rolls, coconut tarts, sweetbread with raisins and rock cakes. His stomach rumbled.

A woman with three children came and sat on the pavement close by. Seeing the tears running down his face she asked him if he was lost. He was not lost. It was his mother who was lost. And his father, and Shanti, and Mr Compai. Everybody was lost and he did not know how he would get home. The tears ran faster.

The woman repeated her question and asked about where he lived and who his parents were. It was his parents who were the cause of this. It was his mother who brought him and left him and it was his father who caused his mother to come. His father and his stupid costume. It was because of the costume and mas' that he was going to die from starvation right here on the pavement. The feeling of utter hopelessness was complete.

The woman's children, a boy younger than him, a girl about his age and a toddler gazed at him with curiosity. The mother gave him a sweet biscuit which he refused. He was going to die to spite them all. She pushed it closer to him and he smelled it. He took it and bit into it and the sweet taste mixed with the salt of his tears and his mouth felt as though it was filled with cobwebs. It was dry and made a lump but would not go down.

'Ma, I want a snow-ball,' the girl said.

'Me, too,' said the boy. 'And I want one with red and green syrup and with condensed milk.'

'Me, too,' echoed the toddler.

'And all-you just had ice cream?'

'But Ma, it hot and we thirsty.' They looked at him all the while as they spoke.

Their features appeared as a blur until he blinked then they cleared somewhat but the blur soon returned.

The woman rose and led them away for the snow-cones and he slumped to the pavement. It was still hot from the midday sun but it was in shadow. From his vantage point all adults looked the same height and he could scarcely make out one feature from another yet he scanned their faces through his film of tears. He was hot, hungry, tired and sleepy, and he was sure he was going to die. That would serve his parents right. They would cry for him and say how they were sorry. He had a faint recollection of his grandfather dead and lying in a box with white lilies round him. They had carried him away walking into the coconut palms with the sunlight making a mist, and he always thought that they had left him near the clump of wild heliconia and that he would return any minute. Whenever he had gone back to his grandmother's he would look at the heliconia to see if his grandfather was there. When you died you were just taken somewhere else and you could come back when you wanted secretly because he had heard his mother saying that her father had visited his grandmother because the old lady had said how she heard the door creaking.

He could see the waves of heat rising from the asphalt. How nice it would be to have Stalin sitting beside him on the river bank in the cool of the cocoa field with the water lapping at your feet, with a guava or a mango in your hand watching the small fish in the clear water playing round your hook.

Someone was touching him and calling him by name. It looked like Gabi but he did not believe his eyes.

'Boy, you harden, yes,' Shanti was saying. 'I tell you wait and I ain't go for two minutes and you run off. I really feel I could tap you up, yes.'

But he was not hearing a word. He was looking at his friend, Gabi. Or maybe it was not his friend but a dream he was having. Maybe he was dead and visiting his friends. But he stared unblinking at the blur that looked like Gabi. No matter how much he rubbed his eyes his vision would not clear.

'So how you goin', palits?'

It was Gabi's voice.

'Don't tell me that you forget you' pardner already.' Gabi was running his fingers through his hair and pulling him up by the shoulders. 'Wha' happen, you ain't playin' mas' like daddy?'

'Gabi,' he said in a croak. 'Gabi, Gabi.' It was still difficult to believe. Gabi had grown taller and he was wearing shining brown shoes above which were brown nylon socks over which hung long brown pants sharply creased and a multi-coloured shirt with dragons. His hair was combed differently: the muff had given way to a low cut plastered with vaseline. A comb with a tin clip and a pen were stuck in the pocket.

'Man, you had Shanti and me worried. We look for you all about.' He had one arm around the girl's shoulder.

Mangal thought it nice that Gabi and Shanti were friends and understood why the girl had left him. She had gone to look for Gabi.

Gabi stretched out his hand and found Mangal's hand clammy with sweat still clutching the six-cent piece.

'You ain't spend the money?' Shanti asked. 'So you ain't eat nothing? Poor fellah you must be starving.'

Gabi brought him hops bread and fried fish. It was a whole herring hot and golden. Shanti opened it and took out the bones in the centre. He bit into the crunchy tail that stuck out of the round loaf.

He had almost completed the sandwich when his mother arrived. He could see streaks of dried tears on her face. 'Where all-you went? I look all about. Mangal, ain't I tell you to stay under the sign at the corner?'

The boy was too busy eating to explain all that had happened to him.

'What happen, Shanti?'

'Nothing,' the girl replied.

Gabi had taken his arm off Shanti's shoulder. 'Miss Samdaye,' he said.

'A-A Gabi, is you? How are you, boy? How you run away so quiet, quiet? You had all of us worried. You well?'

Gabi nodded. 'I OK.'

'You workin'?'

Gabi nodded again. 'I get a job wit' Huggins.'

'You lookin' rich.'

Gabi smiled. 'How Dads? I lookin' for him.'

'He well. He in Sangre Grande lookin' at mas'. He miss you but he ain't sayin' nothing. You must come and see him.'

'I comin' tonight if I ain't see him in Sangre Grande.'

'I goin' home now, Shanti. Come, let us go.'

'You go ahead,' Shanti said. 'I will come with Miss Martina.'

'You come with me and you should go back with me. I don't want nothing to happen to you. Your mother send you with me.'

'Nothing will happen,' Gabi said. 'I will stay wit' her until she meet Miss Martina.'

'Just tell Ma I comin' wit' Miss Tina. Don't tell her nothing more.'

'You sure you not comin' with me?'

Shanti shook her head.

'I gone, then.'

Chapter 19

Manu entered the town, his mask pulled over his face. Every few yards he cracked his whip. It sounded like a gunshot. In order to show that he had nothing to protect his skin he had unbuttoned the top part of his costume. Other 'diable' players often tied leather or layers of cardboard around their backs and chests to absorb the effect of the whips.

He walked alone unlike other players, unlike earlier times. A lone 'diable' was very vulnerable. Others could gang up on him. Tasso was the only one who would do this but he would leave his face uncovered so that he would be recognized. No one then would be foolish enough to challenge him and bring down the anger of the entire band that he led.

Manu wanted it to be known that he had arrived and that he was alone. He would be recognized by his voice and by the fact that he was the only one foolhardy enough to walk alone with his chest bared. He had come to prove that he was the best. 'One day for a man to dead,' he roared. Crack! went his whip.

In the rum-shops the day before he had listened to the talk from followers of the sport that he was in big trouble. The whole of Manzanilla was out to beat him. Manu knew why he was now being seen as an enemy. While he was in Manzanilla he was part of the Tasso band. He was the best but he was always in the shadow of the old man who had to let everyone know that he was the undisputed master. Now that he had left the area he was expected to go to Tasso and ask to be allowed to play with the band. They knew where he was and could have sent him messages at any time. But he was supposed to beg to retain his place. Well, he would show them. He had also heard that other groups of devil masqueraders were out to avenge their many whippings.

He smiled grimly behind his mask. 'When Ah dead bury me deep,' he sang. It was an old stick-fighting song. Pedestrians on the road scattered as he swung the whip in the air and pulled it back sharply making that gunshot blast again and again. Sometimes he pulled the whip back on himself and let it crack across his back and snake around his middle but he knew how to turn his wrist and to give the whip some slack so that the middle of it would make a loud slap on his loose shirt and the end would wrap itself around him without causing any hurt. He saw the looks of fear and admiration.

'Man Man! Aye, Man Man.'

'Is Man Man in town, boy.'

'Lord, is today you goin' to see rope.'

'You too early, boy. Why you come so early?'

He laughed loudly. It was more hysterical than filled with humour. That was the feeling! He pulled himself to his full height and walked along the street moving from side to side in a diagonal path. He loved the expression of alarm on their faces and the occasional shout of his name. This was not the 'yes-sir no-sir' of the estate, no bowing and scraping and hanging down your head like a dog. This was not having to mind wife and children with a few measly dollars every fortnight. This was the time when he was king and when he stood in a ring no dog could bark. When he put on the costume it was like putting on a new skin shedding the old one with all its cares and its million humiliations.

He reached the junction by the police station but had met with no challenge. There were only a few little boys playing dirty devils and some in sailor costumes waiting for the rest of the band to arrive. The street and sidewalks were overflowing with people who had come from the small villages to spend the day in the town. It was really too early.

Leaning on a wall near the doorway of Singh's rum-shop was a 'diable' with his mask hanging round his neck and a beer in his mouth. Manu felt like rushing up to him and dealing him a few blows just for the excitement. As he neared the 'diable' he recognized the fellow as one from a group on the Toco Road. They just played for fun. He went right up to him – 'Aye, feller, buy me a beer, nah man.' Manu saw the boy's eyes widen for he was still in his teenage years. The boy had recognized him. 'You could give me the one in your hand while you go for the other one.' The boy quickly handed over the half-empty bottle. He soon returned with two beers.

Manu looked at the young man's whip which was a length of cheap rope which he had wrapped around his waist.

'It cold enough, Mr Man Man?' There was an excitement in his voice. He could imagine telling his friends later how he had a beer with the great Man Man.

'So, you like playin' this mas'?'

'Yeh,' the young man replied.

'Why?'

'Is a lotta fun.'

'Is fun, eh? You ever challenge anybody in the ring?'

'Me? Nah. I don't want to fight nobody.'

'And if somebody throw down a challenge for you –'

'Nah, I ain't fightin' nobody. It ain't have no one in our band who like fightin'. We like to dress up for Carnival and we pretend to fight among ourselves. We like to look at you, though. Man, you really great.'

'You right, boy, you right.' He turned away sharply. The sport was going to hell. Nobody was taking it seriously anymore. It was time for him, too, to give up this business. He had only one more thing to do.

He swung into the Manzanilla Road where he entered a rum-shop. He would wait there until Tasso and his boys arrived.

Chapter 20

A shower of rain had washed the western sky and a pale sun was trapped among the branches of the almond tree. Samdaye untied the cow and followed it to the pen. The clouds to the east promised more rain.

'Neighbour, you say that Shanti comin' with Tina and them?' Mrs Gopaul called. Several times Samdaye had explained that she asked the girl to accompany her back to Dorado but it was too early and the girl wanted to stay a bit longer. She did not mention that the girl had been left in the company of Gabi.

'I try to get her to come, yes. But you know how young people is these days. Besides, a lot of masqueraders was now comin' out so I didn't want to force her.'

'The sun is goin' to set and she ain't come. I gettin' worried.'

'Don't worry. Miss Tina ain't come back yet.'

As if on cue Prince and Martina appeared walking wearily. There was no sign of the girl. Samdaye stood and allowed the cow to go ahead. Her heart skipped a beat.

'Mangal,' Martina called, 'I bring some phulourie for you. Come quick before I eat it up.' She opened the greasy paper bag. 'Mangal, you comin'?'

Samdaye peered round the bend and saw Compai walking slowly. She waited until it was clear that the girl was not with him.

'Wha' happen, girl?' Martina asked. 'Manu ain't come with us. He must be still singin' "One day for a man to dead".'

Almost simultaneously Samdaye and Mrs Gopaul asked, 'Where Shanti, she ain't come with all-you?'

'Shanti?'

218

'She ain't come? She say she was comin' with you.'

'She didn't say anything about comin' with us. She say to go ahead she will come right away.'

'She was with anybody?' Samdaye asked quietly.

'Nah. Who she will be with?'

'She wasn't with anybody,' Prince said.

Mrs Gopaul had begun to quarrel. 'You can't give children a little chance. You give them a little chance and they play the fool. Why the girl didn't come with all-you? You see how children harden? I didn't want to send her, you know. I only send her because of you,' she looked at Samdaye. 'I didn't know you would leave the girl otherwise I wouldn't send her at all!'

Samdaye felt very uncomfortable. She should have insisted on the girl returning with her.

'What happen?' Martina asked.

'Is Shanti. She tell me she was stayin' back to come with you.'

'I only see her one time after you leave.'

'She was alone?'

'Why you keep askin' if she was alone? Of course she was alone. Who you expect she would be wit'?'

'This is not a day for girl children to be out on the street,' Mrs Gopaul was saying. 'Wit' all them drunk people and all o' them have their face cover wit' mas'. You don't know what could happen. This is not a nice thing you do, Samdaye. Not a nice thing at all.'

'You coun say is not a nice thing neighbour,' Gopaul added.

'All-you mustn't blame Samdaye. If the girl didn't want to come Samdaye couldn't drag her home. She is a big girl. She could travel by herself. It ain't have nothing to worry about. Is still daylight.'

The dark clouds had raced overhead and the grey rain had started to erase the hilltops.

'German! Poland! All-you go down by the Junction and wait for your sister.'

'In this rain?' Gopaul asked. 'The girl will come just now.'

The boys stood uncertainly.

'Don't go anywhere, boys, the rain will start in a minute.' Gopaul said.

219

The rain started in a light drizzle the small drops making orange glints from the slanting rays of the setting sun that hung heavy and bloody, its lower half made jagged by the tree-line on the horizon. Some of the trees were yellow-orange contrasting sharply against the blue-purple of the rain-clouds.

Mangal stood with cupped palm holding the fried balls of dough the same colour as the tree-tops. He dipped them into a thick green mush of curried green mango.

'You say thanks to Miss Tina?'

'Thanks, Miss Tina.'

The clouds soon obliterated the sky and the darkness suddenly descended heavy and thick. The rain was now gushing on the roof. In the kitchen, between preparing the evening meal, Samdaye often went to the side of the building straining her eyes through the darkness to see if the girl had returned. Across the road she could make out the figures of the Gopaul family looking anxiously in the direction of the Junction. She prayed for the safe return of the girl. Her anxiety increased by the minute.

'Manu will come, child,' Martina said. 'Why you does worry so?'

'I was waitin' for him, yes,' Prince said. 'But he was too busy beatin' them fellers. You should see him; he was like a madman. He was callin' out them fellers one by one and one by one they run from him. He was like Samson in the lion den.'

'Was not Samson in the lion den, Prince,' Martina said. 'It was Daniel. Samson lick them down with the jawbone of an ass.'

'Well he was like Samson with the jawbone. Those fellers was takin' licks like peas. When I left he was lookin' for Tasso. I just couldn't keep up with him. I was tired runnin' up and down behind him. I tell him to forget Tasso and come home with me but he was deaf like a log. He ain't listenin' to anybody. He just crackin' that whip and singin' how is one day for a man to dead and callin' out for Tasso.'

Samdaye did not want to hear about Manu. 'Is not he I worried about. If he want to kill himself I not worryin'. Is the girl I worried about.' She wanted to ask Martina if she had seen Gabi. 'Compai,' she called, 'You see Gabi at all?'

'Gabi?' Martina asked.

'Gabi?' Prince sounded incredulous.

'Mangal say that he see Gabi,' She knew then that they had not seen the girl with Gabi.

'I didn't see Gabi,' Compai said. 'You know, come to think of it I think I see somebody like Gabi but I say if is Gabi he must come and talk to me. Nah,' Compai shook his head. 'The boy imagine that. Mangal,' he called above the sound of the rain and the wind, 'You see Gabi today?'

Mangal did not seem to hear and Samdaye did not call out to him. 'So you think Manu will win the money?' She changed the subject.

'And I just hear you say that you ain't worryin' about Manu,' Prince teased.

'Is the girl husband, you know. She must worry,' Martina said.

'Well he sure to bring home the prize money tonight,' Prince said. 'And is a lot of money. More people was puttin' up prize money. It should go well over two hundred dollars. He should be a rich man when he come home. He tell me, though, that he ain't fightin' again after this carnival.'

'He say so every year,' Samdaye said. 'Every Wednesday after Carnival he swear that he finish with mas'. Especially when he start to feel all the sting and bruise and cut and when he lookin' for things to rub.'

'So Mangal say he see Gabi, eh?' Compai was still thinking about the boy. 'Nah, man,' he said as if to himself, 'if Gabi was in Sangre Grande he must come and say "howdy". The boy ain't like that. The child make a mistake. He must be see somebody like Gabi.'

The rain was coming in waves driven by gusts of wind. It rose and fell with a rhythm.

Samdaye was finished in the kitchen and she continued her vigil through a space between the boards in the window which was kept shut because of the constant changes in the direction of the wind and the rain. The baby was asleep and Mangal had collapsed on the bed after the day's adventures. The weak flame of the kerosene lamp flickered. It must have been about an hour later, when the rain had petered out into a fine drizzle and shapes had begun to emerge in the dark that she was startled to see a figure a few feet away at the corner of the barracks dipping into the barrel of water. It was a man and he was washing his hands and arms up to his elbow. He then raised his trouser legs and, using his wet handkerchief, repeatedly wiped his legs. He also seemed to be rubbing out spots on his trousers. He then washed his shoes. In the dark and with his head bent the man was unrecognisable but he appeared shorter than Manu. Samdaye watched him transfixed until he slunk back into the darkness. She could not see which direction he had taken and she quickly went to the front of the building and peered between the two halves of the door but she could see no one at first. It was several minutes later that she heard someone call out to Gopaul and recognized the voice of Gomez.

'You ain't pass Shanti on the road, Overseer?' Gopaul asked anxiously.

'Shanti?' Gomez sounded surprised. 'Where she gone?'

'She went Sangre Grande to see mas'.'

'No I ain't see her. And she ain't come back yet?'

'Naw, Overseer. And I worried something happen to her,' Gopaul said. 'You sure you ain't see her?'

'Well, we better go back and look for her,' Gomez said. He was still standing in the drizzle.

Samdaye saw him framed against the lighted doorway and felt certain that it was Gomez she had seen washing himself at the barrel.

While Mrs Gopaul was explaining how her daughter had gone with Samdaye since morning and how Samdaye had returned without her, Manu returned, his footsteps heavy and unsteady. Samdaye let him in and gasped as she saw him with his costume in tatters and his face and hands bloody and bruised. His hair was wet and plastered on his head and his clothing stuck to his body. He was without his whip.

'I throw the blasted thing in the bush,' he explained. Pushing his hands into his pocket he withdrew a wad of bills and gave them to her. She placed the wet notes on the table.

'You ain't countin' it?' His speech was slurred. 'Count it. I cut a lot of people arse for that.' He slumped to the floor against the doorway.

'And how much they cut you up for it?'

Hearing the talking Prince called out, 'You come, Manu?'

'More dead than alive,' Samdaye said.

'The rest of them more badly off than me.'

'You win the money?'

'I win, yes.'

'You beat Tasso?'

'Tasso and the whole lot of them.'

'Boy, you is a real terror. They ain't have nobody to touch you.'

'They think I was easy. They think I was finish and they all come out for me. You should see how they thirsty for my blood, how their eyes get red when they see me. Tasso set them up to soften me up but them fellars too soft.' His speech was slurred and halting and he seemed to be having difficulty keeping his eyes open. He slid slowly into a semi-reclining position on the floor.

'So, pardner, tell me about the fight with Tasso,' Prince sat on the floor. 'I did want to stay with you but you was runnin' up and down the road too fast for me. I was gettin' tired and I know you could take care of you'self. But, boy, I would like to see you take on Old Man Tasso. That man was the reignin' mas' man with a whip for years and years.' He touched Manu on the knee and Manu flinched. 'Come, boy, tell me.'

'It . . . it ain't . . . have . . . it ain't have . . . nothing . . . to tell. It done . . . finish.'

In the dim lamplight Samdaye tried to discover the extent of her husband's injuries. There were scratches on his face made by the tips of the whips but she had no idea where the blood on his costume came from.

'Tasso must be feelin' bad about the licks he get.'

'I think he should go and sleep,' Samdaye said. 'You ain't hungry?'

He shook his head slowly.

'But what about the money, boy, how much you really win?'

'Look the money right there where he put it,' Samdaye

said. 'I don't know what money could pay for all this cuts and bruise and all this brutalising.'

'You ain't count it?' Prince was looking at the money in wonder.

'Is . . . is two . . . hundred . . . twohun . . . and forty . . . I . . . I ain't use one cent for a drink for meself. Ever . . . everybody want . . . want to gi' me . . . want to buy drink for me.'

'You lucky nobody lock your neck and rob you,' Samdaye said.

He dragged himself back to a sitting position and began to remove his painted canvas shoes. His sweated feet smelled.

'You see Shanti on the road?' Samdaye asked.

'Which . . . which Shanti?'

'From across the road . . . Gopaul daughter. You see her anywhere?'

'What happen to her?'

'She went Sangre Grande and didn't come back yet.'

'Well . . . well I ain't see nobody like her . . . nobody.'

'You better take off your wet clothes or you might get cold or pneumonia. What happen to the mas'?'

'I throw that away too . . . mus' be somewhere in the bush.'

Hearing the sound of voices, Mangal woke and, seeing his father, came slowly up to him.

'Don't touch him, Mangal. He wet and ain't smellin' too good.' She turned to Manu, 'Go and change your clothes and bathe and eat something.' She watched him rise unsteadily.

Gopaul, his wife and Gomez had started on the way to the Junction to search for the girl. The rain had stopped but it still could be heard on the hills.

'Come, Prince,' Gomez called, 'Compai, come, let's go and look.'

'In this rain?' Prince asked. 'All-you will find the girl as soon as you bend the corner. Nothing ain't happen to her.'

'The same thing I telling Gopaul. If we wait a little while she will reach and she will have a good explanation. What could happen to her?'

'On a ordinary day is no trouble but today was Carnival and all kind of people drunk and sober on the road with mas' and disguise, and nobody know who is who and I tell you neighbour, the country not so safe again. Is not like when we was children when you could walk all over this island and nobody will bother you. The Yankee come and bring money and all kind of people flock on this island and everybody come to love easy money. And all kind a vice start to come out. Neighbour, this place ain't nice no more. Nobody ain't safe —'

'Come, man, let we ain't waste no time babblin',' Mrs Gopaul marched ahead. 'I have no idea where this child is.'

'Go ahead, boss,' Prince said, 'I comin' in a while.' After they had departed he told Compai that he couldn't see what the bother was about. The girl was big and she must have met some boy in the town. 'Don't trust those quiet, quiet girls, nah. They like zandolie movin' quiet but fast. Just now you will hear them comin' back laughin'.'

'I don't think so,' Samdaye said. 'Something happen to that girl. She wouldn't stay so late.' She only hoped that Gopaul and his wife would not meet her returning with Gabi. She wondered if she should mention that the girl was seen in the company of the boy. Prince, Martina and Compai would understand but the word might spread and it could spell trouble for the boy from the Gopaul family. She couldn't understand why there was so much trouble in the world: if it is not one thing it is the other. Now that her worries over Manu were over as far as the Carnival was concerned there had to be something else to cause concern. When the rain was falling and the wind was rushing through the trees she thought she could hear the sound of waves and she had pictured herself in Manzanilla. But she was not sure now whether a return to the coast would bring any improvement. No longer would she be persuaded to move until she was certain that things would be better. She would have to find some way of improving their income. Tomorrow, when Manu had recovered, she would sit with him and they would both devise some plan. What he needed was a sense of direction; to see some goals ahead. He had the energy but he had no idea where he wanted to go. Now with the Carnival out of his system he could focus all his drive on getting settled. Maybe some simple carpentry skills would be necessary if they were going to build a house. She was glad that he had thrown away the whip and the mask – something he had never done before.

She listened to the water splashing as he poured it over his head with the calabash. She heard him shudder and groan and wondered if he would put soap on his cuts. She smiled in satisfaction. Looking out through the window she could see the fluorescent white of the soap in the dark and imagined his suffering. She had some vaseline in a bottle and took it out so that she could rub it over his skin.

Martina had come over with Compai and they, too sat on the floor with Prince. Compai's forehead was creased with concern. He was still wondering about the extent of Gabi's involvement with the girl, if indeed he was in Sangre Grande. He suspected that Samdaye was not entirely truthful about seeing the boy. She had evaded the question.

'Mr Prince,' Samdaye said, 'You goin' to look for the girl?'

'I don't think –'

'Well, I goin'. As soon as he finish bathing and I give him something to eat I goin' to look for the girl. I feel bad leavin' the girl behind. I feel if anything happen to her is my fault.'

'Is not your fault,' Martina said. 'She didn't want to come.'

'But I should 'a' wait a while. But I really didn't want to remain and see Manu get beat up. I was ready to come home.'

'I find it strange,' Compai said, 'that the girl should want to stay back alone . . . unless . . . unless she had some reason to stay back.' He was looking at Samdaye who averted her eyes.

'And she really didn't look for me, you know,' Martina said. 'Even with all the people, Sangre Grande is too small.'

'And you too big,' Prince said. 'Nobody could miss you.'

'I still interested to find out why Mangal should say that he see Gabi,' Compai said. 'The boy can't make that up just so.'

'You think that she meet the boy and they stay back?' asked Martina.

'That is what I feel,' Compai said.

'You think they run away together?' Prince asked.

'Don't be foolish, Prince,' Martina said. 'Them is two children.'

'It ain't have children nowadays. These days as soon as they reach twelve and thirteen they feel they is man and woman.' Prince stabbed his stubby fingers on the floor. 'You can't time young people no more.' After a while he added, 'Is them damn Yankees that cause this change. Is them who bring all kinds of rude books and magazines and films. And all that cussin'. Now everybody want to look like American with zoot suit and long chain hangin' from their jacket, and cigarette at the side of their mouth. From the time them Yankees come in the Base this island change.'

They spoke slowly and with long pauses. The urgency was in their voices but their speech was unhurried.

They heard Manu come up the steps.

'Oh God, Sam, you have Vaseline?'

'So is vaseline you want now? What happen you' tail burnin'?'

'I not makin' joke, nah. You ain't have vaseline?' He emerged in his underpants. He sat on the small bench near the table and rubbed his hands over his skin hesitantly.

She took the bottle and went over to him. 'Let me see what you do to yourself. Oh Lord,' she exclaimed, 'You look at yourself?'

There were cuts, weals and scratches all over his back; there were scratches on his face and long, red bruises on his chest. His left arm still bled. 'I don't know what devil does get in you all to do this thing. Look at you!' She started to apply the jelly gently. 'I have a mind not to do anything for you. Let you rub it yourself. Is you went and damage yourself let you fix it.' She mumbled as she continued to look for the places to put the vaseline.

His eyes had cleared. 'You ain't put that money away yet?'

'I ain't touch your blood money.'

'You ain't want it? I know a place where I could enjoy spendin' it.'

'Japan shop?'

'You right. Japan shop. Just tell me if you don't want it.' He was smiling and grimacing alternately. 'Oh God, Prince, this is real foolishness.'

'Well,' Samdaye said, 'I glad you find out at last.'

'So you done with Mas', then?' Prince asked.

'I done.'

'He throw away the whip and the mas',' Samdaye said.

'Pity,' Prince said. 'You was good, real real good.'

'The best,' Manu said.

'The best.'

'I want to hear him say that next year,' Samdaye interjected.

'This time . . . this time –' Manu's statement froze as a long, piercing scream, unending, rent the air.

Chapter 21

The red dress made a vicious gash in the dark of the green grass underneath the umbrella of the low-hanging coffee trees. Flashlights and flambeaux flickered in unexpected focusing and the faces and figures, illuminated from below, took on unusual shadows creating a drama of the unreal. The girl's body lay straight with the dress pulled over her knees as if it had been arranged. Her hair was wet and loose, and with its dishevelled look matched her face with its open mouth and open eyes still giving an expression of terror.

'Anybody touch the body?' the Sergeant asked. He sounded tired. He had had little sleep in the past forty-eight hours. It was always like this during Carnival with the drunks and the brawls, and the accidents; with the stick-fights – that violent 'game' that provided more headaches for him than for the victims who suffered split heads – with the 'diable' bands whose rivalry was expressed in bloody fights with whips; with the noisy competition of the steel-bands that often resulted in pitched battles; with the excess of wife-beatings and reports of infidelities; with full jail-cells and policemen sneaking a drink from some friendly reveller ending sometimes quite drunk by evening. But not this. He could have done without this. In his two years in Sangre Grande there had never been a case of rape-murder. This was a very quiet town where the Carnival was the only excitement and this came only two days a year.

'The mother touch the body?' He looked at the woman who was nearly hysterical. She was babbling and screaming, and crying sitting on her haunches crouched near the girl. Of course she would have held the girl and probably fixed her clothing. When asked directly if she had touched the body she nodded weakly.

He saw that the wet grass had been trampled to the ground and the footsteps of the onlookers would have obliterated any evidence of prints.

'Henry,' he called, 'Come and get the pictures taken before any more damage is done.' He turned to the people, 'Now everybody fall back. Make room for the photographer. Go back! Sorry, madam,' he said to Mrs Gopaul resting his hand on her shoulder, 'is nothing you could do now.'

The police photographer moved around the body taking pictures from different angles. The blinding flashes reduced everything to white.

'The ambulance people reach yet?'

'Yeh.' Two men moved in with a stretcher.

'All right, take her away.'

Mrs Gopaul's shriek, loud and long, startled him. She rushed back to the body and flung herself on it. He allowed her this further outpouring of grief. It must be an extremely distressing experience to find one's daughter like that. He halted the removal of the body for a while then, after what he thought was a decent interval, he motioned the stretcher bearers to continue. 'I want all of you to remain – all except the police. Henry, I want you to remain with me. We might still need photographs. Sukhlal,' he addressed the other policemen, 'you go back in the ambulance.' He watched them depart. 'Now, I don't want anybody to move about. Just stand still.' Breaking two sticks off a coffee branch he stuck them on the ground where the head and feet of the body had been. He then took out his tape and measured the distance from the road. It was twenty feet. He had observed that the heels of the girl's shoes, which were open at the back, contained more mud than the front indicating that she had been dragged. Moving back to where the body was found he searched for signs that would support his theory. It was not easy among all the evidence of tramping but he soon found the spot where the assault took place. It was no more than fifteen feet from the road. He rubbed his chin over the growth of beard from the morning and listened to the murmuring of the people, the constant lamenting of the girl's mother and the occasional slapping of stinging mosquitoes.

The perpetrators of rape were, as far as his experience went, always persons who knew the victims; who had watched them for some time and waited for their opportunities. His killer was among these people or someone from the village. He flashed his light into their faces and immediately dismissed four of them: the girl's father, of course, who stood quietly with tear-stained face mumbling softly to himself occasionally; the old Spanish man who looked equally distressed and who shivered in the wet; the man called Prince who kept gazing vacantly in disbelief and a man they called Shepherd.

The Sergeant believed in instinct. If he didn't get the right vibrations the person was probably guilty. He could tell at first glance. But he never relied completely on first impressions although he was almost always right. There were two men of whom he had doubts. There was the fellow they called the overseer who stood with a mask in his hand and the Indian man with the wet hair and the scratches on his face and who was claiming the mask as his own.

'I find this mas' near the body,' the overseer offered.

'Aha!' the Sergeant lifted his cap and ran his hand over his balding head which was fringed with grey. He looked at the man intently. 'Show me where you find it.' The man pointed somewhere near the spot where the head of the body was. 'Here?' He asked the man. 'Show me the exact spot.' He got the man to put the mask down where he thought he had found it then he had Henry take a photograph. He looked at the man who claimed the mask. 'Is your mask?' The man nodded. Suspect number one, he told himself. 'Alright, let's move from this wet place. I want everybody to go with me.' He led the way out to the road.

At the Gopaul's house the Sergeant heard from each of them facts pertinent to the tragedy: how the girl went with Samdaye to the Carnival in Sangre Grande and how she did not return with the woman. He realized that she was hiding something. From the parents he heard that the girl had no boyfriends, that as far as they knew, she had not planned to meet anybody. Prince and his wife, Martina said that they

231

had not seen her with anybody. Compai had not seen her at all after they got out of the taxi. He had spent most of his time in a rum-shop with some old friends.

The Sergeant made some notes: the correct names as well as those by which they were known and the most important points in their accounts.

'I want to know who find the body,' he announced.

'We,' Gopaul said. 'We find the body.' He indicated himself, his wife and the overseer.

'No, no. Who actually find the body . . . who see it first?'

Gopaul pointed out the overseer.

'You been looking long?'

'Not long,' Gopaul said.

'One hour? Half an hour?'

'Less,' Gopaul said. 'We start to walk down the road and to look in the bush.'

'Who ask you to look in the bush?'

'I had the torchlight,' the overseer said, 'and I was just flashin' the light about.'

'And you see the body.'

'I see something red.'

'And you know it was the girl's body.'

'Well —'

'Let us talk about the mask — at what point you find it? After you find the body or before?' There was something about the overseer he did not trust. He was too anxious to link the mask with the body. Clues are not that easily left by criminals. Sometimes you have to discount the most obvious clues. Why would the criminal leave the mask at the side of the body, about twelve to fifteen feet from the point where the assault had taken place? He would give him some rope. In the meantime he would take the young Indian man down for questioning. He was the person against whom the evidence was stacked: he had arrived less than one hour before the body was discovered; he was bloody, scratched and he looked exhausted. He didn't believe that the fellow was guilty but he could be wrong. He had also learned that the overseer had arrived not long before the Indian fellow. He would take both of them down. In the morning he would return to the Junction to find out if the girl had travelled back with anyone. The killer would have either travelled with her, followed her, or waited for her. Somebody in the Junction would have seen her and with that shiny, bright-red dress someone would have remembered picking her up in a taxi or seeing her get on or off the bus. Also, and this was most important, she would not travel alone. Someone was with her. That someone might have brought her within sight of her house and then left, thinking that she was safe.

'So tell me about the mask,' the Sergeant turned to Manu. 'Tell me how it managed to be in the bush.'

'I throw it away.'

'You throw it away. You throw it away just near the girl's body.'

'I didn't throw it near any body. I didn't know it had a body where I throw it.'

'You remember exactly where you throw it?'

'No. The rain was fallin' and I couldn't see too far in the dark.'

'You want to say why you throw it?'

'For the same reason I throw the whip.'

'You throw away the whip, too?'

'I throw the whip and the mas'.'

'Which you throw first?'

'I don't — I can't remember. I think I throw the whip first.'

'Why?'

'Why what?'

'Why you throw those things away?'

'I decide I was done with Carnival. My wife used to quarrel too much about me playin' mas'. Every time it was the same story. Besides I didn't have no reason to play again.'

'How come?'

'I win the prize. It didn't have nobody else to beat. I beat them all. I beat everybody.'

'You see anybody on the road?'

'I wasn't lookin' for anybody.'

'I didn't ask if you was lookin'. I ask if you see anybody.'

Manu shook his head from side to side.

'You didn't answer.'

'No I ain't see nobody. And I ain't hear nobody either.'

'But the rain had stop by the time you reach where the girl's body was.'

'The rain stop some time while I was walkin' but I really didn't notice when it stop. My mind was full of all kind of things –'

'Like how you goin' to explain to the police?'

'Explain what?'

'What happen to the girl.'

Samdaye felt that her husband was being cornered. She began to see how he could be arrested and charged for something he did not do. He was not the person to do this. She began to wonder about Gabi. Maybe she should tell the Sergeant about Gabi.

'So tell me again how you travel from Sangre Grande.'

'By the bus.'

'Alone?'

'Alone, yes. I travel alone.'

'And you didn't see the girl on the bus.'

'I didn't look for anybody.'

'And you come off the bus alone.'

'I think so.'

'And you wait in the Junction for a while for the rain to pass?'

'Just for about a minute.'

'You see anybody in the shop?'

'I didn't look. I didn't want to go in the shop so I start to walk home.'

'In the rain?'

'Yes.'

'Anybody see you by the shop?'

'I don't – I think so. I think I remember somebody call my name but I not sure –'

'And then you throw the mask by the girl's body just like that.'

Samdaye could feel the anger rising in her husband. If this continued any longer he would explode and he could say anything. She could see how he was tired. His speech was becoming increasingly slurred and, clad in a sleeveless vest, he hugged himself to keep warm.

'And you want to explain how you get those scratches?'

234

'Playin' diable.'

'All those cuts and scratches?'

Manu nodded.

'How much come from fingernail scratches?'

'Nobody scratch me with fingernail.'

The Sergeant brought the lamp closer to his face and poked his finger at individual marks asking for explanations.

'Sergeant,' Samdaye said with anxiety giving an edge to her voice, 'I sure my husband ain't have nothing to do with this. Ask anybody here; ask Mr Prince, ask Compai –'

'So who see you when you reach here?' The Sergeant paid no attention to Samdaye.

'My wife, Prince, Martina . . .'

'They all see you?'

'They hear when I come and they come over.'

'What time was that?'

'I don't know. I ain't have no clock.'

'So you don't know what time you left the Junction and what time you reach here. And nobody ain't see you. So you could 'a take half-an-hour, one hour, two hours . . .'

'I come straight home.'

'And what you do after you come home.'

'He give me the money he win,' Samdaye said.

The Sergeant waited for his reply.

'I go and bathe.'

'And what you do with the clothes?'

'I drop it by the barrel.'

'So it must be washed clean by now? All the blood must be wash out clean?'

'Rain ain't fall since then so it is how I drop it. But the blood wash out before I reach here. It wash out in the rain.'

'You ain't throw no water on it?'

'Water must be fall on it while I was bathin', I don't know.'

'You know you wash it out, man. The rain can't wash it out clean.'

'Go and look at it. It must be still there.'

'I'll go for it,' Gomez said and left.

The Sergeant sent the police photographer after him. In less than two minutes they returned with the costume dripping.

'I find it in the bottom o' the barrel,' Gomez explained.

'The bottom of the barrel?' The Sergeant looked at the Police photographer.

'I see him takin' it out from the barrel,' the policeman said.

'I ain't know how it reach there,' Manu said.

'Must be a jumbie put it in the barrel,' the Sergeant said.

'Well,' the Sergeant rose, 'I will have to take you down for questioning.' He waited for the man's wife to speak. It was the way to bring pressure on her. From all accounts she was the last person to see the girl alive and, since she was the person with whom the girl had gone, she must know the reason why the girl stayed behind. But she said nothing. He pulled back the sleeve of his thick black serge tunic and looked at his watch. It was not yet ten. There was no need to hurry. The corporal would take care of the station while he was here and, besides, he was enjoying himself playing the detective. Agatha Christie was his favourite writer and Perry Mason his model character. A young rooster crowed a high, broken, tremulous sound and the Sergeant sat down again.

Patiently, he went over the various accounts of their activities of the day. He did not allow voluntary corroboration and asked for support only when he thought it was necessary.

Other villagers were arriving. Some had brought biscuits; some had brought benches. A few bamboo poles had been found and a tent was being hastily constructed. A piece of tarpaulin provided covering. Descriptions of what had happened were whispered to every new arrival, every female of whom was greeted with an assault of wailing by Mrs Gopaul who loudly recounted the good qualities of her daughter and lamented her loss. Someone was pouring bay-rum on her head and patting it and murmuring consolations. Gopaul, looking distracted, shook his head all the while as he echoed his wife's laments. The smell of coffee floated about. A pack of cards emerged and a group of four settled down to play 'all-fours'. Shepherd took out his Bible and would have liked to read a chapter and sing a few hymns but these were Hindus and he was not sure if this would have been allowed. He hummed 'Nearer My God to Thee'. Nobody joined in.

BETWEEN TWO SEASONS

The Sergeant leaned back and pulled out his pipe. He lit it with great ceremony and popped small puffs in the dark above the lamplight. The actions of the overseer bothered him. The man had moved too fast to fetch the costume and he was not sure that it had been found in the barrel. He would have to find out from the policeman what had really happened. How did the man know that the clothes were at the bottom of the barrel? He rose suddenly and indicated to Manu that he was being taken down to the station.

Samdaye wept as she watched them leave.

Chapter 22

The red tail-lights of the car diminished in intensity then vanished completely leaving a vacuum of silence that hung like the liquid darkness, heavy and impenetrable. The darkness seemed to soak into their being; to cloud their eyes and deaden their senses; to suffuse the air with fear, uncertainty, foreboding.

Gomez left to change his clothes which were wet, and promised to return. He spoke in whispers and signs, as they all did, afraid to break the stillness. Little by little the sounds increased with the arrival of more visitors. The card players resumed. They gathered the matchsticks which were being used as 'chalks' because they could not remember who was supposed to deal or how many 'chalks' each team had. After some good-natured argument they settled on a procedure and soon each partner exchanged earnest stares and made signals to indicate whether they had 'high' or 'low' or 'Jack'. A bottle of rum was produced and a shot glass made the round.

The rain started to drizzle gently on the galvanized roof like the ruffling of a bird's feathers and the drops gathered into a stream at the corners of the tarpaulin.

Occasionally a choked sob would come from Mrs Gopaul whose husband would reply with a long moan.

'That child didn't use to trouble anybody,' Gopaul said.

'She was so good,' Mrs Gopaul moaned. 'Now who will cook and do the housework and help me with the children?'

'Is better I was dead,' Gopaul added. 'I done old and sickly. And this child ain't start to live her life.'

'Is this damn Carnival,' Mrs Gopaul said. 'I never like the damn thing and I really didn't want the child to go and mix with all kinds of drunk people.' She looked at Samdaye. 'You don't know what kind of people they have living in this world now. You can't tell about your own neighbours. The child left here good good and look how she end up lyin' down on the wet grass and mud.'

'And she ain't trouble nobody,' Gopaul added.

'What devil could do this thing?' She continued to stare at Samdaye whose silent tears rolled down two tracks.

Samdaye was confident that her husband had not done this act. He was a violent man when it came to the Carnival and showed that he was capable of most things because of his quick temper but he would not, unprovoked, commit any act of violence. At no time did he show any interest in the girl other than to smile and talk to her as he did with the other Gopaul children. In the confusion resulting from her fear she had sat quietly and allowed the police to take him away without even a protest. Manu, himself, had not said anything to defend himself. He had kept his head lowered as he was being taken away. He looked tired and resigned as if he did not care what happened to him. The eyes of everyone had followed him and it was only Prince who had said that Manu was not the man the police wanted.

Mrs Gopaul had convinced herself that the right person was being held. She had never liked this man. From the time he came he showed that he was rebellious and that he could attack anybody. She was sorry for Samdaye but the woman was also to be blamed. She could not find a reason but that was not important. The woman was as much at fault as the man. Her hate began to well in her stomach like boiled breadnut seeds. It started to rise slowly then to rush through her veins like a drink of puncheon rum; it gathered in a knot at the base of her skull at the back of her neck and from there it flashed through her eyes. 'The man is a beast, yes,' she mumbled.

'A dangerous animal. You coun say that,' Gopaul agreed.

'You don't know the man do it,' Prince said.

'Don't take up for any criminal, Prince,' Mrs Gopaul said the hate coating her words thickly.

'That is not no criminal, and you know it Ma Gopaul.'

'And the police take him away?'

'To question him.'

'Well, why the police didn't take you or me or anybody else?'

'They know why they doin' that,' Prince said.

'I don't know where all you get those kinda people from, Mr Gomez. How allyou could choose these people to come and live in this good place and mash it up. In the whole history of Dorado we ain't have one murder much more this nasty crime. 'This is a —'

'A nasty nasty crime,' Gopaul assented. 'The man who do that will pay, I tell you.'

'God don't sleep,' Mrs Gopaul shook her head sadly. 'O God, O God, how you could let this happen to my poor child?' She emitted a loud scream and her body was convulsed with sobbing. Someone put more bay-rum on her head and muttered words of comfort. Shepherd's voice rose with the hymn 'Abide With Me' and Martina joined in. The card-players were startled into remembering that this was a wake and their exuberance vanished for a while.

Gomez, who had changed into dry clothes, was back and now put his hand on her shoulders. 'The police don't make joke, Ma Gopaul, they will do for the killer.'

'They hold the wrong man,' Prince said.

'They hold the right man,' Gomez said, 'they ain't foolish.'

'This time they foolish.'

'And what about the mask?' Gomez asked. 'And they find it near the body?'

'You find it near the body,' Compai said quietly. He had been watching everything silently. He was surprised about Manu's absence of protest. If Manu had made some noise others would have joined in and the police might have left him alone. He had lived long enough to be able to read the character of a person and this was not in Manu's character. But the police would like to solve this crime quickly and they did not give one damn who paid. And Manu fitted into their picture well: he should be at the scene about the time the crime was committed; he was all scratched and bloody; he went and bathed as soon as he reached home and he washed his clothes. Also his mask was found at the scene. He felt that Gabi was involved somehow. The fact that the child had said

240

that he had seen Gabi was still to be explored. If Gabi had met the girl then that might have been the reason for her staying back. He would have to get Samdaye to say what she thought had happened. 'Mr Gomez, you didn't say what time you come from Sangre Grande.'

'Everybody know what time I come. I stop off right here by Gopaul. Straight from Sangre Grande I come and I stop here. I didn't go by anybody. I didn't leave the road. Not for one minute, not one second. I only stop by Gopaul to say hello and then, when I hear that the girl ain't come home yet and that they goin' to look for her, I didn't ask no question, I just go with them.'

Compai glanced at Samdaye whose wide eyes became locked with his with an expression, that in the dim light, betrayed something. Was it surprise, disbelief, alarm? He saw that Gomez had also seen her expression and had caught their involuntary communication. What was it that the girl knew? 'So you come straight from the Junction and you didn't see nobody.'

'Not a soul,' Gomez said.

'And you ain't hear nothing?'

'Nothing,' the Overseer replied with a laugh that sounded nervous and dry. 'Wha' happen, Compai, like you playin' detective or what? How you askin' so much question?'

'Is not that I playin' police, but while we sittin' not doin' nothing we could try to find out exactly what happen –'

'The Police know what happen,' Gomez interjected.

'Because they hold Manu?'

'They know why they hold him.'

'They ain't know one dam' thing,' Compai said. 'They only playin' a game. They only guessin'.'

'The evidence will prove –'

'You right. The evidence will prove. All the evidence ain't come in yet.'

'Look, old man, from the time this fellah come here you could see he got bad mind. From the first day he want to chop me up. It didn't have a good week he want to lead strike. Every week he drunk and threatenin' to chop up somebody.' He spoke as though Samdaye was not present.

'That is no proof of nothing,' Compai said. 'We have to deal wit' why and who and when.'

241

'We know why – the man was drunk. We know when – it was tonight. And we know who –'

'Why you keep sayin' "we know who" because we dam' well ain't know who. And don't tell me is that boy. I older than you and I see a lot more than you and I could tell you about character,' the old man's voice was rising cracked and unsteady. 'That boy got a bad temper, yes, and he like to drink but he ain't the one –'

'Unless is your boy,' Gomez waited for that to sink in.

'Who boy?'

'Your boy. The one who run away. I see him in Sangre Grande.'

'What time?'

'How you mean "what time"? I see him.'

'Wit' the girl?'

The overseer hesitated before replying that he had not seen him with the girl.

The man was lying, Compai thought and once more he looked at Samdaye whose face betrayed the same expression he had seen before.

'Yes, yes,' he corrected himself. 'I see him wit' the girl.'

'O God,' Mrs Gopaul groaned, 'they kill me child.' She resumed crying and moaning, and enumerating the good qualities of the girl. Someone coaxed her into rising and she was taken into the house.

Shepherd and Martina were softly singing 'Rock of Ages'. Prince was humming until Shepherd started calling out the words after each line then he, too, joined in the singing. Someone on the card-table hung a Jack and there was loud shouting and celebration 'Bullseye!' someone shouted. 'High Low Hang-Jack Game! Six to go! Move, man, all-you fellers is jokers. Bring on the next pair!' He called for replacement of the losing pair. The playing resumed and, now that Mrs Gopaul had retreated into the bedroom the level of their voices rose.

'You say you see Gabi wit' the girl in Sangre Grande?' Compai asked once again glancing at Samdaye.

'Yes I see him. Was about nearly six o'clock.'

'And you leave them in Sangre Grande?'

'Listen, old man,' the overseer said firmly, 'I had enough

of this questioning. I don't want to talk about this again unless the Police ask me and you ain't no Police.'

Compai moved closer to Samdaye. He wondered why she continued to stay there and thought how she looked like a manicou transfixed by the light of a flambeau not being able to move in the presence of danger. She had sat in the fierce glare of the accusing eyes of Mrs Gopaul and had said nothing even when they were taking her husband away. Her only expression of emotion had been the silent tears rolling down her cheeks and the winding and unwinding of her short fingers. He admired her strength and knew that he could get her to say what was bothering her.

More people arrived. Mrs Gopaul's sister and her husband from Central Trinidad had their arrival marked by another crescendo of crying. Columbus had come out from the forest for the Carnival and he stood unsteadily in a corner watching at the bottle that stood in the middle of the card-players. Mr Jordan, tall and bent, greying and balding came pushing his bicycle with a few cedar boards and his bag of tools. He had made every coffin in the village for over forty years and never waited to be asked. Ezekiel Mohammed was accompanied by Rachel, the teacher. Some of the wild, Blue Indians, still in costume, sat on the roots of a mango tree in Gopaul's yard. Their thickly greased bodies did not feel the occasional drop from the leaves above. Some were villagers from beyond the school; others were relatives who had been given the hurriedly spreading news and some were strangers who were there to lend their presence as it was the decent thing to do. Coffee and biscuits made another round, and another bottle of rum emerged in the middle of another group of 'all-fours' players.

'Now, child, tell me what you know,' Compai said to Samdaye.

'I see Gabi in Sangre Grande,' she said quietly.

'With the girl?'

She nodded.

'That is why she stayed back?'

'She wanted to stay back although I tell her to come with me.'

'Is not your fault. Like they had their own plan.'

'I didn't talk because I didn't want him to get in trouble. I didn't tell Ma Gopaul that I left Shanti with Gabi because she would quarrel too much. She would 'a' left right away for Sangre Grande. And she would blame me.'

'But you know is not Manu who kill the girl.'

'Is not Gabi either.'

'You suspect –'

'Gomez.'

'You sure?'

'He say that he come straight from the junction. That he ain't come off the road. Well I see him washin' his hands and face at my barrel. And wipin' his pants with a handkerchief –'

'You sure is him?'

'It was dark and I ain't see his face clear clear. But it was him.'

'How you so sure?'

'The man was short and he had a long-sleeve shirt . . . and it was not Prince or you –'

'And it was not Manu?'

'It can't be Manu. This man was shorter and bigger. And he had a white, long-sleeve shirt. And Manu come about half an hour after all bloody-up. He didn't wash himself.'

'Well, we can't prove nothing. The man too smart. He went over all the ground with fresh footprints. And, let me tell you, no police will charge the overseer. Even Gopaul will never believe that it is Gomez.'

'And they make up their minds that is Manu.'

'We don't know how Gabi is mix-up in this business but he will talk. He must see something.'

'You think it might be some stranger . . . some mas'-man.'

'And you just say how you see Gomez washin' himself secretly? And you know that he lyin' when he say he didn't leave the road? And you see how he find Manu mas' so easy so everybody could point finger at Manu? But we have to get proof.' He turned to Shepherd. 'Sheppy,' he said, 'lend me your Bible. We want to find out somethin.'

'You want to do a "By Saint Peter"?'

Compai nodded. 'Yeh,' he said loudly so that Gomez could hear. 'I want to find out who is the real criminal. The Bible don't lie.'

'I don't like my Bible to be used for any foolishness, you know. This is a holy book and you must not play games wit' it.'

'This ain't no game, Shep. And you know it. I serious. And I want you to take part.'

'Not here.'

'We will go across the road under the almond tree. Only me, you and Prince.'

'I comin' too,' Martina said. 'I always hear about this thing but I never see it done.'

Compai nodded and they walked to the tree from which large drops occasionally fell. He found a bench and sat astride it and invited Shepherd to sit on the other side. At first the preacher refused but then he sat down reluctantly. 'We want a key and a piece of string.' None of them had keys. Martina remembered seeing an old rusty key hanging from a string in a corner of the room that she and Prince occupied. She brought the key and a longer piece of string. 'I always thought that this key had some use,' she said.

'Is to open the door of truth,' Compai said solemnly. He opened the middle of the Bible and inserted the key which he tied firmly, wrapping the string around the book so that it could be suspended by holding the key. Having done that he closed his eyes for a while. An owl fluttered heavily as its grey underside flashed white in the overhead gloom. In the Gopaul house the drama there seemed unreal as if it was taking place on some stage lit dimly for the occasion. The illuminated figures moved and spoke isolated from the surrounding darkness.

Compai stuck his middle finger under the head of the key and invited Shepherd to do the same but he refused. 'Let Prince do it first,' he said.

'Wha' happen, Shep?' Prince asked. 'You is a real coward, yes. This thing is no obeah, you know. You dealin' wit' the Bible. Come, Compai let me hold the thing.' He stuck out his middle finger and, between the older man and himself, they balanced the key.

Compai admonished them to be silent and reminded them that it was a very serious undertaking. After a brief quiet period he began, 'By Saint Peter, By Saint Paul, Prince

William kill the girl.' He asked Prince William to repeat it. Twice he said it and twice Prince repeated it. 'We will say it one more time,' he said and they did it once more.

'I ain't feel nothing,' Prince said. 'And you suppose to feel the key turn in your hand?'

'And sometimes the Bible does fall,' Martina said.

'How you know so much about it?' Prince asked. 'Like you used to be a see-er woman?'

'Hush,' Compai said.

'By Saint Peter, By Saint Paul is Pablo Oliviera kill the girl.'

'Who is Pablo Oliviera?' Prince asked.

'Lord, Prince,' Martina rolled her eyes upward, 'is Compai.'

'A-A I forget Compai real name, yes.'

'Come on, Prince, do the thing serious and stop the foolishness,' Martina said. 'And I don't think you could call your own name when you doin' this thing. Ain't so, Compai?'

'You right, yes,' Compai said. 'I forget that. So we have to do that again.'

'Well it make no sense to call my name,' Prince said. 'I ain't do it.'

'No,' Compai disagreed, 'You have to call the name of people you know innocent.'

'How you know Prince innocent?' Martina asked, 'You don't think Prince able to do something like that?' She laughed suggestively.

'The same thing I didn't want all-you to use my Bible,' Shepherd protested. 'Look how all-you makin' joke wit' the Bible in you' hand. That is not something to make joke wit', man.' He stepped closer, 'Gimme my Bible, eh. And all-you stop this foolishness right away. You will bring sin on you' head and on my head too. When you put Bible in you' hand you must do it wit' reverence.' He had heard that line somewhere before and he repeated it. 'Reverence,' he said, 'reverence.'

'Relax, Shep,' Compai said. 'Go sit down. I know what I doin' and this is no sin.'

'But is frightenin', eh,' Prince said. 'Look how the hair stand up on my hand. This thing have me scared.'

246

'God,' Compai exclaimed

'And don't use God name in vain,' Shepherd admonished. 'And you still holdin' the Good Book.'

'All right, all right, calm down,' Martina said. 'Come get over this business before mornin' come.'

'We better cut down on the names,' Prince said. 'Otherwise we will remain here all night.'

'You 'fraid to hear your name called?' Shepherd teased.

'True,' Prince said. 'I feel the key start to turn in my hand when my name call.'

'You must be guilty,' Martina said with a laugh. 'Don't tell me you guilty, Prince, boy.'

'I feel if you scared and nervous the thing does turn in your hand,' Prince said.

'That is why everybody must be calm,' Compai said. 'Come on, let's start fresh. Shep, let you and me do this thing. Prince makin' me nervous.'

Reluctantly, Shepherd moved over to the bench. 'I never do this before, eh. And I not sure I believe in it —'

'Well don't take part, then —'

'Nah, I feel that I could do it. I make up my mind,' the preacher said and sat down.

They called Prince's name twice but the key remained firm. In quiet tones with measured syllables they spoke and gazed with deep concentration to see if the Book would move. They called several unlikely names before they decided to call Manu's.

'By Saint Peter, by Saint Paul Manu Hanuman kill the girl, Shanti,' Compai said. Shepherd repeated it. A second time the old man said it more slowly this time. Shepherd lifted his head sharply.

'You feel —'

'Hush,' Compai said and waited for the preacher to repeat it. Shepherd's voice trembled as he spoke and they could see the key move slightly but the Bible did not fall. Three times they did it calling Manu's name and three times the Bible shook.

Silently, they looked at each other then they decided to call Gabi's name. Once again the Bible shook. This time it almost fell from their hands.

'We'll try Gomez, now,' Compai said. 'By Saint Peter, by Saint Paul Ignacio Gomez kill Shanti –'

'So all-you really believe that I had something to do with rapin' the girl?' They had not heard Gomez arrive and, startled, they turned in unison to look up at him. 'Eh, Old Man,' he rested his hand on Compai's shoulder. 'You sure is me and you tryin' your best to make everybody believe is me.'

'We callin' everybody name –'

'Well, I don't want you callin' my name, you hear!'

'We tryin' to find out –'

'Not with my name. You ain't goin' to put no blame on me. Give me that damn Bible,' he snatched at the book and examined the tied key. 'All-you so damn backward . . . believin' in all kind of obeah and nonsense,' he flung the book at Shepherd. 'Take out the damn key from the book and stop this thing at once.' With that he strode out of sight.

'You see what I tell you?' Shepherd said. 'The man blaspheme with my book in his hand.'

'If you ask me, the man guilty as hell,' Compai said.

'How you so sure?' Prince asked.

'I sure.' He turned to Samdaye. 'Ask her to say what she see this evenin'.'

Samdaye recounted what she had observed and they shook their heads slowly and clicked their tongues and wondered what they could do.

'From the time I see that man I say that he was evil,' Shepherd said. 'The man's eye always rovin' and roamin' and lookin' wild. The man is like some animal.' He paused thoughtfully and then became agitated. 'And . . . and you ain't see how the man grab the Bible . . . the Bible . . . MY Bible . . . with his stinkin' sinful self . . . that . . . that criminal. The Bible is not something to play with, you know. I should never let you all get my Bible involve in this thing. And look what happen now.'

'Why you don't hush you' mouth, Shep,' Prince said. 'Nothing happen to you' old Bible –'

'Old Bible . . . OLD Bible . . . Is the word of God, you hear me? The word of God that is gettin' polluted.' He liked the word and repeated it. 'Polluted. It get polluted.'

BETWEEN TWO SEASONS

Samdaye heard her baby crying and left. In a few minutes the crying stopped and she reappeared at the doorway the upper part of her body dimly lit from the faint glimmering of the pale flames across the road. The small group under the almond tree was still there speaking in hushed tones while the card-players gave an occasional shout in celebration of their little achievements.

Chapter 23

Samdaye rose when the sun was still somewhere behind the thick, dark line of trees on the low hills to the south-east and the sky a pink bowl washed with milk. She was not sure that she had slept. All night she had rolled about the bed her head filled with thoughts about the disturbing events of the day before. Occasionally she muttered a half sentence or groaned or sighed, or ground her teeth in her tightly clenched jaw. The morning was cold and damp with dew.

The Gopaul house looked empty and deserted with chairs and benches scattered about at odd angles. It was some time before she noticed Gopaul, chewed twig in his mouth, gazing with a fixed look down the road as if he expected his daughter at any moment. Both his arms kept moving as if he was in a strait-jacket as he scratched the various parts of his body: his calves, behind his thighs, his head, at the back of his neck, between his legs, under his arms. They seemed to have minds of their own and he bent his body, twisted his torso and lifted his legs to meet their demands.

As she stepped outside she caught his eye and she mumbled a greeting to which he grumbled a reply. She wanted to talk with him; to explain what had happened; to say how sorry she was and how much she regretted all that had passed. She was sure that he would understand and show some sign of forgiveness unlike his wife whose accusing stares stripped her bare and whose pointed remarks were like knife wounds. In the mistiness of this milky dawn she imagined he looked like her father who would stand like that in the early morning – minus the scratching, of course – with brushing stick in his mouth gazing out to the sea mesmerized by the rolling waves.

If her father were here he would tell her what to do, how to cope with these myriad troubles, how to still the pandemonium in her mind. She could feel the rough stubble of his beard as he would rub his face on hers and the sting of his pinch as he held both cheeks between fingers and thumbs saying how he was squeezing his 'kaimit' – his star-apple. She leaned on the post and poured all her love through her eyes at Gopaul whose stare went past her round the bend.

The tears started to run as she was enveloped with a feeling of alone-ness. They were tears of mourning for her father whose loss she now felt more than on the day of his cremation, and her shoulders began to shake with her sobbing. Fear held her and despair as she felt herself in a vast void endless and empty, silent as this morning without the reassuring noise of the sea. In this village far from her mother and her sisters, without her father and distant from familiar sights and sounds and smells there was nothing that she could hold on to.

In front of Gopaul's house was the polished taxi which was an indication that Mrs Gopaul's sister was here with her husband. This was soon confirmed as the women came out from the house. They were joined by another woman who was also a sister and Mrs Gopaul began speaking in a low voice as she saw Samdaye and indicating in her direction with her head. Through her tears Samdaye saw the women looking at her with the same kind of stares she had got from Mrs Gopaul. 'He in jail,' she heard Mrs Gopaul say. 'The police done take him down already.'

'O God! How some people nasty and wicked,' one sister said still looking in her direction.

'And the woman ain't have no shame standin' there and watchin' as though she have business here,' the other sister said. 'If was me I woulda bury meself wid shame. I woulda go and jump in the sea and drown meself. Shame, sister, shame is not a thing everybody does have.'

'And the child was such a good child,' Mrs Gopaul said. 'How she was a sweet child. Ain't all-you know how that child used to help me.'

'Yes, everybody know how she was so quiet and nice nice. Whenever I come the first thing she used to ask was "Mausi,

251

you want some tea? Mausi, you want some cocoa tea? I could boil some now now." She used to hug me up and kiss me, and ask for the children. Each one she use to ask for – all seven a them. She use to remember all their name and everything.'

'I tell you, there ain't have no child like that nowhere.'

'You so right, "didi", God does work in a mystery. Nobody could understan'. He does give and He does take, and it ain't have rhyme nor reason.'

'I remember how she used to make a tomatoes "chokha",' Dolly, the youngest sister said. 'How she used to roast the tomatoes on hot coals in the "chulha" and the skin would get thin and black and wrinkle, and it wouldn't burst, and how she used to mash it up with garlic and pepper and chop fresh onion fine fine and mix it, and she used to put sweet-oil over it and when she make a thick "sada" roti with one side crispy and the other side thick and fluffy, and she give you that to eat you used to bite your tongue.'

'And wit' all that cookin' she used to see about the children like a mother and do all the housework. The poor child couldn't finish school because of all the work it had to do in this house. And she was no dunce. She never came less than fift' in test. She used to get up before daybreak and make the tea and make lunch for everybody in time for me to go to work. Ah God,' Mrs Gopaul sighed, 'I lost my right hand.'

'The nasty man rob you o' you child. They will hang his backside for sure for sure.' Dolly spoke the last line more loudly.

Samdaye dropped her head when she saw that there was no opening for her to cross the road and explain. Blinded by her tears she stumbled to the pen to tie the cow out in the field and to busy herself with chores. She wanted to go to Sangre Grande to find out what had happened to Manu but she had to wait until Mangal had gone to school. She could then leave with the baby.

She was returning from the field when she heard Gabi's voice and she went anxiously to meet him. She was sure that the boy could provide some answers to her many questions.

'Look the other one come,' Mrs Gopaul said. 'The other criminal. They come to make more plot.'

The boy turned and began a greeting to Gopaul and his wife but he saw the venom in the eyes of the woman and stopped.

Compai, Prince and Martina all came outside and Mangal, hearing Gabi, rushed down the steps. They all huddled at the back of the building away from the eyes of the Gopaul family and, after the initial greetings, questioned him.

At first Gabi was embarrassed to talk with Compai and shied away from him but the old man rushed up to the boy and embraced him with unreserved warmth. To the many questions simultaneously asked, Gabi related his story.

After Samdaye left Gabi and the girl went towards the Police Station just past where, in front of the court house, the stick-fighting competitions and the whip-swinging clowns with devil horns staged their fights. Gabi wanted to see Manu in action. They were in time to see him defeat the last three of the band and then challenge Tasso. But it was getting late and dark clouds had started massing in the east and the girl insisted that they leave for home. Reluctantly, he had agreed.

Because of the threatening rain there was a great rush for the few taxis and a large knot of people had already gathered at the bus-stop.

'You didn't see the overseer?' Samdaye asked.

Gabi nodded. 'We pass him outside the door of Uncle Sam bar. He had a beer in his hand.'

'He see you?' Samdaye asked.

'I call out to him. I say, "Overseer" and he wave.'

'He see the girl?'

'He not only see the girl, he come up and talk to her. He say how she lookin' nice and he ask if we want beer.'

'How he look, drunk?' Prince asked.

'Not drunk but a little tipsy. You know how his eyes get small and red when he drink a few.'

'So he went and buy the beer?'

'Nah. We left to get transport.'

'He didn't follow?' Samdaye could not conceal her anxiety.

'You know, all-you askin' so much question and I ain't know as yet what happen to the girl. All I hear on the radio this mornin' that a girl was found murdered in Dorado and

253

they give the name. I couldn't believe it but when they say it a second time I decide to come right away. In the Junction they sayin' that they think somebody rape her and kill her.' His voice caught and he swallowed. 'But that couldn't happen. I left her right here. Just round the corner. We could see the house. And because the rain was startin' to drizzle again and we could hear it comin', Shanti tell me to run fast before it catch me. I left her standin' watchin' me run.'

'Well, the poor girl well dead, eh,' Samdaye said. 'And somebody kill her.'

'I hear they hold Manu,' Gabi said.

Samdaye merely lowered her eyes.

'But that can't be true. Manu couldn't have nothing to do with that. We left him in Sangre Grande and he was still lookin' to fight Tasso.'

'And you had to wait long for the bus?' Prince asked.

'Yes. The first bus come and full up before we could get on. But we didn't have to wait too long for the second one.'

'Where you sit in the bus?' Samdaye asked.

'The last seat in the back.' He looked abashed. 'We keep lookin' back to see if we see Manu because I wanted to know if he win.'

'But you didn't see him.'

'No. But we see Gomez. He come in the bus.'

'The same bus?'

'The same bus. And he sit down in front.'

'He see all-you in the bus?' The questions were tumbling from Samdaye.

'He could see us all the time if he wanted from where he was by Uncle Sam Bar. Is not far – just about a hundred yards from where he was to the bus-stop.'

'Tell me what happen at the Junction.'

'Nothing. He get off and started to walk home.'

'In front?'

Gabi nodded.

'Fast?'

The boy's eyebrows raised.

'He was walking fast?'

'Faster than we.'

'So you didn't see him again.'

'Yes. I could see him in front. In the dark it was not hard to see his white shirt with the long sleeve.'

'He was walking just slow enough to stay in front.'

'It look so.'

'He was looking back?'

'It was too dark to see.'

'That is the criminal, I tell you, that man is the real crook,' Samdaye said excitedly. 'And you didn't see Manu on your way back?'

'Nah. I run full speed to get away from the rain. Nah, I didn't see him.'

'You see?' she said. 'Manu was nowhere by this thing. Is that dog, Gomez.' She turned to Gabi. 'His clothes was muddy?'

'Whose clothes?'

'The overseer.'

'Muddy? How you mean "muddy"?'

'Muddy, man. Dirty with mud.'

'Nah. He was neat and clean as usual.'

'The man come and wash himself by the barrel. He wash out the mud from his clothes and he wash out his nasty self.'

'But we have to prove it,' Prince said.

'They want to put the blame on my husband but we will prove who do it.'

'They want to put blame on you, too, Gabi,' Compai said quietly.

'Me?' Gabi looked at the old man in amazement.

'You was the last to see her alive. You better don't hang around here or they will arrest you too.'

'Let them arrest me. I ain't do nothing.'

'That not easy to prove. They will charge either you or Manu.'

'I want to go and see how Manu is.' Samdaye said.

'I will go with you,' Gabi said.

'You better don't go to Sangre Grande,' Compai advised. 'That is the last place you want to go. They will hold you for sure.'

'I innocent so I don't 'fraid police.'

'Innocent don't mean nothing,' Compai said. 'They want to hold somebody and they will hold somebody.'

'But what about Gomez?' Gabi asked.

'What about Gomez?' Compai looked at him. 'You too young to know, boy. Nobody will hold Gomez. They will believe anything Gomez say. And we ain't have proof Gomez do anything.'

'But if is not my husband . . . and is not Gabi . . .'

'Could be anybody. Could be some mas'man drunk and lookin' for excitement. It ain't bound to be Gomez.'

'Wha' happen, Compai, like you takin' up for the dam' 'pagniol overseer?' Samdaye asked.

The old man did not reply.

Mangal was alternately holding Gabi's hand and running round him saying 'puck puck puck-a-a-a' and trying to get the boy to notice him. He could not understand why everybody was so serious and why they were speaking as if they were sharing a secret. In his sleep, it seemed, he had heard wailing and crying the evening before. He did not see his father come home and he suddenly realised that his father was not among them. 'Where Pa?' he tugged at his mother's arm. 'Eh, where Pa?' But they all ignored him. Without much enthusiasm he made several more attempts to get Gabi to play with him or even make a joke but Gabi was very serious. He sensed that something was wrong and that it had something to do with his father. His father was probably still in bed but when he ran back into the room he was not there. Neither was his costume nor his whip. Maybe he didn't come home the night before and he then began to get worried.

Later that morning when he was ready for school he had waited for Stalin but the boy had passed by without looking at him and his brothers had given him a look of loathing. In his hand he had a mottled green marble which he had borrowed from Stalin and which he was waiting to return. He was shocked when, on running after the boy and giving it to him, Stalin had flung the marble in the bush. 'Son of a killer!' they said. 'Son of a murderer!' 'You' father does rape people and kill them!' It sounded like 'rip'. He could not imagine what his father had done. 'They have him in jail.' They drove him away from the group and he had to fall some distance behind. When someone threw a stone at him he stood for a while then he returned home where his mother was getting ready to go out. She had on the dress which she wore the day before. 'You goin' back to see Carnival?' he asked. She did not reply but asked him what he was doing back home and when he explained she then told him what had happened the previous day and how the police had taken his father. But it was all a mistake and she was going to bring him back home from the police station. He was not to go to school but could stay with Compai. Prince and Gabi were going with her.

The jail cells – two of them – were in a sort of concrete box separate from, and behind, the police station. Each had a heavy wooden door rough and mildewed with a small rectangular opening screened by iron bars. Accompanied by a policeman, Samdaye, Prince and Gabi were allowed to approach the door.

'Hanuman!' the policeman called. 'Hanuman! People to see you!'

From the dark and windowless room that was about six feet by eight feet Manu's face appeared streaked by the bars. His eyes were red and his face hollow and unshaven. There was a look of bewilderment and incomprehension, and his mouth hung slack and open. A number of other faces crowded the opening. A heavy stench of vomit and a sharp scent of urine came through the cracks and, from the bottom of the door, the mixture could be seen oozing on the broken concrete.

Samdaye did not know what to say to him and his look of utter hopelessness filled her with pity and sorrow, and she began to cry. She offered him the small paperbag with roti but he refused it saying that he could not eat. Not in that crowded room and with the nauseous smell. She urged him to keep it. All the questions that had filled her mind had now vanished and she just stared at him with the tears echoing the bars on his face.

He smiled. 'Le Branche flowin' again.' He greeted Prince and Gabi and asked what they were saying in the Junction. He was to be interviewed by the District Superintendent and then they would either charge him or let him go.

'But they can't charge you,' Gabi said.

'We will know when he come. He expect to come about ten o'clock.'

'What the Sergeant sayin'?' Prince asked.

'He don't believe I do it.'

'Well, why he don't let you go?'

'He have to wait on the Super.'

Gabi congratulated Manu on winning the big prize and said that he was sure that Manu was innocent because he left him in Sangre Grande and did not see him on the way back.

'We think is Gomez,' Samdaye said.

'Hush,' Prince advised. 'Don't call name.' But he nodded in agreement.

They were still talking when the Sergeant appeared and, looking closely at Gabi, asked his name. 'Ah, boy, you save me some worry,' he said on hearing the name. 'We woulda have to look for you. Come with me.' He beckoned and Gabi followed.

'Sergeant,' Samdaye called. 'Sergeant, when all-you letting my husband go?' She followed him closely.

'That is not up to me.'

'But everybody know he not guilty,' she pleaded.

'That is not for me to decide. That is for the Superintendent.'

'All-you will charge him? And you know that he didn't do it? All-you went and find out from the overseer where he was and what he do? Just straight so all-you decide is my husband without findin' out from anybody what happen – without makin' proper investigation? Is just so dry dry all-you does lock up people. Just because is poor people.' She was at his heels. 'So all-you ain't sending nobody to find out from the Junction who see who. All-you decide just so case solve.'

'Lady, gi'me a chance,' the Sergeant said. 'Nobody ain't decide nothing yet. The Superintendent ain't come yet and he is the man to make any decision.' He looked at her tear-stained face, 'I glad you come, yes. You better follow me and let me get your statement one time.' He motioned for Prince to follow also.

They walked round to the front of the building where an arc of a driveway cut the 'Y' of the junction and separated a tiny grassy semi-circle in which a huge poui tree grew. The tree was almost leafless with clumps of yellow flowers many of which lay on the ground. From the branches hung the long straw nests of yellow-tails that squawked and screeched, and fluttered noisily. They walked up the wide concrete steps. To the left was a door which led to a small room with a desk. Samdaye was motioned inside. Prince was asked to stay out in the yard while Gabi was led to the counter where his answers to questions were written in a large book.

Before the end of the questioning the Superintendent arrived. He was a stern and imposing man taller than the Sergeant and blacker. A fringe of white hair ran round his cap. Frowning, he looked at Samdaye who cringed. She brought up her right arm and held the baby as if to protect it from attack then she rose quickly.

The Sergeant quickly explained who she was and the Superintendent, without taking his eyes off her, turned wordlessly and walked out of the room. The Sergeant followed. Samdaye could hear them talking as though nobody was within hearing distance. They discussed the case for some time then she heard the Superintendent say, 'Good work, good work. I glad you hold the culprit without trouble.' Then there followed an argument in which the Sergeant was saying how he was doubtful that the right man had been arrested.

'Sergeant,' the Superintendent said, 'guilt or innocence is not for me and you to decide. Our job is to hold the suspects. The court will decide who guilty and who innocent.' He looked up at the noisy birds. 'That racket don't trouble you?'

The Sergeant shook his head.

'If I had to work here I would cut down this damn tree long time.' He listened to the questioning of Gabi for a while then returned to Samdaye to whom he barely paid attention while she explained. After a while he dismissed both Samdaye and Prince and ordered that Gabi be detained also.

Samdaye pleaded for her husband and was supported by Prince but the Superintendent would not listen. He curtly turned her away and closed the door of the Sergeant's office.

Chapter 24

The Sergeant did not like this case. There were some things that bothered him, the most important of all was the fact that the Superintendent was too eager to close the book on that silly fellow who was not helping by remaining so quiet. All the man was saying was that he knew nothing about the charge. And he would say it in a soft resigned way as if he knew that there was no use in trying to put up a defence. The Superintendent continued to interpret this as a sign of guilt and latent malevolence. He was firm in his belief that they had caught their man and that there was no need to pursue any further investigation. But he had doubts. The fact that the man was so passive might be because he blamed himself for being in that predicament. He did not seem to care what happened to him. He had made no attempt to seek legal advice.

The Sergeant had questioned the man's wife and had to pry out the fact that the girl had been left in the company of the boy, Gabi, who readily admitted that they had arranged to meet. The Superintendent was prepared to lock the boy up also but he had to decide which of the two was more vulnerable to the charge.

The woman seemed more eager to protect the girl's reputation than to save her husband. Maybe she was certain of his innocence and his eventual release.

It was the overseer who bothered him most as he thought about it – more than the attitude of the Superintendent. He was very interested in the man's wife's account of the figure that washed himself in the rain-barrel. Even then the woman was very forthright in declaring that she was not sure because it was dark and she had suspected nothing as the alarm had not yet been raised. Although the Superintendent had told him to get witnesses to support the charge against the man, he was still keeping an open mind and would try to get material sufficient to hold the overseer. The Sergeant knew his instinct never failed. The overseer was the culprit. He would send the Indian man down to the jail in Port of Spain as he had been instructed but he would himself go to Dorado to conduct the investigation. First he had to check with the doctor who did the post mortem. With cases like these you might be wrong about the cause of death. You have to be very careful. He was under pressure to release the body as soon as possible. The parents and relatives had been going back and forth from the hospital to the police station and needed to make arrangements for the cremation.

He phoned the doctor and was surprised to learn that death was due to asphyxiation. She had been choked to death. The killer must be a madman, he thought. That surely put a different light on the matter. He would wait till the funeral was over then he would go back to investigate.

In Dorado a pall seemed to have settled on the village. People spoke in hushed tones even though the cremation had taken place and the tent at the Gopauls' had been broken down. Gopaul's humming in his hammock had taken on a funereal tone and he no longer called out his morning greeting to the neighbours.

Compai, sitting under the almond tree, felt a heaviness in his heart although he was relieved that Gabi had been released and had visited him on his way back to Port of Spain. He looked across at the Gopaul house and imagined the girl standing as she always did with the baby astride her hips and a coconut broom in her hand sweeping the yard around the house. How sudden had death come to the child. Death held no fears for him now for the death of each person he knew diminished his life and made death more acceptable. It was not difficult to imagine his lifeless body stretched out in a box with a few villagers standing round the graveside and Shepherd leading the group in a few hymns. There would be few to mourn him.

As he thought about his lifeless body he remembered Chhotu. It was in Cedros when Compai was still a young man that Chhotu, then about forty, fell ill and died. They tied his big toes together and put a bowl with a clump of grass – its bunch of fine roots still intertwined in a clod – on his belly to prevent it from swelling. A pundit had come and said prayers, and a wake had started with some of the young men beating bamboo joints and dancing the bongo. It was after midnight when most of the people had gone that Compai had heard Chhotu's wife bawling. She was running around the rain-barrel at the back of the house alternately crying and shouting, and all the while trying to push it over. 'Chhotu! O God, Chhotu! What you tryin' to do?' She cried. When they ran to see what was happening they discovered that Chhotu was down in the barrel head first and his feet sticking out on top. Quickly they pushed the barrel over and pulled the man out wide-eyed and spluttering, 'Leave me, leave me, man. I want to dead.' When he had been taken out and dried properly Chhotu explained that since everyone thought he was dead, and since he felt that he was not going to get better, he might as well be dead so he was trying to drown himself. Compai smiled at the story. He could imagine how the man felt. It is possible that Manu was feeling the same way. The boy was committing suicide and Compai could see little reason for it especially with a wife and two children. He had a lot to live for. Chhotu had lived for over twenty-five years after that incident. He was sorry that he was too young to ask Chhotu how he felt when he knew that his life was at an end. Long afterwards he had heard the man say that 'death don't mean nothing' and that 'life ain't have no beginnin' and no endin'.'

Compai recalled a kind of opaqueness in Manu's eyes; an invitation-to-death quality in his recklessness; a 'brave danger' in the ease in which he was ready to resort to violence; and the unprotected way in which he faced the most violent of the 'diable-diable' men. What had caused the boy to become like that? Was it because his father had been rootless and that he himself had no relatives? But he had his wife and children. And that was such a gift, such a blessing, something that filled the great emptiness that Compai felt. How could he not prize that? Was there some way he could save this boy against himself?

He had observed Samdaye moving in a daze with tear-filled eyes wordlessly seeking some advice — some words of hope. She had forced her son to go to school and face squarely the badgering and taunting of the children. She had related what had happened to his father and had explained that what he was told was all lies and that his father would be out soon and would show them. He was not to retaliate but if he were physically attacked, he should tell his teacher.

Compai had seen the manner in which she had faced the accusations of the Gopaul family and the relatives. Bravely, she had walked up to the coffin and gazed at the girl then she had walked right back to her room after shooting a glance of pure hatred at Gomez who was offering consolation to all while expressing his grief and regrets. The man had even spoken to some of the now unemployed labourers who had gathered around him concerning the state of agriculture and the future of the estate. Now that work had been stopped, he, Gomez had to perform a variety of tasks. Nearly all the animals had been sold and he had to walk all over the fields chopping off a dead branch here and pruning an excess sapling there. The bananas were being left to rot on the trees and the birds were having a great time with the ripe fruits. The squirrels, too, were roaming freely attacking the cocoa pods and leaving holes in all of them. He was trying to elicit some sympathy for his loss of dignity in having to do all the menial work.

'So I hear that the estate up for sale,' someone had asked.

'Well, who will want to keep a cow after the milk done dry up,' he had replied. 'I think Mr Pierre fed up with the system. You work the land, reap the crop, prepare it then sell it to some company in Port of Spain which ship the beans to England where they make cocoa powder and chocolate and all kinds of things then they send it back and you have to pay about ten times what it cost you.'

'He get a buyer?'

'He get a buyer, yes. And all-you see a strange feller come two or three times already? That is the feller.' He was dressed in a brown suit with a black bow-tie and his hair parted on the side glistened with vaseline. He was trying desperately to put some expression of sorrow in his small, sharp, shifty eyes. 'I meself don't know if by next week I will have a job. I could be like anyone of you, yes, with no place to go.'

After the funeral the Superintendent had come and was seen talking and laughing with Gomez as if they were old friends. They might have known each other, Compai thought. In that case the old man saw no possibility of Gomez being suspected far more arrested.

A few days later the Sergeant had returned and had questioned several persons at the Junction. He had gone back to the scene of the crime and had also questioned Compai and others. When asked about bail the Sergeant had said that bail was not possible and that the matter was out of his hands. He would like to find out more about Gomez; where he worked before; whether he had any previous history of sexual interference with estate women.

Compai had laughed. 'You ever hear of any overseer who didn't rush women on the estate? Must be one in every hundred who was decent.' He looked at the Sergeant and thought that the man was really trying. 'You have a good idea. I hear that he came from a estate in Rio Claro. Is good to find out why he left.'

'It had too much people on the road on Carnival Tuesday for somebody not to see something.' He rubbed his chin and removed his unlit pipe. 'I want the names of all the people who pass here that evenin'. I don't think I talk to everybody. I will be back soon.'

The Sergeant had not returned.

Samdaye had watched the Superintendent come and go and the Sergeant questioning people. The days were passing and her husband must be starving in jail. He must be rotting in that stinking place. Several times she had gone to see him. After waiting for hours she was brusquely told that she could not see him. They had taken the food she had brought and had poked and prodded the paper-bag opening it and examining the contents. She did not know if their hands were clean. Every time the gate had closed she felt the sound deep in her belly where there was now a permanent hollow. The thick stone walls rose way up and tiny barred windows made dark holes. Somewhere inside that dungeon was her husband alone with his thoughts. She could not imagine what he thought. Seeing a lawyer's nameplate on a street as she walked she had ventured in. There she had met a grey-haired man in a crumpled black jacket who listened to her while examining her worn clothes and sandals and the broken nails in her fingers. He enquired about how much money she had and whether or not they owned land. 'This will cost a lot of money,' he said. 'I don't know if you could afford it. A murder case is big, big money.' She did not know if she was imagining the way he looked at her as she stood but his eyes were running up and down her body. 'Maybe something could be worked out,' he said. 'Come back when you have a deposit.' He asked for five hundred dollars.

She felt her head swelling. Five hundred dollars! And that was just the deposit! She had his prize money of over two hundred. If she sold the cow which was now in young she could get a couple hundred more. But that was just the deposit. Where would she get the rest. Her mother had come when she heard the news but she had shown sympathy only for Samdaye and the children. She expressed little surprise saying that she knew that he would come to a bad end. She made no offer to help. She wanted to take them all away from Dorado so that they could make a fresh start. Especially Mangal who must be having a difficult time in school.

The more Samdaye thought about her predicament the more she felt that she had to do something. She sought the opinion of Compai and Prince knowing that her mother had only one suggestion which, to her, was unthinkable. Increasingly, she began to be filled with a fear of Manu breaking out of jail. She knew that he was not one to stomach confinement and to meekly take orders. She had to talk to him. If he only ran away they would surely shoot him.

She would go to Rio Claro and conduct her own investigation. 'I goin' to Rio Claro to find out more about that crook,' she announced loudly to a startled Prince and Martina. 'I hear that is where he used to work before they throw 'im out.'

'Hush,' Martina said. 'Why you talkin' loud loud so?'

'I want Ma Gopaul and them to hear.'

'They will tell the man and you don't know what he could do.'

'He can't do worse than what he do already. In any case he can't do me one dam' thing. I ready for him.' Her voice became louder, 'If they kill my husband he dead! He ain't livin' one day longer than my husband!' Her lips trembled.

'You only invitin' trouble,' Martina said.

'Miss Tina, I in plenty of trouble already. I ain't backin' out from no more trouble.' She felt that she was beginning to sound like her husband. 'I feel like a balloon ready to burst . . . ready to explo'. You see me quiet quiet I don't eat nice, nah.' She was beginning to enjoy this feeling of power. 'I could use cutlass just like anybody else.'

As if infected by her anger the yellow-tails screeched more noisily.

'You better don't do anything foolish,' Compai said. 'Better wait till tomorrow.'

'You should do as Compai say, girl,' Martina said. 'Wait for a day or two.'

'Waitin' won't help,' Samdaye answered. 'You know my husband. He will break out. He ain't stayin' lock up for long. And I don't want him get kill for something he ain't do. If he break out they will kill him – shoot him down like a dog. And the longer this crook stay outside the crazier I will get. So as soon as possible I leavin' for Rio Claro or Biche or where the hell he used to work before this blight . . . this witches' broom fall on the head of this village.'

'You ever went to Rio?' Martina asked.

'Nah. But it ain't hard to find out.'

'You can't go and come back the same day unless you have you' own car.'

'Is not like it in Venezuela.' It was almost as if it was her husband talking. She thought for a moment. 'If I don't go you have any other plan?'

'We could do for him,' Compai said quietly.

'How?'

'We could put a light on his head.'

'You mean work obeah?'

'Obeah voodoo jingay . . . those things ain't so foolish as people think.' Comapi was whispering. 'The things I see

266

already will make you believe anything is possible. Yes, all-you never see nothing yet. If we get the right man he could make Gomez stand up in the Junction and confess. I know a Pundit in Arouca who is a giant in fixin' up anything. You should see his house. Everyday it have more people there than the warden office. They come to fix date for wedding, find out about their future, get their husband or wife to come back, fix up a case in the magistrate court, get police to drop cases . . . anything, man, anything. The man really good.'

'Well I is Hindu,' Samdaye said.

'And he don't charge nothing.'

'So how he live, then?'

'You take him some gift . . . chicken, clothes, money . . .'

'Is how long this thing take to work –'

'I know another feller. He come from Venezuela. Now that is a place where they have obeah. British Guiana, too. People do a lot o' strange things in those places. Well, as I was sayin', this thing happen in Cedros . . . about, le' me see . . . about twenty-five years ago. It had a man called Ezekiel – we use to call him Ziki for short. Ziki couldn't get along wit' his neighbour, Rebecca. Rebecca was a lovely girl from Venezuela who was married to a feller from San Fernando but they lived in Cedros after Becca mother died. They move in the house where Becca grow up. To tell you the trut' I don't know what cause the quarrel. Ziki was a married man and much older than Becca. Too, besides, he was a black man – blacker than Prince. And big-chested. I don't know if he used to like Becca mother and was vex Becca move into the house or if he like Becca and was jealous. But they lived across the road from each other and almost every day Ziki use to provoke a quarrel wit' the girl. Every day, almost I tell you. Was a quarrel and a quarrel never done until one day Becca come home and find her pot on the fireside with mess in it. Somebody come and mess in the girl pot and put it back just so on the fireside. And the place stink like hell. Well,' Compai paused to look at their faces.

'Oh shi-i-it,' Prince exclaimed.

'Is that self,' Compai said.

'You mean the man was so wicked?' Martina asked.

'Nobody say it was the man. I ain't say was Old Man Ziki. Anyway,' he raised a crooked finger, Becca call everybody in the village to see, then she put the pot down on an old coconut stump behind the house and she announce loud loud that she goin' to do for the man who mess in she pot. She goin' to see the Venezuelan man they use to call Papa Zeno and off she went. Late that night she come back and she say to everybody that the person who do it will never go to the latrine again, he will die from constipation, and that will happen before nine days finish. Then she light a fire behind the house and put the pot on it. And in the pot she put . . . I don't know what she put, but she put all kinds o' powder and flowers and thing, and then she walked round the pot I don't know how many times then she light the fire. Well, I swear to God, I hear a scream from across by Ziki. I hear the man bawl out like his backside on fire!'

'And what happen?' Martina eyes were wide. 'He dead?'

'Not right away. For nine days that man groaned and bawled. And he never again go to empty his bowel. On the nint' day he close his eyes . . . dead like a nit!'

Samdaye's eyes glowed. 'And the old Spanish man – he still livin'?'

'As far as I know.'

Samdaye was silent for a while. 'And you say the pundit from Arouca don't charge for what he do? That he will take anything you give him?'

The old man nodded.

'But first I have to go to Rio Claro,' Samdaye said. 'And nothing . . . nobody will change my mind. I have to make sure about this man here.'

Chapter 25

One pale-green star stuck unblinking in a shell-pink haze over a whitening horizon as Samdaye hurried outside to tend to the cow. A cool wet wind came through the trees. The cow, pregnant now, moved slowly out of the pen and seemed reluctant to put its feet in the dewy grass. She wondered if Gomez would still insist on their paying for the bull. Although she had the money now she was not going to pay. Her shouting to Mangal had wakened them all and Martina stuck her head over her door to warn her about embarking on a senseless journey.

'I tell you, girl, you too stupid and harden. You ain't know where you goin' and you goin' alone, too. You ever heard about Madinga Village? You ever hear about them Madinga Tigers? Eh? Well you have to pass through that village and them fellers bad like hell. They will beat you up and kill you for nothing. Them fellers does make their own guns and they does walk wit' bull-pistle round their waist for belt. They don't make joke, eh. You only trouble them and you gone. I hear if you only look at them hard you in trouble.'

'Miss Tina, me ain't trouble nobody and nobody should trouble me. I mindin' my own business.' She raised her voice, 'I have to know more about this devil . . . this red devil. I find he was too anxious to point his finger at my husband. Findin' mas' . . . findin' mas' . . . and tellin' everybody is my husband that commit crime? And all the time he well know that is he do it?'

Martina withdrew from the door. She did not like the way the woman was announcing her intentions so that the man would hear.

'I goin' to Rio today and today I will find out what he was

269

up to before he come here. Is so he think he will make people pay for what he do? Is bad he think he bad? He like woman, eh? Well, when I finish with him I will alter him like they alter male pig to get them fat. I will cut out his –' she cast a quick glance at the Gopaul house and saw Gopaul looking at her and she bent her head. Somehow she felt that the man understood.

She cleaned out the pen, washed her hands and feet, fed the baby, wrapped Mangal's lunch in a piece of brown paper, and took the baby to Martina. 'Here, see after the child for me till I come back,' she said.

'You comin' back today?' Prince asked.

'How you mean? The place so far?'

'You see you ain't know how far you goin'.' Martina said. 'Tell her, Prince. Tell her how to get there otherwise she will get lost and put everybody in confusion.'

Prince explained the route she would have to take. She would have to travel to Sangre Grande then take a bus to Biche where the bus ends its journey. Then she would have to get some transport to travel the next ten or twelve miles to Rio Claro. He had no idea if there was a bus service on that side. There might be taxis. She had an alternative route through San Fernando but it was much longer. She would have to change too many vehicles. 'But when you get to Rio how you would know which part to go? How you goin' to travel to wherever the estate is? This is really spinnin' top in mud but is your business.'

She told them that they should not worry and left as the sun was rising. Both the star and the pink haze had vanished and the sky was a glowing white.

She had not travelled very far when she was suddenly confronted by Gomez who emerged from behind a coffee bush. His tall rubber boots were wet and gleaming and stuffed with the ends of his trousers. He wore a khaki shirt and a large straw hat. In his hand was a riding crop. Striding up to her he came within a few feet and she could see his blazing eyes level with hers. Her fear rose and vanished in a flash and she gazed at him steadily.

'So I hear you sayin' that is I kill the girl. You know is I kill the girl?'

She did not shift her gaze but did not reply.

'You want to blame me for what your husband done?' He repeated the question stressing 'me'. He tapped the end of the crop into his palm as he mentioned her husband. 'What happen . . . you hate me or what?' He stepped closer and she could smell his night-old stale maleness. 'Why you hate me so? I do you anything wrong? Look how much I do for all-you. I give you work and your husband is not a easy man to work with. As soon as he come he start to make mischief wit' talk about strikin' for more money or some kind of foolishness –'

'He does fight for his right.'

'Right? **Right?** That man don't know right from wrong –'

'Look,' her eyes were still riveted on his. 'If you have something to tell me say it and say it fast. I –'

'And look how I give you all place to stay even wit' the trouble –'

She saw the wavering in his eyes. 'I ain't have time to waste. I have business to do.'

'Listen,' his eyes became hard again, narrowed and blazed, 'I tryin' to give you a chance but you just like your husband. Don't play wit' me, woman.' He stepped menacingly closer and she could almost feel his hot breath. 'I could make life easy for you, yes.' His gaze travelled down her face to her breasts. 'I could do a lot for you.' She felt that he might grab her and she started to back away. At that instant she saw Columbus moving unsteadily up the road. Gomez followed her gaze and, noticing Columbus, stepped aside slowly and continued on his way. 'Lady, don't play the ass wit' me. eh. If you make trouble for me you might end up like the girl. I could break your neck like a piece of stick, yes. Just like that.' His fingers opened and closed. 'If you know what's good you will keep your ass quiet and stay at home. Don't push me.'

'Wha-what that old crook tellin' you? Eh?' Columbus, his clothes rumpled, his matted hair sticking out from under his hat which was set back on his head, looked as if he was already drunk. 'The . . . the man troublin' you or wha-what? How you' face lookin' worried so? A nice . . . a nice wom-woman like you, eh?' She had never had a conversation with him before but she was grateful that he arrived when he did.

'Nah,' she said shaking her head from side to side. 'He ain't –'

'But he was loo-lookin' as if he was troublin' you. Heh heh,' he chuckled. 'You . . . you too nice to be walkin' about so early in the mornin'.' He smiled crookedly and as he staggered away he said in a mutter to himself, 'I see him, yes. He ain't know that I see the bastard. I see him comin' from the bush . . .'

Samdaye hurried away. She did not like how the morning started. The encounter with Gomez troubled her. She felt that he might have attacked her if Columbus had not happened along. She smiled when she thought of the drunken man. He always seemed to be in a state of intoxication and wondered how he could be in such a condition so early in the morning.

She got a bus to take her to Sangre Grande where she did not have to wait long before getting another one to take her to Biche. A middle-aged man with a long beard sat next to her and made no attempt to start a conversation. The road was narrow, winding and hilly, and on both sides of it the vegetation hung to the very edge. Several cocoa and coffee fields interspersed with bananas succeeded one another and there were few houses. The cultivated areas soon gave way to thick forest and tall trees that almost met each other across the road leaving a thin jagged strip of sky. Through the trees she could see nothing but an almost impenetrable dark with only here and there shafts of light shot through. The bus rattled along the rutted road and ground laboriously up the many hills. Only occasionally did a passenger get on. After almost an hour with the absence of conversation weighing heavily on her she decided to ask the man about the infamous village of which Prince had spoken.

'You know where Madinga Village is?' she asked.

The man turned to her wordlessly and she saw that both of his eyes were red, almost bloodshot.

'I hear so much about Madinga Village –'

'Why you want to know?' his voice was not friendly.

'I just want to know. I never pass on this road before and I hear –'

'What you hear?'

'– that the people don't make joke –'

'You mean they don't laugh?'

'Nah. I hear they bad like hell.'

He was silent again.

'I hear them Madinga Tigers —'

He turned sharply to her then he smiled with his mouth hanging to one side to hide the two missing teeth on the left. 'You know anybody in that village?'

'No,' she answered. 'But I just want to know when I pass the village.'

'Well, I hope that you pass the village safe and that nobody kill you —'

'I hear they nearly beat a feller to death when he run over a chicken wit' his car. Imagine killin' somebody for a chicken!'

'You sure it wasn't a child he bounce?'

'Nah. Is a chicken, I hear. They say you mustn't stop for nothing in the village.' She looked at him more closely. He was not as old as he appeared at first. It was all that hair on his face that made him look older. He could be Muslim. 'I hear that all the people in Madinga Village is Muslim.'

'Yes. They does kill any other people. Hindu and Christian don't have a chance!' A smile seemed to play around his eyes.

The bus approached a village of a few houses in the middle of which was a mosque with a small dome. The bus stopped and the man got out. 'Don't forget,' he said. 'Be careful if you goin' through that village.' He laughed as he walked away and then she saw the thing that looked like a rope around his waist. As the bus started she asked the driver the name of the village.

'Madinga Village,' he answered.

Quickly she turned and looked at the few simple wooden houses and the man standing gazing at the departing bus.

'I hear you talkin' to the man about that village,' a woman turned to her from the seat in front. 'You must know how you talkin'. That is the worst of the Tigers. That man bad for spite!'

She thought about the man. He did not look like any criminal. It was the same thing people said about her husband — how he was a bad man and how he had no pity when he had a whip in his hand. This man had actually smiled and

273

was even joking with her as she now realized. In any case she vowed not to talk too much. She wanted to find out about Gomez but this experience kept her silent for a long while. Although the engine of the bus made a continuous noise she felt the absence of conversation weighing heavily. As soon as the bus stopped she moved to the seat with the woman.

'You must not just say things about people so,' she admonished. 'Especially when you ain't know who you talkin' to.'

'I really ain't know anybody from round here.' She looked at the woman to determine whether she should continue.

'And where you from?'

'Dorado. But I from Manzanilla, really.'

'You far from home.'

'I want to find out something.'

'You lookin' for the Baptist see-er man? The man who does do all kinds o' things?'

'And what he could do?'

'He does help people in trouble, tell them about their future. Put spirit on people – if somebody troublin' you he could put a spirit on them.'

'He could get somebody out o' jail?'

'I don't know if he do that yet.'

'He could get a man to confess if he do some crime?'

'Maybe.' The woman gave her a long stare. 'You in some kind o' trouble?'

Samdaye thought for a moment. 'I lookin' for some information.' The word made her sound as if she was a census-taker. 'I want to find out about a overseer we have who used to work round here or round Rio Claro somewhere.' She explained about her husband and how they all thought that the overseer was the man who committed the crime but they had no real evidence against him. She had taken it upon herself to find out more about the background of the overseer to see if there had been a pattern of this kind of behaviour.

'What the man name?'

'Gomez –'

'Ignacio?'

'You know him?'

274

'Know him? Who ain't know him?'

Samdaye became excited. 'He used to work 'round here?'

'That man move about from place to place all about these parts. He get run out from almost every place. You never hear about the Los Bravos Estate murder case? About the young woman they found raped in the bush wit' her neck broke? It make the *Guardian* papers and all kind of police come from San Fernando and Port of Spain. The police ain't find no clue but everybody suspect Ignacio. That happen about ten . . . twelve years ago. That was the first we get to hear about him but some people say he had a history before he came around here.'

Samdaye listened with growing amazement as the woman related the many suspicions many people had of Gomez. 'Well, it look like he done something like that in Dorado. And it look like he will get away again like before.'

'He didn't get away every time,' the woman said. 'One time, right in this village he nearly get killed. He started to run after some woman from Madinga Village. Girl, that was the worst mistake he could ever make. You ain't know but that place have only Muslims livin' and they very strict wit' their religion. You don't go messin' about wit' the women and worse of all you don't mess about wit' nobody wife. And to top all that not only you ain't a Muslim you'self but you is some half breed!'

'Was somebody wife?'

'Somebody? **Somebody?** Was the wife of one o' them Tiger! I tell you the man poke he head in some jack-spaniard nest when he interfere wit' them Tigers.'

'What they do?'

'What they do? About six o' them come down here one evenin'. Was a Friday and they finish their prayers and, man, they come down here in a rage wit' bull-pistle flashin'. They catch Gomez in the rum-shop and they only had time to drop about two on him. I wasn't there but I hear he jump about six feet in the air and he take off like that black man who win the Hitler Olympics. Soon after that Gomez left for some place near Arima, I hear.'

'That must be when he come to Dorado.'

'Must be.'

A few houses began to appear more frequently and soon a small village came into view. The woman said that she would get off soon and that the bus was only going a short distance further and would turn back for Sangre Grande after about one hour wait. Samdaye was to enquire at the Junction for an old man named Clarkie who could give much more information about Gomez. 'But you might have to buy a drink of rum for him.' And to her quizzical gaze she added that the old man was always under the eaves of the rum-shop sitting on a bench. After some thought she said that she might as well accompany her to the Junction. 'I have a few things to buy, anyway.'

'A-A! It still have woman lookin' for Ignacio?' the old man said as he scratched his grey uneven stubble on his chin. 'I can't believe woman still runnin' that 'pagniol down.' His rheumy eyes glinted between small slits. 'Mus' be the Brilliantine he does put in his hair ... or must be the Palmolive soap ... or mus' be something I ain't even know about.' He chuckled. He spoke as if to a crowd and seemed not to be looking at the woman. 'All this talkin' does make a man thirsty, yes.'

The woman nodded to Samdaye who went to the counter and indicated the old man with her head. She was given a drink of white rum the fumes of which rushed up her nostrils and she caught her breath. The shopkeeper handed her a bottle of water to take to the old man who downed the drink in a gulp and washed it down with some water.

The woman related Samdaye's story to the man who chuckled intermittently for some time. 'You can't teach old dog new trick,' he said. 'And the old dog still up to his old tricks.' He opened his eyes wide and looked at Samdaye. 'Girl, it ain't have nothing I could tell you that all the people in this village couldn't tell you. And all the people in Tabaquite couldn't tell you. And all the people in Mafeking couldn't tell you. The man is a wicked man ... a Satan. But only wit' women.' He adjusted the faded US Army cap which was sideways on his head. 'You know how many men will swear that Ignacio is a good man? He is a nice fellah, they will tell you. He does buy drinks for everybody in the shop. And he always used to have a little "all-fours" game at this house on a weekend. Is only that women used to drive him crazy. He was mad, eh. Something used to go wild in his head when he see a nice woman. And when he had a few drinks in his head and his eyes get little so,' he demonstrated by squeezing his eyelids almost shut, 'any woman look nice.' He paused and Samdaye was about to fetch another drink when the woman nudged her and she hesitated. 'The police could never hold him. He does make them believe anything he tell them especially after he offer them a little scotch and coconut water and when he put on his long-sleeve white shirt and he slick back his hair and he trim his moustache and smile at them smellin' of Brilliantine, they never believe he does drink anything harder than milk.'

'That man smart, yes,' Samdaye said.

'Too smart,' the man said. 'But every rope got a end.'

'I hope he run out this time.'

Clarkie raised the empty glass to his lips and held it for a while until the last drop was drained. Samdaye pretended not to notice. She had no more money to spend on liquor.

'I could give you some advice,' he was now looking intently at the empty glass.

'You does drink too dam' much,' the woman said. 'You ain't see that the girl in trouble.'

'Me throat does get dry wit' all this talkin'.'

The woman motioned to Samdaye to ignore him and she entered the shop followed by Samdaye. 'Don't waste your money. You ain't goin' to get anything mo' from 'im.'

But Samdaye saw him with the glass in his hand and felt that she owed him for even speaking to her. Taking the glass she had it refilled then she heard the bus returning and she crossed the road.

'You ain't want the advice?' Clarkie shouted.

The bus stopped in front of the shop and the driver came out. He went into the shop and bought a drink of rum.

'The bus ain't goin' right now, lady.'

She was about to enter the bus when she asked, 'What you think I should do?'

'Obeah,' Clarkie said and laughed. 'Put something on his head. Light a candle.'

Chapter 26

Between the hushed whispers of Prince and Compai the shrill buzzing of crickets filled the night air.

'You say that Shep comin'?' Prince asked.

'How much time I will tell you that Shep comin'?'

'He mus' be preachin' some place.'

'He ain't preachin' tonight. How you so anxious, Prince?'

'I want to make sure before we do anything.'

'But we sure,' Compai insisted.

'We ain't sure sure.'

'You think Manu do it?'

Prince shook his head.

'You think Gabi do it?'

'Don' be foolish. How Gabi will do a t'ing like that?'

'You t'ink a stranger do it?'

'That not impossible.'

'So when Shep do his t'ing you will be sure?'

'And you say Shep bringin' a seer-man?'

'So the seer-man will make you believe?'

'He might.' Prince fidgeted. 'I really don't like to dabble in this business, you know. You can't tell what could happen.'

'What business?'

'This black magic . . . or obeah . . . or whatever. I hear about a feller who raise a spirit in the cemetery to do something for him and it turn round on him and he catch the same spirit and for the rest of his life he used to hang around cemeteries every night. They say the spirit could not find its body because they disturb it and it used to have this man goin' from grave to grave.'

'Jesus!' Martina interjected. 'Prince you could talk foolishness, yes. Is the Bible all-you dealin' wit'.'

'But you remember what Shep himself say? He say that you should not mess about with the Good Book.'

'Prince, if you don't believe this thing it won't work. You will cause this t'ing not to work, yes. You better get you' tail out a here and let we do what we doin'.'

'Compai right, Prince. You have to put your mind to it.'

'But I jus' talkin' me mind. I want to make sure that nothing bad happen to me ... or Compai ... or any innocent body.'

'You is just a coward, Prince. I sure millions o' people do this already. You ain't meddlin' wit' no spirit and no dead people in no cemetery. You askin' Saint Peter and Saint Paul.' Martina chucked him playfully.

'So Peter and Paul livin'? Them dead, too. Is them spirit you callin' just like the feller in the cemetery. It ain't have no difference.' He stuck his thick finger in the air and wagged it while he beamed at the cleverness of his response.

'We ain't doin' this because we hate Gomez, you know,' Compai explained. 'We feel he guilty but we ain't know for sure. All the evidence pointin' to him, though. What we know for sure is that they have the wrong man in jail.'

'That is what have me frighten',' Samdaye joined the group. 'I have a strong feelin' he will run away from jail. I can't sleep thinkin' about that. The more I think about that the more I believe he will break out. I know the man.'

'He will be really foolish to do that,' Compai said. 'He will spoil all that we tryin' to do.'

'If he break jail and the police hold him they will beat up his tail —'

'— if they don't shoot him dead first,' Martina said.

'Breakin' out will do him no good,' Compai said. 'He can't do nothing to clear his name. He will make things worse.'

'He might head for Gomez.'

'But he don't know for sure if Gomez frame him,' Prince said.

'He know,' Martina continued. 'Everybody know that. And seein' how he don't like Gomez already ...'

They heard footsteps approaching and fell silent. Shepherd came in through the back accompanied by a gaunt, bearded man wearing a shabby jacket several sizes too large for him.

On his head was a faded black bowler hat. He held a long stick curved like an umbrella handle at the top and painted in rings of red, yellow and black.

'Papa Zeng,' Compai whispered.

Samdaye had never seen this man of whom so much had been said. With long slabs of matted hair sticking out below his bowler and the whites of his small sunken eyes shining in the dark he looked as fearsome as he had been made out to be.

Papa Zeng lived on the way to Toco in a shack made of bits and pieces of packing crates, flattened tins and oil-drum tops. A few sheets of rusty corrugated iron as well as various kinds of tin formed the roof. On both sides of the earthen track leading to the shack on the hill he had erected numerous crosses that were planted in a disordered mass around the house and on which were written in crude black letters various lines taken from the Bible. He wore long gowns of jute rice-bags and on his hat he wore a crown of vines and leaves. He sometimes wove thorny twigs into the crown which would be placed on his head and he could often be seen with trickles of blood running down his face. Although his reputation as an obeah-man was well-known few people from the village around him sought his advice. They left him severely alone. However, every day persons would come in cars to consult with him. But he would take no money. He would accept white chickens and flowers which he would place at the foot of a cross he would have them plant. And so the entire site looked like a graveyard. No one but Shepherd could have made him leave his house to see someone who needed help.

Before they could sit down Shepherd said, 'All-you ain't hear about how they finally charge Manu?'

'Nah. When?' they asked almost in a chorus.

'This evenin' it come over the radio. I hear it in the shop at the Junction.'

'What happen – they get new evidence.' Prince asked.

'The radio only say that a eye-witness come out and say that he see Manu.'

'Who?'

'Who you think?'

'Gomez?'

'He 'self. And they charge Gabi, too.'

'Gabi?' Compai said in disbelief.

'Gomez say he see the two a them.'

'But the Sergeant —'

'The Sergeant ain't have nothing to say. If the Super say he have the evidence who is the Sergeant to disagree?'

A dry sob escaped Samdaye's lips. It sounded like a gasp.

'That is why we here,' Shepherd said. 'Right away I decide to go for Papa Zeng. He didn't want to come but I beg him. Now, you know me — I don't go for this kind a thing but this is water more than flour and I think this thing call for more than just prayin' and singin' hymn.'

'So what all-you want to see happen?' Zeng's voice was surprisingly soft.

They looked at each other in the flickering light of the kerosene lamp. 'We want to see them boys set free,' Compai said.

'And we want to see the guilty get punish,' Martina said.

'But we must make sure who guilty,' Prince added.

'Tell me the whole story,' Zeng said.

'I already tell him ... but ... but maybe he want to hear it from you.'

'I want to hear it from them.'

There was some hesitation then Compai related what had happened with Prince, Martina and Samdaye adding details.

After they were finished Zeng sat silently then he asked, 'What about the girl's parents — they ain't want to take part in this? They know about what you doin'?'

'They believe the police catch the criminals. They believe the overseer tellin' the truth and that Manu and the boy guilty.' Prince said.

'And all-you sure them boys innocent.'

There was a concerted nod.

'I don't want to do nothing if I ain't sure about what I doin'. I only doin' it if I sure sure because this thing could backfire and it will be bad for somebody — bad bad.'

'We sure,' Compai said.

They sat silently for a while. The crickets had almost ceased their buzzing and somewhere an owl hooted. Across the road

Gopaul's dog barked a few times. Zeng had kicked off his tyre-sandals and was rubbing one unkempt big toe against the other.

Zeng looked at each one then asked, 'Who will take part in this business?'

Samdaye quickly said she would.

'This is dangerous business, eh,' Zeng said. 'Things could go wrong and bad things could happen.'

'I will do it,' Compai said. 'What bad? Nothing can be bad for a old man like me. I live my life already. I could dead anytime. That ain't mean nothing to me. Man' I would give anything to see Gabi out of that mess. I know the boy. That boy wouldn't do this nastiness. No, not Gabi.' With a toss of the head he added, 'Anytime you ready I ready.'

Zeng rose and walked about the kitchen area. He returned and paced the room. Stepping out into the yard he walked slowly around the building. They followed him as he went about. From Gopaul's house they could see the Gopaul family looking on with curiosity. Gomez was also there.

'It will take more than obeah to get them criminals out of jail,' Gomez said. 'Is only God could save them now.' He spoke loud enough so that they could hear.

'Some people can't get over their jungle habits,' Gopaul's wife observed.

To Prince's enquiry Zeng said that he was looking for a clean place. 'I could feel it when it clean. But this yard got too much evil vibration. It comin' up through my foot.' They then noticed that he was walking bare-footed. 'I ain't goin' to do nothing tonight. But I must find a spot to work.'

'You have white cock, Prince? Compai?' Gomez called out. 'That is a white fowl man, yes. He don't do nothing unless he get white fowl.'

'He does eat well,' Gopaul's wife added. 'Better than me.'

'What about by the mango tree?' Samdaye suggested. They headed in that direction.

'That is the wrong direction,' Gomez said. 'You have to go at the place of the crime.'

As Zeng turned to Compai and raised his eyebrows he was told that the speaker was the overseer and the man they all suspected.

'Conscience is a helluva thing,' Compai said just loud enough so that Gomez could hear.

'We goin' to hear about conscience from the police,' Mrs Gopaul said, 'from the hangman. Jest wait a while and everybody will hear about who have conscience.'

'Don't mind the woman,' Compai said to Zeng. 'She lost her child and she still upset so she hittin' out at anybody.'

'The evidence gone in,' Mrs Gopaul called out. 'People done give witness to the police.'

Samdaye, standing at the side of the building looking at Compai and the others as they headed towards the mango tree, could contain herself no more. Since she heard about Manu being charged as a result of Gomez declaring that he was a witness, she had felt a buzzing in her ears and the heat of the blood in her face. 'I hope the witness confess – that damn lyin' crook.'

'A–A, but look at trouble! Now the witness 'come crook! I wonder who else is crook,' Mrs Gopaul called.

'One set o' lyin' beast,' Samdaye said.

'So the witness is a beast, now,' Gomez said.

'Monkey say "cool breeze". Everything will come out in time. As God is above the truth will come out. God ain't sleepin', you know. He watchin' at all this nastiness.' After some pause she said something she used to hear her father say, 'Bhagwan is great and He will see to justice.' She did not want to continue the argument and went inside.

When Zeng had departed with Shepherd saying that he was not going to return for a day or two because he had some rituals to perform for which he needed the names of all the people connected with the murder, Samdaye sat silently on the back step contemplating her position. Tears of frustration were building.

The departure of Zeng and Shepherd seemed to get Mrs Gopaul more agitated and she and Gomez continued a loud conversation for the benefit of the people in the Barracks. 'Is not one witness who see the deed, is two. Two people see and they come out and give evidence.'

'Who is the next one – you?' Samdaye shouted.

'You want to know, eh? You well want to know.'

'For you' information,' Gomez called, 'is Columbus!'

In spite of herself Samdaye laughed and in this she was joined by Martina and Prince.

'Columbus?' Prince exclaimed. 'COLUMBUS?'

'That po' drunken man?' Martina said. 'Lady, nobody would believe Columbus!'

'Columbus say he see Manu?' Prince could not contain his laughter. 'You think he could stay sober enough to give evidence?'

'I wonder how much rum they give him to make him say that,' Samdaye said. 'Boy, they really scrapin' the barrel.'

'You know why they call him "Columbus"? Eh?' Prince asked. 'Everybody know why they call him that. Is because he ain't know East from West! He ain't know mornin' from evenin'. He ain't know if he goin' o' comin'.'

'And that is when he sober!' Martina laughed uproariously.

'If they put him on the stand case finish one time!' Prince said. 'The judge goin' to dead with laugh!'

'Boy, that is a thing! Imagine Columbus goin' as witness!'

'All-you will hear who drunk and who sober,' Mrs Gopaul said. 'The man will say what he see.'

'Or what they tell him to say,' Samdaye said.

The baby began to cry.

'All-you makin' too much noise,' Compai said.

They discussed, in hushed tones, the new developments. Gomez had got Columbus to agree to give evidence and that was serious indeed. Two EYE-witnesses. Out of the hearing of Samdaye, Prince began to wonder aloud if Manu was not really guilty. What if the overseer and Columbus were speaking the truth. For all his frequent drunken state Columbus was quite harmless and he would not make up a story just like that. They decided to wait on word from Shepherd who would get the information from Zeng whether or not they should proceed with some sort of action. Zeng was known not to waste time on matters he did not himself believe.

Samdaye's humming was punctuated by frequent bursts of laughter from Gopaul's house where a quieter discussion was taking place.

The baby asleep, Samdaye lay awake in the dark thinking over the events of the day. All that she had heard about

Gomez in Biche amounted to nothing if it could not save her husband. Any crime he had committed in the past was of no use in this trial. The bed felt hot under her and she turned about restlessly. She would have to get some legal advice if Manu had indeed been charged. From all accounts this would run into thousands of dollars and there was no way she could raise that kind of money. She may be able to get something from her sister but she doubted that her mother would mortgage her few acres in Manzanilla in order to save Manu whom she always thought would get into serious trouble some day. Her main cause for anxiety at this time was trying to get Manu to refrain from trying to escape. He should stay in there and they would fight it out. She had to go to him as soon as possible.

It might have been about midnight when, half asleep, she thought she heard the floorboards creak but she was too sleepy to mind. Sometime later she thought something had brushed her face and, thinking that it might be the wind seeping through the window cracks, pulled the thin sheet over her head.

Chapter 27

Samdaye was startled by a heavy pounding on the door and shouts of 'Police, open the door!' She jumped out of bed and, for a few seconds, stood confused then she ran to the door and turned the wooden latch. Immediately she was blinded by flash-lights and a gun was shoved in her ribs. She backed into the room.

'Where he hidin'?'

'Where you' husband?'

'Come on, woman, talk. Talk quick. Where you hidin' 'im?'

The Gopauls' dog was barking furiously and others had joined in a raucous chorus. Prince, Martina and Compai were calling out questions but were shouted down by the policemen three of whom rushed into her room. In a glance they could have seen that Manu was not in the room but they lingered, peering repeatedly under the bed in turns. Their boots made such heavy thuds that the baby woke and began to cry. Mangal also stared wide-eyed and open-mouthed until he too, began to whimper.

One of the policemen pushed open the back door which had not been latched. Samdaye quickly looked where Manu kept his machete. It was gone. So was his hat. His ankle-length rubber boots were also missing as was a pair of trousers and a shirt which had been hanging on the nail in the corner. She half-remembered a creak and something brushing her face. He had been there.

'He was here, not so?'

'He just run out? Don't lie. He was here and he run out when he hear the vehicle!'

She began to gather her senses. 'Who-who you talkin' about?'

'Don't pretend that you ain't know. The man was here. Look, the back-door was not locked. It was not even pushed in properly.'

The one with the gun, a corporal, poked the long barrel into her belly and shoved her towards the back-door. 'Which direction he run, eh? So?' he indicated with the gun. 'He run so?' he pointed in another direction.

'I ain't know what all-you talkin' about. What happen? Why all-you askin' about my husband? And all-you know he in jail? And all-you put him in jail? And now I hear all-you charge him wit' some crime he ain't know nothing about?' Her voice had risen in an attempt to work up some anger.

'He escape this evenin',' one of the policemen said.

'How?' she asked.

'Lady, you is not the one to ask question! You is the one to answer! Now, gi' we some answer. Your husban' come here tonight?'

'So he escape!' she almost smiled. 'An' you think he will come straight here so you could catch him? You think he so stupid?'

'He must come here.'

'He will come here but not right away.'

'He come here already,' one of the men said. 'I know that.' He gazed about the room following the beam of the flashlight with his eyes. 'What missin' from the room?' He flashed the light in her face. 'You missin' any of his things?' He seemed to be in some thought. 'Where his cutlass?'

'Cutlass?'

'Yes, cutlass. And where the case for it?'

At that minute Prince came into the room. 'And you say you lost it?' he asked Samdaye.

'Yes it lost a few days ago –'

'Who is you?' the policeman asked Prince.

'I live next door.'

'Anybody ask you anything?'

'Well . . . I –'

'Listen, mister, go back to you' room. When we want you we will call.'

Prince then asked what was happening.

'It look like Manu escape,' Samdaye said.

287

'When?'

'Mister, mind you own business, you hear? Now leave the room.'

'You ain't see him?' Samdaye asked Prince. 'Martina,' she called, 'you see my husband this evenin'? Look, the police say that he escape. But if he escape he ain't comin' here –'

'Lady, don't try to confuse anybody,' the Corporal said. He seemed to be in charge although he had asked nothing up to then. He was just standing and looking at everything quietly. He pointed his flashlight here and there then he directed it across the field. It was then that Samdaye saw that there were a couple of policemen at the edge of the cocoa-field already. They were carefully searching the ground and poking into the bushes.

The policemen were moving swiftly. Samdaye could hear them in the other rooms searching and questioning. There must be five or six of them and they seemed to be everywhere at the same time. She could hear Martina's voice loudly answering the questions and her complaints about their being present in her room. Compai had gone outside under the tree and had given them free access to search.

'So none of you see anything?' the Corporal asked. 'You know that soundin' strange! Because we know that he headed this way. We know that he hopped the train just outside Port of Spain and that he jumped off between Arima and Cumuto. So where he goin' if not here?'

Samdaye felt that the man was making this all up. How could he know where Manu had got on and off? If he had known why had they not caught him? They were only guessing. She felt a bit of excitement as she thought of him coming into the room and touching them. He must have kissed the baby. She passed her finger-tips lightly over her face. Then the fear of what might happen to him if he were caught gripped her and she wondered where he was. He knew the cocoa estate thoroughly and, with his experience in the forest, he would know where to hide.

Gradually they learned what had happened. Having been charged finally, he was being transferred to another prison when he just wrung his hand free and ran down the street. He had not been hand-cuffed so his limbs were unfettered.

Like a deer he had taken off showing them the soles of his bare feet. No one had attempted to assist the police in holding on to him so he had just scampered down the street. The police had spent a long time interrogating various persons in the direction in which he had run but the one or two vagrants that were hanging around the train station and the few vendors of fruits and peanuts as well as passers-by were not too inclined, as usual, to help the police. They did not care too much what he had done and enjoyed the occasional chase by the police. An escaped prisoner provided much excitement.

Samdaye imagined Manu dashing down the street like some frightened squirrel. Pretending to scratch her nose, she hid her smile. He would never grow up, she thought. He would always be impulsive. Now he would be in trouble. She had always felt that, somehow, he would be freed. God was not that cruel. But his running away had only made everything worse. Once more she felt thoroughly confused and, as she looked at the menacing, long black guns there was a dryness in her throat.

'I don't want anybody to think that this is a joke, eh,' the corporal said. 'Harbouring a criminal is a serious crime. Anybody who knowingly conceals the whereabouts of a criminal is guilty of an offence.' He paused to let that oft-repeated policeman's warning sink in. 'That is a crime, you hear? That could bring arrest and jail. Jail for everybody who take part in it. It ain't have more guilty and less guilty. So if you know something, talk. And talk fast. I don't want to have to take everybody down to Port of Spain.' He spoke loudly and waved his finger which appeared and disappeared as it caught the rectangle of weak light coming from the room. 'If I have to I will arrest everybody so make up your mind who goin' to talk. I will wait here until somebody say something.' But he did not stay long. The Police van returned soon after and they all left after the Corporal gave several more cautions and threats.

When they had gone Samdaye thanked Prince for coming to her rescue.

'Is nothing,' Prince said. 'We all have to stand together. And Manu is my pardner.'

Martina, hearing the low voices called Prince inside. 'Prince,' she said, 'I don't want to get mix up in anything, you hear. And I don't want you to get mix up either.'

'I ain't mix up in nothing,' Prince said.

'Don't lie! I hear the whisperin'. You know something. You hear the man and you didn't talk.'

'He come in, yes.'

'In my room?' she asked incredulously. 'He come in my room?'

'He ask for my bottle.'

'He ask for the rum?'

Prince nodded.

'And you give him?'

'The man in enough trouble. What is a little bit of rum?'

'But the man bold, yes. He damn bold. To walk in my room – to break in the room and ask for rum.'

'He didn't break in. He knock on the door –'

'And you didn't wake me?'

'For what? You was sleepin' strong.'

'Prince, you know what you doin'? We can't get mix in this business. If the man could break out the man is a criminal. Who know whether he really guilty? You know for sure? We ain't know these people. They come here just the other day and already they bring so much trouble. Look here, first thing in the mornin' I goin' to the Police and I will tell them everything.'

'Don't be foolish.'

'I ain't makin' joke. Before this man come we was goin' good. The estate had work. The overseer was goin' good. We had nothing against him. Now we treatin' him as enemy and we believin' all kind of things against him. Suppose Gomez tellin' the truth and suppose Manu lyin' you ain't see what trouble we lookin' for?'

'We not in no trouble. We ain't hidin' nobody –'

'But you know the man was here and you lie to the Police –'

'How I know he break away from jail?'

'That is not the point. You lie to the Police.' Her voice was getting higher.

Samdaye heard the argument develop and now she could hear what they were saying. Compai was sitting quietly on his steps. Suddenly he said, 'All-you hush all-you mouth. Nobody know if some policeman still in the bush. Martina, what happen, happen already. We will stay quiet. The only person they will suspect is Samdaye and she, poor thing, ain't know nothing. She didn't see him at all. Let this thing remain just so. I have my own plan.'

There was a chorus of cock-crowing. Samdaye had no idea what time it was. It could be midnight or it could be four in the morning. But no one was going to sleep. Even the Gopaul's lamp was lit and their figures could be seen moving occasionally as they listened. She wondered what Compai's plan was. Maybe it was the same foolish obeah he had been talking about. The baby started to cry once more and she brought it to the doorway where she sat and hummed and rocked absent-mindedly. Her mind flashed from subject to subject: now Manu, now her mother, now the children. She had to get a hold on herself. She could not let her husband continue to do whatever impulsive thing he wanted to do and then try to adjust her life. She had two children and one was just a baby and this was no way to bring them up. Mangal, since his father had been taken away, had become restless. He would often stand by the window looking out as though Manu would be shortly coming round the bend. His interest in his school-work was non-existent. All he did was draw with his crayons on whatever paper he could find. His pictures were almost always of the sea. He must miss Manzanilla. One day he had said that Dorado was a place you couldn't see far. The mountains and the trees blocked everything out. But Manzanilla was no solution. Not even her mother's place where she had an open invitation to live, with or without her husband, presented an attractive alternative. She was not going to return to Manzanilla and appear defeated.

'What plan you talkin' about, Compai?' she asked.

'Don't worry. You will see.' He rose slowly and went inside after complaining about the dew falling.

She could hear Martina still mumbling and quarrelling about their involvement. Across the road Mrs Gopaul had quieted down after expressing fears about a killer running about and complaining about the quality of people who had come to live in the village and how they were 'low-rating' the place. And that this village where she had lived all her life had taken a turn for the worse and could never get to be the same place it had been.

In Dorado, Samdaye thought, she could expect to have to fend for herself. She could get some support from Compai and Prince but their ability to help was severely limited. When Manu was in prison the problem was how to get him out on bail. But there was no way in which she could help him now. In the forest that stretched across the entire north of the island, blanketing the mountains and valleys for about forty or fifty miles from East to West and about eight miles from North to South, a man could hide forever. But she was not prepared to live in the forest like a wild animal. She had to think about the children and their future which was more important than that of her's and Manu's. He would come for her. Of that she was certain but she would have to be very firm. She imagined him sleeping under some lean-to he had left when he was burning charcoal. Other charcoal burners would help him and keep him warned of Police movements so that he could live in there indefinitely. If he could ever extricate himself from this trouble she would have to talk to him seriously and have him live up to his responsibility even if it meant leaving Dorado.

She took the child to the bed and lay down but could not sleep. She went back to the doorway so that if Manu was hiding within view he would see her. A wave of sympathy for him swept over her. He was so much like a boy but she could not understand what madness possessed him to behave in the way he did. Life was so simple; it had to do with working, feeding yourselves and your children and seeing about the children's future so that they could have a better chance than you.

In the morning her mother would surely come. By then she would have got the news of the escape. Her sister might also come. She imagined the embarrassment and dreaded their coming and the old arguments about how, if she had listened to advice, she would not have found herself in such a predicament, and how it was not too late to return to Manzanilla and begin life anew. But life was not like a line in Mangal's drawing book that you could erase and start afresh. Each day brought its load of experiences with its problems and solutions, and this burden gets greater day by day. You couldn't just throw it down like a bag of charcoal and walk on.

In the confusion going on in her mind she failed to notice the faint lightening of the sky and the approach of dawn.

She was mesmerized by the decreasing darkness and the growing intensity of the colours and the glistening grass. The birds were darting and flitting and streaking by, and whistling and making all their peculiar noises. But the morning held still wet and heavy. Rain might have fallen from a passing cloud.

Glancing at the children, she was about to tend to the cow when she heard a loud shouting and the tremendous explosion of a gun. Gopaul's dog added to the din. Gomez was striding with his short legs, his hair stiff and uncombed, and sticking out in all directions, waving his gun and complaining about something. 'I will kill them! I will shoot him! So help me God! They want to terrorize me. Is so they think they could terrorize me? With their nasty obeah? Let them come – one by one, two by two – I will fix them up. Blow their ass to hell!' He reached Gopaul's house and, above the din of the dog, the conversation could be heard.

Prince and Martina ran out but Compai merely peeped over the lower half of his door.

'It must be the man – the madman who break jail! He think is so Ignacio will get frighten. I just want to set my eye on him and his goose cook, his dog dead, he ain't goin' to see another minute. I will blow his tail away!'

'Wha' happen, overseer? You coun say you lookin' well vex this mornin'.'

'Vex? VEX! Who wouldn't be vex if he find a frog on his doorstep with a piece of paper in his mouth and you' name write in blood and a piece of wire pushed through the frog mouth to keep the paper in place. And three piece of candle and flowers and God know what else. Is terrorize they tryin' to terrorize me!'

'But who will want to do –'

'I just want to catch the crook and he dead!'

'Is not obeah, Boss, is some mischief,' Gopaul tried to reassure him. 'Must be some little boy prank.'

'Little boy prank? This ain't no little boy prank. They tryin'
to drive me crazy. Make me confess!'

'Prince,' Martina asked quietly, 'You know anything about
it?'

'Tina, you foolish o' what? And you was wit' me all night?'

'I feel you and Compai have somet'ing to do wit' it.'

Prince chuckled nervously. 'Woman, you talkin' foolishness . . . and don't talk so hard. Me ain't want the man to
aim his damn gun in my direction.'

A faint smile played about the corner of Compai's mouth.

'Compai –' Martina started.

'Hush you' mouth, Tina!' Prince ordered.

Gomez loaded another cartridge in the double-barrelled
gun. Slowly he swept the gun across the front of the Barracks
causing the occupants to disappear. Another explosion
blasted the stillness and some pellets fell like raindrops on
the roof.

'If is not that jail-breaker, if is not that killer, is somebody
from this village. And if is not somebody from the village
who really do it, they pay somebody to do it!' He strode
past then turned back all the while shouting accusations.
'Nobody ain't brave enough to come to my face and tell
me I done anything. So they hidin' behind crapaud. But I
will mash them up just like how motorcar mash up crapaud
on the road.' Bang! He reloaded the empty chamber. Again
the pellets fell on the roof.

'That man will kill somebody, you know,' Prince said.

'That is against the law,' Compai said. 'You can't shoot off
no gun on the public road. You can't walk wit' no loaded gun
on the road.'

'Go tell 'im that, nah,' Tina said.

'Prince,' Gomez shouted, 'Is you? Is you who do the obeah,
Prince?'

'Nah, is not me Boss.'

'Well, show you' face, Prince, don't hide behind the door.'

'You know me, overseer, I never would do somet'ing so.'

'Like what, Prince?'

'Like what you say . . . like puttin' crapaud on you' step –'

'How you know is crapaud, Prince?'

'And you just say –'

294

'Hush,' Martina said. 'Don't answer. If you don't talk he will go 'way.'

'Eh, Prince, how you know is crapaud?'

Prince did not reply.

Samdaye, standing in the cowpen behind the animal, did not move. She observed the wildness in the man's actions and his unusually unkempt appearance as he walked briskly back and forth in front of the Barracks.

'Compai! Old man! What you know about this thing, eh? You have anything to do wit' this? You, too against me? You, too workin' obeah against Ignacio? Eh, Compai? Eh, Old man?'

There was no reply from Compai.

While he was reloading the gun after letting off another shot a heavy rolling was heard and a police van ground into the gravel. Ignacio immediately broke the shotgun and pulled out the cartridges but before he could put them in his pocket he was surrounded by about five policemen who ran up to him and began to struggle with him to get possession of the gun.

'What the hell you t'ink you doin'?' one of them asked.

'Who is you?' another prodded him with a rifle.

Pushed about and bereft of his gun, Gomez looked small and defenceless. He began to mumble apologetically. The policemen handed him back his gun and listened to his story about frogs with messages written in blood. They looked at one another and seemed to question the wisdom of returning the gun.

In a few minutes they were all over the Barrack yard continuing their questions of the previous evening. They gathered everyone under the almond tree and tried to bully them into giving answers that they expected.

'And after he left here w'ere he go?'

'But I just say he didn't come here.'

'How you know he didn't come here?'

'I didn't see him.'

'Because you didn't see him don't mean he didn't come here.'

'What he take from his room?'

'He didn't take anything from the room.'

'How you know he didn't take anything from the room?'

'I didn't see him take anything.'

'So you see him –'

'I didn't see 'im.'

The questions kept being repeated and asked in different ways in an effort to confuse Prince and the rest. The policemen would ask a number of questions at once then at the other sometimes without waiting for the answer.

The Corporal arrived in a jeep. 'Arrest the woman,' he ordered. 'Take her down.'

One of them grabbed Samdaye by the arm and pulled her to the van. Mangal started to cry and ran to his mother who was being pushed up into the vehicle. The boy grabbed his mother's skirt and began to follow her.

'What foolishness all-you doin'?' Compai asked.

'Shut up, old man.'

'You tryin' to frighten everybody so they could tell you something?'

'You want to go down wit' her?' the corporal asked. 'Look, if you say one more word I will put you in the van, too. I really have a mind to put everybody in and take them down.'

Martina was heard to mumble something and Prince glared at her.

'You sayin' something, lady?' the corporal asked. 'You know something you want to talk about?'

'She ain't know nothing,' Prince said.

'Nobody ask you!' The corporal looked hard at Martina. 'You was sayin' something. What you was tryin' to say?'

Samdaye stared at Martina who was gazing at the ground. She felt that any minute Martina would say what she knew and what she suspected. Samdaye started to scream and beat her breast. She began to call out loudly for her baby. She made such a commotion that the corporal went to her and told her to be quiet. Martina disappeared into the room and brought out the baby.

'This is what I was grumblin' about,' Martina said. 'All-you ain't have no heart. The lady got a little baby and all-you treatin' her so. What happen, all-you ain't got mother?'

Samdaye continued her screaming and asking for her baby. 'You will have to jail my baby . . . and jail my son too.'

Mangal had not got up into the vehicle. There was terror in his large eyes. His father had gone and now his mother was to be taken away. He looked at the increasing crowd of people in the midst of which shifted Gomez his outsize head looking even larger with its stiff mass of hair.

'And what you doin' about that crapaud on my steps?' Gomez asked the corporal. 'I ain't takin' that easy, nah. Somebody have to get arrested for makin' obeah on me. Eh, Mr. Corporal? You listenin' to me? Because if you ain't doin' nothing I will take the law into my own hand! Yes, sir, I takin' the law —'

'Why you don't shut up!' The Corporal was getting exasperated. Nothing seemed to be going how he expected. It was while Manu was under his charge that he escaped and it was a matter of pride and self-respect that he catch Manu himself. And he had to do it soon.

Another police car arrived and a superintendent emerged in short khaki pants, long khaki socks and a baton under his arm. He enquired what was happening and told Samdaye to get out of the van. He then gathered them and began questioning all over again. Seeing Gomez with the gun he asked who he was and why he was walking about with the weapon. Nobody mentioned about the shooting but his sharp eyes saw the two empty cartridges at the side of the road. He picked them up and sniffed at them. 'You been shooting this morning?'

'He was out huntin' squirrel,' Compai offered.

The Superintendent told Gomez to go and put the gun back in the house as he did not want unnecessary shooting. He went back to Samdaye.

'Super,' Compai said, 'this lady sit in front of her door whole night. Right there she sit down whole night I tell you without one wink of sleep. You t'ink she would do that if the man was here. She do that to see if she could get him to give himself up as soon as he come. This lady watch out all night lookin' out for her husband.'

The Superintendent gazed at Compai. 'So how you know that?'

'I see how she sit all night.'

'You stayed up all night? You didn't sleep?'

297

'I get up now and again.'

Gomez looked at the old man with a questioning expression. His head jerked back and forth from the officer to Compai. He was trying to determine on which side the old man was having come to his defence with the excuse of hunting squirrels and now protecting Samdaye. There was something strange about this. He was now certain that Compai had something to do with the frog on his doorstep. He shuddered in an attempt to shake off the experience. 'You wake up whole night?' he asked Compai.

The officer seemed surprised that the overseer was still there and ordered him to go and put the gun away.

'Super, they tryin' to put obeah on me,' he said. Then he explained what had happened and how if no investigation and arrest was made he would take the law in his own hands. As the Overseer he was entitled to some protection.

The Superintendent barked at him to leave at that instant or he could lose his gun. He would not tolerate any threats coming from a man with a gun in his hand. He wondered what the story was behind the obeah attempt. 'Come back here when you put the gun away. I want to talk to you.'

He called the Corporal and, moving away, spoke in whispers.

'Is too late for dogs,' the Superintendent said aloud.

'Unless we could get some recent prison clothes that he had.'

'Or unless he made a change of clothes here. You check the clothes?'

'He didn't change clothes here.'

'You don't think he reach here yet?'

'I think he reach here and I think the Barracks people see him and I think he is somewhere in the bush either around here watching or he gone deep inside to hide.'

'He dangerous you think?'

'He is a violent fellah . . . and he strong . . . and fast.'

'I better send for the dogs,' the Superintendent said. He gave the driver of the van instructions to go back for dogs. He studied the villagers. He hated dealing with people from the countryside in criminal matters. For no reason they would hide things from the police whom they did not trust. They would readily protect each other. He thought that he should reason with them. 'So none of you see this man. I have a feeling you all see him but you don't want to talk.' He continued telling them how the man was a criminal and how they should do their bit to keep the village safe from people who would harm their own – people who would rape and kill: how it was the duty of every citizen to co-operate with the Police so that the entire country could be safe. He could see that they were looking at him curiously and guessed that they had never had dealing with anyone of his rank and that they were not really listening to him. Finally he said that they should help to recapture this man without any bloodshed. They should try to get him to give himself up.

At the sound of the word 'bloodshed' Samdaye began to cry. She offered to go with them so she could call out to him and get him to surrender. She began to beg them not to kill him; that he was not dangerous and that he was really innocent of the crime with which he had been charged; that they should talk to the overseer if they wanted to find out the identity of the criminal.

At that the eyebrows of the Superintendent went up. What did she mean by that? Was it not that the overseer himself who was the accuser and the main witness?

'Ask him,' Samdaye continued. 'Let him tell you the truth.'

Tapping the side of his cap with his baton, the officer pondered on this advice. He began to see the connection with the frog with the sewn mouth.

At that point the Sergeant from Sangre Grande arrived. The Superintendent drew him aside and they spoke out of earshot then the Superintendent left for Port of Spain after instructing the Corporal where to conduct the search. 'You better find this man before evening,' he said on leaving.

The Sergeant rushed over after his superior had left. 'What happen to Hanuman – he mad or what? How he actin' so stupid? I was workin' on the case and I was sure he innocent. I was goin' to call the CID people today to tell them what I find out and what I think. They jump the gun and charge him but that was no problem. I was goin' to get him off. And the boy too, for sure. But look how he complicate matters.' He looked at Samdaye. 'You can't get him to give himself up? He will be charged for escapin' custody. But if he get a good lawyer he could get away from that charge especially if they release him on the rape charge.'

'I don't know where he is, Sarge,' she said.

'He come here last night?'

She nodded.

'And where he went?'

'I don't know, Sarge. I didn't even know when he come.'

The Sergeant looked puzzled and she explained what had happened omitting to implicate Prince.

'He is a smart man, you know – your husband. But if he come get him to give himself up otherwise the Police could shoot him. He embarrass them and that Corporal don't make joke. He is a CID man.'

Samdaye begged him to intervene but he just nodded and advised the rest of them to co-operate.

Prince, in an effort to keep Martina from the Police had gone into his room. Only Compai was still on his doorstep. In one corner sat Mangal his drawing book in his lap, his underlip between his teeth and the corners of his mouth crinkling. He was drawing the policemen. He drew them with their hats floating above their heads and the long guns suspended in front of them. In the background was the sea.

Chapter 28

Manu hugged himself in the early morning dampness. He had spent the night with two St. Lucian coal-burners. They knew nothing of the death of the girl and of the drama being played out in the village. They had built a huge pit and had lit it the previous afternoon. Carnival was not a celebration that excited them so they had not left the forest in more than two weeks. They knew that Manu was trying to build a pit and had promised to give him a hand in the final stage of packing it with dirt and twigs to ensure an even burn. This would be done as soon as they had opened their pit and had started to pull out the coals.

The aroma of coffee filtered slowly through the wall of palm fronds and mixed with the smell of burnt clay. A light drizzle had fallen in the early dawn and the leaves still leaked drops to the forest floor.

Manu had wrestled with the thought of telling the men about his predicament. It was unfair to them if he kept his problems secret. They would feel used.

'Reds, boy, I in some trouble,' he said abruptly.

Reds looked up from mending a hole in one of the bags.

'I in a real mess.'

'What happen, you light the pit and it bust?'

'I wish it was only that. This is bad business.'

'So what happen to the pit?'

'I ain't have no pit. This ain't have nothing to do with makin' coal-pit.' He paused. 'I break out from jail and I runnin' from the police.'

Reds broke into a loud laugh but cut it sharply as he saw the earnestness in Manu's face. 'What happen?'

Manu related the story to the two men whose eyes grew

larger and larger and their mouths hung lower and lower with increasing disbelief.

'You crazy o' what, boy?' Reds said. 'You in big trouble, yes. And you makin' it worse every day you stay outside. What happen, you have **caca-poule** for brains? You ever sit down to imagine how this thing could end? Wit' you damn **caca-poule** brains makin' ants nest on the ground? **Bon Dieu**, boy sit down, you hear, and think out this thing.' Reds looked at his partner. 'Eh, Registe, you ever hear anything like this?'

'Give you'self up. Give you'self up. That is all I could say. You could stay in the ranch here and I will go out and tell the police they could come for you.' He stared at Manu. 'No no no, Reds, he ain't have choice. Innocent or not he in a real bad position and police wit' gun is nothing to play wit'. Come on, have a cup of coffee and sit down right here and we will do something to make things right.'

Manu shook his head slowly. 'Nothing could get this right.'

'Don't be stupid,' Reds said. 'You have wife and family. And, again, you innocent.'

'Innocent don't mean nothing. Not when you up against authority. You think I have a chance against the overseer? Man, they will have my tail on a rope in the mornin'. The will have to shoot me first.'

'That is what they will do. That is what they will do.'

'You too young, boy. You have your whole life in front o' you.'

'To do what? To rake and scrape for my whole life? You think that is livin'? The estate close down and soon they will kick everybody out from the barracks and I will have to move again. And I tired movin', you hear? I ain't movin' again.'

'Well, makin' the police shoot you ain't solvin' nothing.'

'If the police shoot you and kill you outright is one thing. But if they shoot you in you' mouth somewhere and you paralyse and you' face disfigure, you ain't think that worse than death?' Reds had stopped his mending.

'I goin',' Manu said suddenly.

'How you mean you goin'?' Registe asked. 'Sit down, man, sit down. We have to look hard at this thing.' He quickly brought out a cup of coffee. 'Take some coffee first.'

Manu took the large enamel cup. The warm smell of the coffee cleared his head and he sat down on a small up-ended log, and for a long time nobody spoke. The only sounds were the heavy thuds of drops on the bed of dry leaves, the blowing of air into the cups and the sucking of the hot liquid. A light breeze rustled the leaves resulting in a raining of drops.

Manu rose with his cup and went closer to the pit. He could feel the warmth of the pit and imagined the red heat inside like a volcano. He hoped that the heat from the outside would join with the hot coffee inside his stomach. From the afternoon of the carnival a chill had entered his body. It had seeped into every bone. From the time he had faced Tasso a coldness like death had enveloped him. He had enjoyed taking on the young players, watching their bravado turn to fear. But when Tasso finally entered the ring and the hush of anticipation hung thick in the air he had to steel himself to face the old man. Tasso was his 'guru' and one held one's teacher second to God. Furthermore Tasso had pulled his mask over his face to conceal what Manu thought he saw as an expression of pain. But he knew that when Tasso took up his whip in earnest he would show no mercy. And that is what Manu wanted. The old man had taunted him from the moment he had arrived from Manzanilla. He had really poured scorn on him so Manu drove pity from his mind. In any case this was a competition and he needed the money.

The coldness had increased after Tasso, his costume in tatters with the dark stains of blood mingling with those of sweat, had thrown down his whip and turned away in defeat. Manu had felt no elation of victory. The prize money had been pressed into his hand and he was lifted and carried into a rumshop. Drink after drink kept appearing before him.

The drinks had not brought an end to the cold and, as he walked away from the bus toward his home, the rain made him shiver.

He recalled throwing away the whip then the mask and remembered entering the room. But the rest was like a dream. The dead girl in the red dress, the police interrogation, the small, crowded jail cell, the journey to the prison, the escape, and now these days in the forest were like experiences

303

involving someone else. There was a numbness in his mind and body. He really did not care anymore.

In front of him the pit seemed like a pyre and he imagined himself in it. This thought did not even produce a shudder.

'I ready for anything,'

'To leave your wife and children to catch hell? You ready for that? You ready to kill your self?' Registe's voice had risen.

'You ain't makin' no sense at all. Eh, Reds? We can't let the boy waste his life just so.'

'Is his life, yes.'

'But we could give him some advice. He must listen to advice.'

'The most we could do is talk. We can't tie him up.'

'We could tell him what is best ... what is best. Eh, Reds? We older and have more experience.' Registe turned to Manu.

'So you not goin' to play mas' again. Well, that is one problem solve. So the estate close down. That ain't no big problem. Look how Reds and me makin' a livin'. When the American base close down we didn't run back to St. Lucia. We decide to make it here. We didn't know one thing about coals and coal-pit but we decide to do something together about it. Man, you believe cocoa estate work is the onliest thing to do. It have plenty other thing to do besides that.'

Manu thought about working on cocoa plantations. It was the job he knew best. It was what his father knew best and he had been initiated in it in his early teens. There was a kind of freedom in the many activities that changed with the seasons. There was the brushing of the shrubs between the trees with the long-handled swiper; the picking of the cocoa pods with his rod, hooking and slicing with the sharp knife; the pling of his razor-sharp cutlass which swung from a leather case that hung from his belt on his left side, and which was drawn with his right hand like a sword. There was beauty in a tree laden with yellow or red pods or a coffee tree in bloom giving off a sweet fragrance. There was pride in a tree well trimmed of excess branches or witches' broom. There was always movement and change. Unlike producing charcoal which involved hacking away at some mora log with an axe then loading the wood in a pit, then sitting and watching it burn. It was boring and unexciting. It was slow drudgery.

'So they charge you for something you didn't do,' Registe continued doggedly. 'That is what they have court for. To decide who guilty and who innocent.'

'You know what lawyer cost?' Manu asked. 'Let me tell you, court have nothing to do with who guilty and who innocent. It have to do with who could hire the best lawyer.' He had heard that statement expressed by many a prisoner in the few days he had spent in prison. There had been many a tale of wrongful arrests and of the innocent being convicted, some of which he suspected were exaggerations. They couldn't all be true. But some of them sounded believable.

The mention of his wife and children stabbed at his conscience. There was no doubt that he loved his wife. From the first time he saw her he became attracted to her and her large eyes so quick to fill with tears when she was hurt or upset, melted his anger every time. But she had changed into an irritable and quarrelsome woman filled with impatience and anxiety to own what they could not afford. Maybe, she thought that he was a failure. And the children – especially the baby – of course he loved them but there was little he could do to improve their lives.

He thought of his father. There was not one memory of his father hugging him or showing any affection unless he was drunk. And then he would bemoan his fate. It was always work. 'You sharpen you' cutlass, boy? You fix the spade handle?' Only in the rumshop was there any camaraderie.

His mother was always busy as far as he could recall. In the mornings she would move like a shadow rising before his father to cook roti and fry vegetables, and leave before dawn with him to work on the plantation. He spent more time with other children of the barracks than with his parents.

Manu rose. 'I goin'. I really goin' this time.'

'Stay and have something to eat, man,' Registe said.

Manu shook his head. 'Good luck,' he said. 'Good luck with the pit.' He quickly disappeared in the bush.

It was too early for the police to be out so he was moving briskly but not running. When he was out of sight of the coal-burners he turned north towards the mountains.

It was past midday when he came across a small stream with its clear water making hundreds of small eddies round the many smooth rocks. In one place there was a deep pool. He sat on a rock for some time then he removed his clothes and entered the pool. The water was so cool and fresh that he stayed until the tips of his fingers began to wrinkle. It was so easy, he thought, to go under and stay until he drowned. In this way he would have picked his place to die but there was no part of the pool deep enough to cover his height. He lay in a shallow area and listened to the gurgling sounds. Close to his ears they made a great rushing roar.

After a while he rose and walked up the stream in case the police came with dogs.

He thought he heard someone calling his name and he stopped and listened but the sound was not repeated and he dismissed it as a forest noise. It sounded like Samdaye but it might have been his imagination. He must have been travelling in a half-circle because he suddenly heard voices and before he could hide, he was confronted with a surprised policeman who was swiftly raising his rifle. In a flash Manu was upon him with his cutlass using the flat side of the blade to slap away the gun. He saw neither the flash nor did he hear the report of the gunshot. There was just a tremendous roaring and rushing and flashing as though he was at the centre of all the storms of the earth.

Chapter 29

Starting where the coal-burners deposited their bags of charcoal for the trucks from Port of Spain to pick up, and where the loggers left their mora and cedar and other forest-tree logs to be transported to the saw mills, Samdaye ran into the forest. Oblivious to the deep-rutted, muddy tracks along which the logs had slid and the oxen had left hoofprints some of which held water like cups; ignoring the small stumps and the wild palm prickles, her bare feet slapped and slid, her dress and hair followed her flying figure deeper and deeper into the gloom. She had to get to him before he was shot. 'Manu', she called, 'MAANOO!' Wild heliconia leaves and stumps and clumps of bushes deceived her and mocked her and several times she swore that she had seen him. 'MAAN! MAANOO!' She had fed the children and, dismissing the protests of Prince and the others, had run off saying that she had to find her husband first.

She did not know her way in the forest and she paid no attention to the direction in which she was going. She just kept following the track which began to branch in several paths each as wide as the other. The drag-lines made many tiny criss-crossing streams and she could see where logs had grated against standing trees. Now and again she would see the boot-prints of the policemen. She changed her direction as she did not want to run into them. 'MAAN-OHHH!' Her echoing voice rolled, it seemed, for miles. It was as though she was shouting into a steel drum.

The trees were still wet and large drops of water fell on her hair which was now wet with perspiration. Startled birds flashed in yellow or red streaks and a few times she heard scurrying through the undergrowth.

At times she felt that she was being observed and, standing still, peered around but she could see nothing. She could hear only the brushing leaves in the silent wind and the heavy drops from the leaves. Occasional shafts of sunlight shot through the thick foliage above and made flashlight beams ending in ellipses on the ground.

The land began to rise and she knew that she was climbing the foothills of the Northern Range. Logging tracks still crossed each other and, occasionally, she came upon some used-up and abandoned coal-pit where, greener than the foliage around, would be an old clump of banana plants and dasheen with large heart-shaped leaves. Sometimes there would be strands of string-bean vines hanging from stands of dried twigs.

She kept running and calling, and standing still and listening but there was no reply. She did not know for how long she had been travelling except that the shafts of sunlight had straightened and were now slanting in the other direction. Suddenly, her throat dry, and her feet bruised and bleeding she sat heavily on a log. For a long time she sat in a silence light as mist and listened to her pumping heart and heavy breathing. A few times she called weakly then she began to cry. It was a tearless sobbing with a dry cobweb-filled mouth soundless and despairing. She pounded the log with her fist and prayed in broken sounds.

Suddenly she rose and brushed her dress with her hands. She was going back to her children. She had to take care of her baby herself and not leave her to the kindness of Martina. She would return to the barracks and be prepared to face whatever happened. She had lost her way among the many tracks but she knew the general direction from which she had come and she set out with a determined expression.

She had not made a few steps when a shot rang out and, involuntarily, she started towards it but stopped after a few yards. She was not sure it was a shot; it could have been a branch snapping. Dry branches breaking off made the same kind of sound. For a little while she listened but heard no more sounds; there was no shouting, no cries and no other noises like the one she heard. Probably she just thought she heard it. But a panic returned for an instant before she suppressed it and continued her way.

She had not realized that she had gone such a long distance into the forest and several times she thought she had been travelling in circles. She began to doubt that she had walked that far but the sun, occasionally glimpsed, was still in the same direction only dropping lower. The road lay ahead. She just kept the sun to her right and hurried along. Tiredness was creeping up her calves and her arms felt weighted.

She reached the road which had become hot with the late afternoon sun and soon the mud caked on her bare feet. Nearing the barracks she became anxious for the children. As she rounded the bend approaching Gopaul's house she could see her mother, her sister and her brother-in-law standing under the almond tree. At first her mother did not recognize her and stared at her with a question in her eyebrows. Samdaye did not hurry any faster but her mother and sister rushed to her. Her mother looked at her red-rimmed eyes and her bare feet now white with dry, cracked mud.

'We was worried about you, **beti.** When we hear how you gone in the high-wood and all them police and them in there too, we really was worried.' She put an arm round Samdaye who was also being hugged by her sister. 'Child, this is not the place for you. You ain't have no place here. This place will drive you crazy. It will kill you.'

'Is true,' her sister said.

'You hear? Even you' sister say is true. And this place will kill not only you but me for sure. Every day I think about you and I worry. And I worry about the children. Because I don't know who seein' about them wit' you' husband runnin' wild and you runnin' behind 'im. What kind of life is this, eh? Tell me what kind of life you livin'? And what kind of life you givin' these poor little children?'

Samdaye realized that neither her mother nor her sister had asked about Manu. It was as if he was not in trouble – was not in danger of losing his life. It was as if he did not exist. So she stopped listening to the woman who continued decrying the level of her existence and was offering the same tired advice. Her sister was alternating between turning round her thin gold bangle and touching the filligreed cupolas dangling from her ears.

Martina stood by her door keeping her distance from Samdaye's mother who she knew was open in her condemnation of not only the barracks but also of the people who lived in it. But she was anxious to find out what had happened in the forest. Prince and Compai also stood quietly by.

The argument moved with Samdaye as she went from the tree to the steps in front of her room then back to the tree. She went in and brought out her baby which was kissed by her mother and her sister who wrinkled her nose at the stale smell of the child.

They were still standing in a group as the police van sped past. From the back two feet stuck out from someone lying on the floor. A policeman, bleeding from the shoulder, was being cradled in the arms of one while another was fanning him with a leaf. The jeep followed soon after and the news that Manu had been shot came with it. He was dead someone said.

For a long time Samdaye stood and stared as though the van was standing still then she screamed a long, piercing cry and sat on the bare earth. Someone took the baby from her as she bent double on the ground. A low bench was brought and she was made to sit on it while her head was bathed with bay-rum. Her mother hugged and rocked her and said things to console her. All the neighbours gathered – even Mrs Gopaul, who immediately began to speak well of Manu. Gopaul, a half-made crown dangling from his hand stood in shock while his children came to look for Mangal.

Samdaye's brother-in-law jumped in his little British Ford and offered to follow the van. She wanted to go with him but she was held back. The car also sped away with Prince.

It was already dark when the car returned and Prince confirmed that Manu had been shot dead. He had been cornered he was told and was asked to give himself up but he had shouted abuse at the policemen and swore that he was not returning to jail. They would have to take his dead body. 'Is one day for a man to dead!' he had said and had rushed up to the Corporal wielding chops with his cutlass.

BETWEEN TWO SEASONS

The Corporal had received two chops before Manu was shot. The body was in the Arima Hospital Mortuary and a post-mortem would have to be done in the morning before the body could be released. This news started another round of wailing.

Broadcast over the radio, the information spread rapidly and immediately people began to gather. A tent was hurriedly erected with bamboo poles and tarpaulins from some truck-driver. Bottles of rum and paper-bags of biscuits arrived. Card-players gathered and arranged benches and candles. Shepherd organised hymn singing. Old Jordan came with his bicycle on which were tied a few cedar boards. Everybody knew how tall Manu was. 'So high' they said and showed a few inches above their heads or level with their eyebrows. And Jordan took his measurements from them. The air was filled with the singing of hymns, the shouting of card-players, the sawing and hammering of Jordan and the occasional laughter of those who were recounting stories of Manu's prowess as a wielder of the whip.

People had come from Arima and Sangre Grande and even as far away as Manzanilla. Most of them left way past midnight but a few stayed till morning.

By noon the body was released and the funeral took place that afternoon. An agency from Sangre Grande transported the body free because Manu had won their prize the year before.

Samdaye had not accompanied the body to the cemetery. Holding Mangal's hand and clutching the baby to her breast she had silently watched the hearse go out of sight.

Samdaye's mother had brought the pundit who had chanted prayers and had strewn flowers in the coffin. A garland of marigold and ixoras was placed round his neck and shone against his white 'kurta'. Someone, it might have been Tasso, insisted that his clown-devil costume be put in the coffin and another rolled the whip and placed that too. Prince put a 'nip' of rum, a small pack of cigarettes and a box of matches at his side and Compai just watched and thought what a waste this was. To have this young man in his prime, with his skin taut and all his organs in healthy condition, throw away his life for no reason was a great tragedy.

311

In the days that followed Gomez behaved increasingly as though he was losing his mind. Every night the frogs appeared on his doorstep and every morning he would walk to the Junction in various states of disarray, Bible in hand. On the ninth day after the first frog was found he appeared with blood streaming down his eyes and his face, falling in big drops on his chest. He was chopping his forehead with a machete, making, not deep cuts, but enough to break the skin. He began to confess to many crimes some of which people thought were imaginary. On that morning with the villagers hiding in their homes and peeping through cracks and behind curtains fearing that Gomez might be violent, the police came and took him away to the Mental Asylum in St Ann's in Port of Spain. He had meekly given up his machete and had willingly climbed into the back of the van. He left smiling and waving with his handcuffed hands.

For days his condition was discussed and many reasons were offered for his madness: the 'obeah' of Papa Zeng evidenced by the frogs on the doorstep; a guilty conscience resulting from his various crimes; but most of all, the fact that the estate had been sold from under him and he had been asked to move. Although the land had been sold and the new owner had been moving around with surveyors, Gomez had continued to walk about in his tall rubber boots and his pith helmet, pulling black pods from the cocoa trees and lopping off unwanted twigs. On late afternoons he went after squirrels with his gun until the police came and took the gun away on instructions from the last owner.

Petit Pierre never returned to the estate. The sale had been handled by an agent. It was said that Pierre had migrated to Barbados where he had bought or was building a hotel. He was disturbed by the new political party that was holding mass meetings throughout the island on a platform of immediate independence. Removed from British rule the government might just disintegrate. The rule of law might vanish. The anti-colonialist speeches sounded anti-white. Some said the leader was communist. Even some priests were saying that. The future did not look promising.

The new owner soon completed the task of surveying the land and offered for sale small plots along the road